FIDDLIN'

Charlie Bowman

FIDDLIN'

Charlie

AN EAST TENNESSEE OLD-TIM

THE UNIVERSITY OF TENNESSEE PRESS / KNOXVILLE

Bowman

With an Afterword
by Archie Green

USIC PIONEER AND HIS MUSICAL FAMILY

BOB L. COX

Copyright © 2007 by The University of Tennessee Press / Knoxville.
All Rights Reserved. Manufactured in the United States of America.
First Edition.

This book is printed on acid-free paper.

Library of Congress Cataloging-in-Publication Data

Cox, Bob L.
Fiddlin' Charlie Bowman : an East Tennessee old-time music pioneer and his
musical family / Bob L. Cox ; with an afterword by Archie Green. — 1st ed.
    p. cm.
Includes bibliographical references, discography (p.   ), and index.
ISBN-13: 978-1-57233-566-0 (pbk.: alk. paper)
ISBN-10: 1-57233-566-1

1. Bowman, Charlie. 2. Fiddlers—Tennessee—Biography. I. Title.

ML418.B64C69 2007
787.2'1642092—dc22
[B]   2006039177

*To my late grandmother, Ethel Bowman Carroll, the youngest sister of Fiddlin'
Charlie Bowman, known affectionately as "Aunt Ethel" and "Granny Gord,"
who instilled in me a love and an appreciation for old-time music and my
multitalented family's musical heritage.*

No ordinary mortal ever felt the raptures of a fiddler; the fiddle is his bride, and the honeymoon lasts forever.

BOB TAYLOR
Tennessee governor (1886–90, 1896–98)

CONTENTS

ILLUSTRATIONS

ACKNOWLEDGMENTS

I am most grateful to my cousin Dr. James Bowman for mulitple readings of my manuscript, offering numerous suggestions for improvement, and providing continuous encouragement. I also want to thank other family members and friends who contributed their remembrances: Ray Bowman, Tony Bowman, Robert Bowman, Wanda Bowman Church (deceased), Mickey Church, Joann Bowman Jones, Jean Bowman Moore, Dorothy Bowman Haugh, Melba Bowman Jones, Pauline Bowman Huggans (deceased), Linda Cain Head, Jasper Bowman, Howard Bowman (deceased), Mary Lou Weibel, Atlee Barnes (deceased), Evangeline Bowman Eyer, Martha Bowman Bost, Leota Carroll Cox, Weldon Bowman, Wayne Whittimore, Carl Whittimore, Ray Reaves, Mary Neil Rader, Ralph Blizard (deceased), and Clint Isenberg.

I also wish to thank Art Powers, publisher and vice president of the Johnson City Press, for permission to use several vintage newspaper clippings from the *Johnson City Chronicle*. I further appreciate the many suggestions, guidance, and moral support offered to me by Dr. Wayne Daniel, author of *Pickin' on Peachtree*. Last and certainly not least, I want to thank my wife, Pat, for putting up with me during the many long hours I labored over the manuscript. To each of these individuals, I am grateful for their assistance and understanding.

INTRODUCTION

This book is the realization of a lifelong dream: to author a book about my multi-talented great uncle, Fiddlin' Charlie Bowman and his Upper East Tennessee musical family. I am a Bowman in that my grandmother was the youngest of Charlie's eight siblings. I grew up knowing this legendary entertainer, seven of his nine brothers and sisters, his first wife, Fannie Mae, and eleven of his thirteen children.

I warmheartedly remember the musical talents of my family. Saturday evenings were reserved for a family gathering at the home of Elbert Bowman, Charlie's youngest brother, in Johnson City, Tennessee, to fellowship, dine, and listen to music. From these get-togethers, I recall listening to various family members and friends produce a wide spectrum of music, from old-time pre-bluegrass Appalachian style to western swing to southern gospel.

Although I have always been engrossed in the Bowman family history, it was not until I took early retirement from Eastman Chemical Company in early 2000 that I embarked on an exhaustive effort to document my relatives' musical past. My focus was on completeness, detail, and authenticity. With the help of numerous family members, some of whom are now deceased, and the scholarly research efforts of several old-time country music historians, I accomplished my ambitious goal in about five years.

Charlie Bowman is referenced in numerous publications that document the history of early country music; however, there currently exists no book written exclusively about him and his family. I vowed to rectify that situation by writing a book that examines his life from an insider's, or family member's, perspective. Although Charlie is noted for his association with the Hill Billies (the first assemblage to apply that name to characterize early old-time music), his musical profession goes far beyond this group, spanning about a quarter of a century.

The Charlie Bowman story is not just about an individual; it entails a large colorful family: the Samuel Bowman descendants; a close-knit community: Gray Station; a geographic area: Upper East Tennessee; and a specific musical genre: old-time traditional Appalachian style pre-bluegrass acoustical music. It addresses the acquaintances of our family and the musicians who performed with them in concerts and on stage. As alleged by the East Tennessee Historical Society in Knoxville, Tennessee, this account is about how "the Bowman family brought the East Tennessee hills alive with the sound of music."

Within these pages, the reader will observe the harsh yet idyllic life as it existed in the dense mountainous region of East Tennessee in the early part of the twentieth century. Several musical groups of that era will be introduced that Charlie served either as leader or member. Many well-known old-time performers will be unveiled as we travel to fiddle contests, ice cream suppers, tobacco auctions, political rallies, and end-of-school celebrations. We will pause long enough to make some 78-rpm records for Brunswick, Vocalion, and Columbia Records. After that, we will travel on the road with the Hill Billies and journey all over the Northeast, performing in vaudeville shows at numerous theaters. Along the voyage, I will acquaint you with Charlie's two oldest daughters, Jennie and Pauline, who joined him when he began performing with a musical ensemble known as H. M. Barnes' Blue Ridge Ramblers. We will revisit the Northeast, performing on the stages of the Loews Metropolitan Theatre Circuit and the Smalley Time Circuit in the waning days of the vaudeville era.

Moreover, you will become familiar with Charlie's brothers, three of his whom performed with him when they were known as Charlie Bowman and His Brothers. I will discuss several other bands he either played with or formed himself as the entertainer continued touring into the southern and western states. This journey will not be entirely smooth. Of necessity, I will present facts about the family he left behind in Gray Station and the many hardships caused by his departure and prolonged absence. I will conclude this extensive excursion with Charlie's resting years, when the aging entertainer was forced to put his fiddle and bow on the shelf for a long overdue rest. I will relate how he stayed remarkably active in the kind of music he loved right up to the end of his life.

Fiddlin' Charlie Bowman has two primary heroes: Charlie, for his myriad contributions to early country music, and Fannie, for her steadfast dedication to her family by remaining at home and raising kids while her musically inclined husband performed on the road far from his roots. When Charlie first learned to play fiddle and other acoustic instruments, little did he perceive that this was the foundation of his legacy. Nevertheless, this farmer-turned-performer would become one of the pioneers who helped shape and develop a musical genre. Fortunately, I have been able to tap into a variety of resources in preparation for this book: family photographs, newspaper articles, death notices, marriage certificates, family Bible, Civil War accounts, government pension logs, family scrapbooks, diaries, and published books and articles. In addition, I conducted numerous taped interviews of family members and friends. It is my sincere desire that the reader find this seventy-three-year musical journey into the world of Fiddlin' Charlie Bowman and his Upper East Tennessee musical family both educational and entertaining.

Buckle your seatbelt, sit back, and relax; you are about to embark on a long musical voyage that begins on a small rural country farm community in Gray Station, Tennessee, and concludes in a small combination grocery store–residence in Union City, Georgia, a suburb of Atlanta.

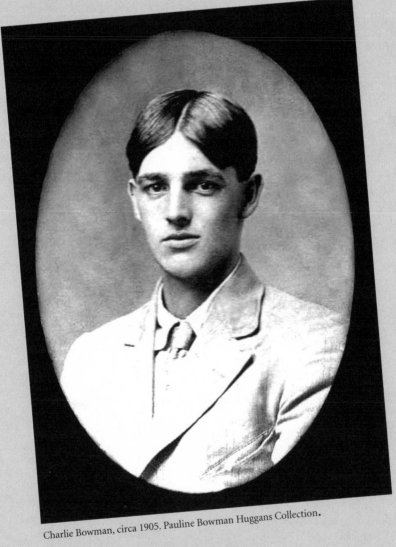

Charlie Bowman, circa 1905. Pauline Bowman Huggans Collection.

Charlie's Growing Years
1889-1910

You must always honor your mother.
Give her gifts of joy and love.
You will always be rewarded.
With blessings from Heaven above.
No friend on earth is so near you.
No one will ever be so true.
As mother who always awaits you.
And has always a smile for you.

Charlie Bowman's "Mother's Love"

Chapter 1

A FIDDLER'S FIRST NOTES

Charles Thomas Bowman did not originate in Grinder's Switch, Tennessee, where Minnie Pearl entered the world, or in Bent Fork, Tennessee, the alleged birthplace of Tennessee Ernie Ford, or in Hohenwald, Tennessee, which produced Rod Brasfield. He was born in an unnamed farm community, later named Gray's Station, located about ten miles northwest of Johnson City in Upper East Tennessee. Nevertheless, like "Cousin Minnie," the "Ole Pea Picker," and the "Hohenwald Flash," Charlie Bowman was a true dyed-in-the-wool hillbilly seemingly from the moment of his birth until his last breath. Whereas a goodly number of Appalachian residents shied away from the word "hillbilly" because of its unflattering stereotyped images, the world-class musician was proud to be called by that name throughout his entire life. Born on July 30, 1889, this future renowned fiddler would later be known by a variety of names: "Fiddlin' Charlie Bowman," "Tenn-O-See Charlie," and "Fox Hunt Charlie." To his family members, he was known simply as "Uncle Charlie." Being born with the surname "Bowman," it was only fitting that this individual would ultimately develop into a fiddler, or "bow man."

To properly relate this old-time fiddler's story is to turn back the clock to October 12, 1834, when fifteen-year-old James Bowman, Charlie's grandfather, married twenty-four-year-old Margaret Mattacks in Carter County, Tennessee. The rural couple would eventually bring eight children into the world, two boys and six girls: Mary, Nancy, Rhoda, Rebecca, Samuel (Charlie's father), Jackson, Elizabeth, and Edna. While little is known about this pioneer family, Charlie later learned from his mother that his grandfather was an old-time fiddler; she often bragged about the fiddling and singing talents of James. She described him as having a long white beard, and when he would play his fiddle and sing the old-time songs, a crowd of people would gather around him, with many of them moved to tears by his plaintive heartfelt music. Charlie recalled how his own father, Samuel, could also play the fiddle, although he provided few details. Thus, fiddling was definitely in Charlie's blood; it would emerge profoundly in just a few short years.

Samuel Bowman and Nancy Carolyn Price were married on January 14, 1872. Three years later, they would start their family, eventually bringing nine children into the world: Jennie, Alfred, Mary, Walter, Nora, Charlie, Argil, Elbert, and Ethel. This family could not have been born in a more beautiful part of the country, being in the Okolona area, within sight of majestic-looking Buffalo Mountain, a section of the Cherokee National Forest within the Appalachian Mountains and close to the 2,100-mile Appalachian Trail. Buffalo Mountain stretches east to west for about seven miles from Johnson City to Jonesborough. Buffalo Creek and Buffalo Mountain are aptly named because herds of buffalo once roamed freely in this region. Although it would tax one's imagination to visualize these beasts in East Tennessee, about 250 years ago only Indians and buffalos were present. The buffalo are regarded as the area's first civil engineers responsible for forming the major roads. These critters regularly traversed along paths of least resistance, pounding the ground with their heavy weight, all along Buffalo Creek and Buffalo Mountain as well as many other trails in and around the area. In 1673, the first white people of the English-speaking race to see the Tennessee River valley passed by the great buffalo trail up Buffalo Creek and around Buffalo Mountain.[1]

Individuals familiar with East Tennessee history will be acquainted with a legendary political campaign from 1886 known as the "War of the Roses." A remarkable fact about this confrontation was that the two candidates, Bob Taylor and Alf Taylor, were brothers who opposed each other for the governorship of the state. Those favoring Bob, the Democratic candidate, adopted the White Rose of York, while those supporting Al, the Republican contender, selected the Red Rose of Lancaster.[2] While Bob Taylor was victorious against his older brother, Alf became governor in 1921, several years after Bob died. Although both men were known as amateur fiddlers, Bob fulfilled his speaking engagements in the daytime and then fiddled at local dances at night. He once said, "No ordinary mortal ever felt the raptures of a fiddler; the fiddle is his bride, and the honeymoon lasts forever."[3] Charlie Bowman would later become a living example of this imaginative comment.

The James Bowman family must have been acquainted with the Taylor family, with their residences being close to each other and with their common interest in fiddling. When Bob and Alf were born, James Bowman was about thirty years old, and Samuel was about five. Charlie later recorded a song on the subject of Governor Alf Taylor going on a fox chase on Buffalo Mountain.

Just a few months before Charlie was born in 1889, Samuel and Nancy moved their family seventeen miles from the beautiful Okolona area south of Johnson

The Samuel Bowman Family, 1901. Samuel *(middle row, fifth from left)*, Nancy *(middle row, third from left)*, Charlie *(middle row, first to left)*, Walter *(top row, third from left)*, Elbert *(bottom row, last to right)*, Argil *(bottom row, first to left)*, Mary *(top row, first to left)*, Nora *(top row, second from left)*, and Ethel *(bottom row, third from left)*. Alfred and Jennie are not pictured. Charlie Bowman Collection.

City to an equally lovely yet unnamed community to the northwest between Johnson City and Kingsport. In 1908, this countryside was named Gray's Station when the Cincinnati, Clinchfield and Ohio Railroad, known as the CC&O, erected a train depot there. The train hauled cattle to market, transported cannery goods from the Gray Canning Company, and provided transportation to nearby cities for a limited number of passengers.[4] Gray's Station was later shortened to Gray Station and eventually to Gray, its current designation.

The rolling countryside around Gray can boast of at least two historical distinctions. One involves the famed pioneer Daniel Boone, who, according to a state historical marker, is alleged to have crossed through the area as a hunter between 1760 and 1769 following the buffalo trails: "0.2 mile along this road is the waterfall under which Boone hid himself from raiding Indians; the falls were then about 4 ft. high." Another marker 1.1 miles along the road indicates the site of the beech tree where "D. Boon cilled a bar in year 1760."[5] The second age-old distinction of this area alleges that Buffalo Ridge Baptist Church was the first permanent church of any denomination to be built in the state of Tennessee. Another state marker offers these succinct facts: "Buffalo Ridge Church, 5.0 miles. This pioneer Baptist Church, established in 1779 by the Rev. Tidence Lane, was the first Baptist Church on Tennessee soil."[6]

Charlie's childhood home in Gray Station was an unpainted two-story wooden structure with an upstairs attic and a large fireplace in the downstairs living room that heated the entire house. Since the dwelling was without electricity, the family used kerosene lanterns; everyone was forced to go to bed at night with the chickens and rise each morning with the roosters. The house included a small guest bedroom that the children used as a playroom, and from which they would precariously climb out of a window and onto the high roof. A moneymaking opportunity for the youngsters was to hoe an adjoining neighbor's garden for a nickel per row. This cash could then be used to purchase such items as a pair of shoes ($1.98), a baseball ($0.05), cereal ($0.12/five packages), cocoa ($0.19/two-pound can), or bologna ($0.10/pound). They also played in the old barn behind the house and swam in the pond adjacent to the barn. The uncomplicated life at the Samuel Bowman home was like that of most of their rural neighbors.

Charlie's life was a mixture of joy and sadness. The earliest known story about him, related by family members, occurred in 1895 when his eighteen-year-old brother, Alfred, needed to go to nearby Jonesboro (later renamed Jonesborough) to purchase fertilizer for the family farm. Six-year-old Charlie asked if he could ride down there with him on his horse-drawn wagon. Since it was a particularly cold day and Charlie wasn't dressed properly for the journey, Alfred refused his request. Consequently, Alfred hitched up the wagon and headed toward Jonesboro, a journey of about ten miles. About a mile or so down the road, he glanced back and was surprised to see his fatigued little brother running toward him wearing an old coat so outrageously oversized that part of it was dragging the ground, and the rest was flapping in the breeze. The coat most likely belonged to one of his older brothers. At first Alfred was amused at Charlie's outlandish appearance, but soon felt sorry for him, realizing just how much he wanted to go with him to Jonesboro. Alfred could have exercised his sibling authority to make the youngster return to the farm, but since Charlie now had on a warm coat, he stopped the horse and allowed the lad to climb onto the wagon. The two brothers then resumed their journey toward Jonesboro. Upon arrival at the feed store, Alfred went inside to purchase fertilizer and other needed merchandise while Charlie stayed outside and walked along the town's main street. Going to the "big city" was a royal treat for the young boy. When Alfred exited the feed store and loaded the supplies onto the back of the wagon, he saw Charlie gazing intently at something in a store window. Upon later hearing this story, family members naturally assumed that the object of Charlie's attention was a fiddle. Such was not the case; the item was a hat, appropriate for the cold blustery day. Alfred jokingly asked his younger brother how much money he had, to which the six-year-old quickly replied, "not a dadburned cent." Chuckling, Alfred again felt sorry for his little brother and bought him the hat.

Music was a prominent component of Charlie's early life. Family members, friends, and neighbors were seemingly always playing it at his home, especially since his father and grandfather were old-time fiddlers. His plunge into the music world occurred in 1899 at the age of ten, when he learned to play a homemade banjo. That instrument came into existence through atypical circumstances. Charlie and Walter were acquainted with an older neighborhood boy known as "Long Jess" (so called because of his imposing six-foot, four-inch height), who had decided to craft his own banjo. After fabricating the hoop, neck, and pegs, he searched for a suitable hide to stretch over the hoop, but everything he found was too thick and heavy. Finally, he spotted the source of the perfect hide material—a stray cat walking in some nearby woods. With little fanfare, Long Jess fetched a hog rifle and killed the animal; Alfred Bowman skinned it for him. After preparing the hide and allowing it to dry for several days, the lad stretched it over his hoop, installed a handcrafted bridge, and placed a set of strings on his newly created instrument. The two Bowman brothers borrowed the banjo and each learned to play it, thus introducing them to old-time music.[7]

It was but a brief time later when Charlie borrowed a friend's fiddle and learned to play a handful of tunes on it. He amazed himself at how quickly he was able to play this relatively difficult instrument. Although Charlie returned the fiddle to his friend, he later borrowed it a second time and learned some additional songs. Within a short time, he recognized that he possessed a natural-born talent for playing the fiddle. He purchased his own instrument in nearby Johnson City for $4.50, later saying that this dark-colored fiddle was the best one he ever owned; it was a prized possession throughout his illustrious career.

September 1905 brought sadness to the Bowman family when, after thirty-three years of marriage and twenty-two years of being an invalid from diseases contracted during the Civil War, sixty-one-year-old Samuel Bowman departed this life. The death of Charlie's father left behind a forty-nine-year-old widow and eight of their nine children, ranging in ages from eight to twenty-eight. Samuel was laid to rest in the Sulphur Springs Cemetery near his oldest daughter, Jennie, who had died five years prior. It would be another thirty years before Nancy joined her husband in death. Most of what is known about Charlie's father was obtained from his obituary in the Jonesboro newspaper:

> Samuel Lafayette Bowman was born June 10, 1844 on Buffalo Creek, in Carter County, Tennessee, and died September 4, 1905. While yet a young man, he worked as section hand on the old East Tennessee, Virginia, and Georgia Railroad. For some time he was brakeman on the same road during which time, while coupling cars in Greeneville, he met with an accident in which he nearly lost his life. During the Civil War, he served with honor in Company I, Eighth Tennessee [Cavalry] Regiment [USA], and participated in many important raids and thrilling encounters. As a soldier, he was brave, unfaltering, and ever ready to go where duty called him; and by the hardships and exposures he underwent for the flag he always loved, he contracted diseases, which ended his life. As a Christian, his record is unsullied. He united with the Dunkard Church at Pleasant Valley and earnestly endeavored to follow the footsteps of Jesus. His life is an example of meekness, honest of purpose, and devotion to God. Never would he let an opportunity pass to accommodate a neighbor; never would he refuse, when in his power, to befriend the needy; never did he falter in his duty to his home. His life was gentle, and the elements so mixed in him that all the world might say, this was a man.[8]

Because he was the oldest male and unmarried, Alfred became the official father figure after the elder Bowman's death. Alfred had already begun easing into a leadership role due to Samuel's invalid condition during the last several years of his fragile life.

The year 1908 was pivotal in the career of Charlie Bowman. He walked to nearby Sherman Adams's farm one day to have some corn ground in his gristmill. During that visit, Sherman showed the teenager his new Edison cylinder phonograph that was a combination player and recorder. Eager to try out the new gadget, Sherman sent Charlie home to get his fiddle. By this time, Charlie had been practicing for about three years, but by his own admission was still a novice. Nevertheless, he somewhat nervously allowed Sherman to record him playing the old traditional fiddle tune "Turkey in the Straw."

> Turkey in the hay, in the hay, hay, hay.
> Turkey in the straw, in the straw, straw, straw.
> Pick 'em up, shake 'em up, any way at all.
> And hit up a tune called Turkey in the Straw.[9]

This ancient fiddle tune is believed to have originated in the mid-South. It is now played worldwide along with its close cousins, "Old Zip Coon," from the minstrel stage, and "Natchez under the Hill," concerning a frontier riverboat scene on the Mississippi. Charlie was rather impressed that he had been asked to play his fiddle to make a cylinder recording. "Turkey in the Straw" was the young amateur musician's first recording, but it would certainly not be his last. Fiddlin' Charlie Bowman was on the move . . . without realizing it.

Charlie Bowman, circa 1924. Pauline Bowman Huggans Collection.

Charlie's Working Years
1911–1946

I've got a good woman just the same.
I've got a good woman just the same.
Woman just the same, Fannie Bowman is her name.
Got a good woman just the same.
Charlie Bowman's "Roll on Buddy"

Chapter 2

FANNIE'S FIDDLER BEAU

The year 1910 found twenty-one-year-old Charlie Bowman as a handsome young man anxious to get married and begin raising a family. While an abundance of young eligible ladies resided in the Gray Station area, the one who undeniably caught his eye was pretty Fannie Mae Mohlar Ferguson. Six years earlier she had become a widow with two young boys, Elmer and Joe, when her husband, Jake Ferguson, was killed in a mining accident in Saltville, Virginia. This unfortunate accident set the stage for Fannie and Charlie to start courting and marry within a year. The young groom would later write "I Can't Say Goodbye," which seems to depict his feelings toward his new sweetheart:

> Seems I have found a sweet maiden.
> I can't get her off my mind.
> All my dreams are about her.
> I'm praying some day she'll be mine.
>
> Her face is as bright as the sunlight.
> Her heart is as clear as the moon.
> And she is as sweet to me right now.
> As the dew from the sweet clover bloom.
>
> *Chorus:*
> If we should say good-by to each other,
> I'd almost go out of my mind.
> For all of my dreams are about you,
> And I'm praying someday you'll be mine.[1]

That "someday" became a reality on January 24, 1911, when Charlie and Fannie tied the knot under a big apple tree located in a field behind Fannie's parents' place. The young fiddler acquired a ready-made family consisting of a lovely young bride and two juvenile boys. The newlywed's first order of business was to find a place to live and raise their family, which would eventually grow from two to twelve. They located a small house near Gray Station's rock quarry, where they resided for about nine years. During this time, Charlie learned a variety of crafts, including carpentry, house painting, and logging with a team of oxen. These experiences resulted in his finding numerous employment opportunities near the Gray Station area.

Charlie Bowman and Fannie Mae Mohlar Bowman, circa 1924. Pauline Bowman Huggans Collection.

It was while Charlie was working in Kingsport that a local movie theater owner approached him about playing his fiddle for silent pictures. This was several years before "talkies" came on the scene and before radio became commercialized. Although these movies mostly utilized the piano or organ for background effects, stringed instruments were more appropriate for some pictures. Charlie, his brother, Argil, and "Wash" Milhorn were hired to play live stringed music, featuring Charlie on fiddle, Argil on guitar, and Wash on banjo.[2] This was the first time Charlie was compensated for playing before a live audience, and it was certainly more satisfying than performing sweaty odd jobs in the surrounding community.

By 1918, Charlie and Fannie Bowman had had five children together: Pauline, Jennie, Lester, Donnie, and Howard. Between 1919 and 1930, Dorothy, Jasper, Hansel, Melba, and Jean arrived on the scene. A neighbor laughingly commented, "It looks like the Bowmans and the sage grass are taking over the County."[3] Charlie and Fannie began a search for a more spacious dwelling to accommodate their ever-increasing family. They purchased property on a hill alongside Roscoe Fitz (short for Fitzgerald) Road overlooking the beautiful Gray Station countryside and just over the hill from Grandma Bowman's farm. When they bought the land, the only thing standing on it was a small barn. Charlie decided to find an existing house and move it to his new place. He soon located and purchased a two-story single-pen log house that had been built about 1818 at nearby Keebler's Crossroads, and had it moved to his family's new property. Relocating the structure was a laborious chore, considering the fact that it had to be transported largely with animal labor. When the family was forced to vacate their first residence, the one-hundred-year-old log house was in the process of being moved, so Charlie erected a tent on their new site for the family to sleep in

Charlie, Fannie, and their six children at the log house on Roscoe Fitz Road, Gray Station, Tennessee. The Bowman Sisters, Jennie and Pauline, are dressed alike and holding musical instruments. Bob Cox Collection.

until the permanent house was ready for occupancy. This was a unique experience for the children, one they thoroughly enjoyed.

The men meticulously reassembled the two-story house log by log on their new property. By this time Charlie had developed into an experienced carpenter, so he actively participated, along with help from family members and friends. The building was obviously not in top shape, but it was the best that he and Fannie could afford at the time. Ironically, Pauline remembered that the barn on their new property was in better condition than the reassembled house.

The Bowman children named their new residence the "Abraham Lincoln house," since Honest Abe was reportedly born in a log cabin. At the time the dwelling was reassembled, it had just two big rooms, one downstairs and one upstairs. The only access to the upstairs was a movable wooden ladder until Charlie replaced it with a safer more permanent stairway. He also added some internal walls downstairs to provide for one small bedroom, a small combination kitchen and dining room, and a living room containing a fireplace. According to Dorothy, the odd thing about the first floor was that its ceiling was only about six feet high, requiring tall people to bend over when they walked through the room. Charlie and Fannie converted the upstairs area into a large loft, or barracks, that provided sleeping quarters for the older children. All the downstairs windows had glass in them but no screens; oddly enough, the two upstairs windows had neither glass nor screens. During the summer months, the windows stayed uncovered, allowing an ever-present number of flies, bees, and other unwanted critters to enter the house. In winter, the large upstairs room with its high ceiling became an ideal location for family and friends to convene and play music. Wooden boards with handles were loosely hung over the windows in an attempt to thwart the cold air from entering. Cracks between the logs where the daub (or mud filling) had fallen out meant that the children sometimes came home from school to find snow covering the floor and their beds. Their remedy was to stuff the cracks with paper, rags, and anything they could find. This situation is described in the first two verses of the old fiddle tune "Arkansas Traveler":

> Oh, once upon a time in Arkansas,
> An old man sat in his little cabin door,
> And fiddled at a tune that he liked to hear.
> A jolly old tune that he played by ear.

> It was raining hard, but the fiddler didn't care.
> He sawed aways at the popular air.
> Though his rooftop leaked like a waterfall,
> That didn't seem to bother the old man at all.[4]

The Bowman children were not oblivious to these adverse conditions, as was the fiddler in the song; they just had to accept whatever fate brought them.

The dining room was barely large enough for its long rectangular table with rustic benches along each side and chairs at each end. Fannie always sat at the end nearest the kitchen, and Charlie sat at the opposite end. Since the family never owned a playpen or a high chair, the younger children were loosely tied to a regular chair beside Fannie so they wouldn't fall off. More often than not they ended up on her lap before the meal had concluded. In the warmer months, one child was designated to wave a "fly bush," a tree branch with leaves, back and forth across the table to keep flies off the food. The provisions for keeping food refrigerated were crude; the "refrigerator" was a cellar along the left side of the house, with a dirt trench that ran its entire length. This ditch usually stayed cool, dark, and moist, but when it became dry, water was added to it. It was here where Fannie kept hams, canned sausage and fruits (peaches, apples, and pears), as well as milk products from their two cows, Blacky and Rube.

The cistern just off the kitchen was an essential item for providing the family with water for their daily needs. It was a deep underground hard clay earthen enclosure with a drainpipe connected at one end to the roof gutter. When it rained, Fannie would initially allow the water to run off the roof onto the ground to wash the bird droppings and other debris from the roof. Once the water was clear, she would attach the drainpipe to the top of the cistern and allow the run-off water to collect inside it. She kept a supply of white flour sacks that she would wash and place over the end of the drainpipe to filter the water going inside the cistern. Occasionally, Fannie would add lime to the water for increased purification. When the family needed water for drinking, cooking, washing and bathing, someone lowered a bucket into the cistern using a rope pulley to bring up the cool refreshing liquid. Once a year, the cistern had to be emptied and the sludge removed; then it was refilled with fresh water from a spring near Lige Adams's store. All the children helped with this time-consuming and laborious chore by carrying fresh water buckets from the spring to the cistern.

In the winter months, the fire in the fireplace was banked before the family went to bed at night. Banking the fire included covering the coals with ashes and adjusting the air draft so that the fire would last well into the night, providing reduced heat for the house. A normal day in the Bowman household began with Fannie rising at five o'clock to build a fire in the fireplace. She would simultaneously build a fire in the kitchen stove for cooking breakfast. Fannie made biscuits for breakfast as well as for the children to take to school for lunch. For making cornbread, she used what she called a "baker," a one-foot wide three-legged black iron pot with a lid that sat in the fireplace over the coals. The lid permitted hot coals to be placed on top of it, allowing its contents to cook evenly on all sides. According to the Bowman children, cornbread made in the baker was immensely tastier than that prepared on the stove. After killing hogs around the end of November, the Bowman family had enough meat until about February. After the supply was depleted, the young housewife substituted lard, although these biscuits did not have the same delectable taste as those made with sausage. Biscuits and gravy is the subject of one of Charlie's fiddle songs, "Black Eyed Susie":

> Love my wife,
> Love my baby,
> Love my biscuits sopped in [sausage] gravy.
>
> Hey, black eyed Susie,
> Ho, black eyed Susie,
> Hey, black eyed Susie Jane.[5]

Pork was not the only meat brought to the table. Thanks to the keen hunting skills of young Donnie, the family enjoyed an ample supply of squirrel meat. The lad was so accurate with his "gravel flipper" that he could kill a squirrel by simply anticipating where it would run and shooting ahead of it. After the children skinned, cleaned, and removed all the hairs from the squirrel—a strict requirement before Fannie would cook it—she combined fried squirrel meat with squirrel gravy and served it along with some of her delectable homemade biscuits.

With twelve children crowded into the log house over the years, the sleeping arrangement for the dwelling was structured so as to be quite practical. The one downstairs bedroom consisted of two double beds, while the upstairs loft had several double beds. Charlie and Fannie slept in one bed in the downstairs bedroom and the oldest girl, Pauline, slept in the other one. When a new child was born, an event, which occurred on the average of every two years, he or she initially slept between Fannie and Charlie. When the next child was born, that infant slept between Fannie and Charlie, relegating the first child into the bed with Pauline. The third successive child slept between Fannie and Charlie, causing the previous child to bed with Pauline. This nightly process meant three in her bed for a while until the oldest child graduated to the upstairs loft. The sleeping ritual for all twelve children was repeated in this identical manner. The older children who slept upstairs were responsible for making sure the younger ones behaved.

None of the beds in the log house had modern mattresses; instead, they used "straw ticks," which were fabric cases filled with straw. After about a year of use, the straw would break down and need replacing. When the men thrashed wheat in the fields, family members would empty the broken straw from the bed ticks and refill the ticks with fresh straw from the wheat fields. At first, sleeping on the new straw ticks was difficult and even painful; the sharp ends of the straw would thrust through the sheets. Fannie corrected that problem by putting heavy blankets over the mattresses until they were sufficiently flattened enough to be comfortable. A few families were fortunate enough to have feather ticks, which were warmer and more comfortable than straw ticks but required a great many feathers just to supply one bed. Plucking feathers was tedious work and consternated the geese. Fannie compromised by using feathers in her pillows and straw in her ticks. The use of feathers for bedding is the subject of "Go Tell Aunt Rhody," an old song that has been traced to a 1752 opera by Jean-Jacques Rousseau:

> Go tell Aunt Rhody, go tell Aunt Rhody,
> Go tell Aunt Rhody, that the old gray goose is dead.
>
> The one she's been saving, the one she's been saving,
> The one she's been saving, to make a feather bed.
>
> Old gander's weeping, old gander's weeping,
> Old gander's weeping, because his wife is dead.
>
> And the goslings are mourning, and the goslings are mourning,
> And the old goslings are mourning, because their mother's dead.[6]

Recent generations of children have heard the perennial lament of their elders' spiel about walking a mile in the snow to school—uphill both ways. In actuality, the offspring of Charlie and Fannie had a jaunt of about three miles to school on the main road, but the trip was about a mile less taking shortcuts across the fields. Weather conditions usually determined which route they chose. The usual fare was for them to join their neighboring friends for the weekday walk. Four area schools figured into their formal education: Victory, Douglas Shed, Gray Station, and Sulphur Springs. The young people walked to the first three schools but rode the bus when they attended Sulphur Springs School, which was not within walking distance. In those days, the students had to furnish their own instructional materials—books, pencils, and paper. The school provided the facilities, furniture, and faculty. Those children who could not afford books were never assigned homework. Some of the more affluent students would lend their books to their less fortunate classmates. The afternoon school bell did not signal the end of learning for the Bowman children; their determined mother further enhanced their education after their daily chores were finished. Fannie would become their schoolteacher, teaching them such things as multiplication tables. This was quite a task, considering the number of school age children she had, but the young mother had enough love to cover each one.

Living with modest income on a farm in a century-old log house in the early 1920s was not without its hardships. However, several of the children later commented just how much fun it was growing up in that rudimentary dwelling. Further, no one could remember ever missing a meal; Fannie Bowman saw to that. During this time, Fannie and Charlie shared the rearing of their offspring in a harsh country environment. That would soon change, with Fannie essentially assuming full responsibility. Charlie was about to go on the road to play music professionally, eventually being away from home most of the time. Big changes, some good and some not so favorable, were on the horizon for the Charlie Bowman family.

Chapter 3
BIRTH OF A STRING BAND

By 1905 the four members of a future string band—Charlie, Walter, Elbert, and Argil—were on the scene. However, it would be several more years before they would be old enough and adequately proficient to form their own aggregation. Whereas most bands are formed with several musicians getting together and then deciding to combine their musical talents, the Bowman brothers string band was literally birthed into existence. Alfred was the lone exception, as he had absolutely no interest in this musical genre. By the time Elbert, the youngest brother, was ready to play an instrument, the Bowman brothers were geared up to entertain the locals around Gray Station. Charlie assumed leadership of what became known as Charlie Bowman and His Brothers. Although each brother specialized in one instrument, all of them soon became sufficiently versatile to switch instruments at will: Charlie on fiddle, guitar, and banjo; Walter on guitar, fiddle, and banjo; Elbert on banjo and guitar; and Argil on guitar and banjo.

The East Tennessee area in the late teens and early twenties was certainly not lacking for old-time fiddlers. Over the years, this region would become a hotbed of some of the best traditional musicians in the country. These were the days before radio and television when many men and women learned to play the fiddle if for no other reason than to idle away the hours. Some were content simply to piddle on the fiddle, while others took fiddling seriously by concentrating on techniques and learning an assortment of tunes. Rough mountainous roads and limited transportation kept these musicians within a relative short distance of their homes. Unlike skilled violinists who read music and take their cues from a conductor, these fiddlers played by ear and carried their tunes in their hearts. While some fiddlers preferred to play solo, others opted to play with other stringed musicians, usually on someone's front or back porch or in the yard. Those with decent singing voices would sing and play their instruments, drawing a crowd of dancers. Skilled fiddlers were routinely beckoned to display their talents at local schools, churches, barn dances, tobacco auctions, political rallies, and ice cream suppers. Buck dancing was popular, and it was common

The Bowman Brothers, circa 1950. *Left to right:* Charlie, Elbert, Alfred, Walter, and Argil. Bob Cox Collection.

to spread salt on the floor for the dancers. Some put metal taps on their shoes. During this time the Bowman brothers were rapidly becoming a major part of this Upper East Tennessee country music scene.

If someone were to ask Charlie and his brothers, or any musicians of that era, to put a label on the kind of music they played, most, if not all, would answer "old-time music." The question then begs to be answered, "What is old-time music?" There can be as many answers as there are respondents to that question. Probably the broadest definition comes from Alan Lomax, folk song collector and developer of the Archive of Folksong at the Library of Congress. In his essay "Folk Song Style," he writes: "The intent of old-time music is to give the listener a feeling of security, for it symbolizes the place where he was born, his earliest childhood satisfactions, his religious experience, his pleasure in community doings, his courtship and his work—any or all of these personality-shaping experiences."[1]

Although Charlie's father and grandfather were old-time fiddlers, Charlie did not inherit his style of fiddling from them. Instead, he learned it from John Mitchell of Fort Mill, South Carolina, who moved into the Gray Station area for a brief period around 1915. Very little is known about this transported South

Carolinian except that he was an exceptionally good musician and quickly became known as the finest fiddler around those parts. He was so impressive that Charlie and his brothers invited him to join their newly formed string band. He obliged them for a short time before moving back to South Carolina. During his stay, John not only influenced Charlie's music but also that of his brothers. John seemed to possess that special touch that all musicians crave, and, thanks to him, Charlie Bowman soon went from being a good fiddler to becoming a great one. In his senior years he often spoke of just how influential John Mitchell was to his music and that of his brothers.

By 1920, music was being played increasingly at the log house. Charlie, Elbert, Walter, and Argil routinely played there, drawing in other area musicians as well as people from all over Gray Station who came to dance or just to watch the merriment. During warmer weather, the musicians played on the hillside along the north side of their log house; during colder weather they moved to the upstairs loft. To accommodate overflow crowds, Charlie's children propped the beds against the wall. In spite of this, there were often so many people in the loft that there was little space for dancing. Sometimes the crowd was so big that the floor would bounce up and down, giving concern that it might collapse, but it never did. Charlie's oldest daughter, Pauline, remembered Fiddlin' Cowan Powers and his three daughters, Ada, Opha Lou, and Carrie Belle, and his son, Charlie, playing music at their house on numerous occasions. Powers was an excellent fiddler who played with a full, rich, liquid tone, as if his fiddle was filled with water. Pauline was more acquainted with Ada and Opha Lou than the others. As a family, they recorded for Victor, Edison, and Okeh records and resided in Russell County, Virginia. Mother Maybelle Carter, who lived not far from them in southwest Virginia, tutored one of their girls.

Charlie also played music with locals Roby Chinouth and Walt Bacon. The latter is rumored to have recorded with the Bowman brothers. Also, the four Bowman brothers briefly played a stint with Roby Chinouth and were called "Fiddlin' Chinouth and the Bowman Brothers," but it was not long before the band was renamed "Charlie Bowman and His Brothers."[2]

While the Bowman boys were not well known outside of Gray Station before 1920, that began to change rapidly as they regularly performed at local venues. The young men labored all day on their farms and then played their music at night, often going well into the wee hours of the morning. It was customary in those days for schools to have a musical show when the academic year ended as a way for both students and teachers to celebrate the upcoming summer break. Sometimes each brother was paid as much as seventy-five cents for making an appearance, but as often as not they just got whatever came in from "passing the hat." Times were so lean that they were fortunate to get their hat back.

Frequently, compensation consisted of a hot cooked meal at someone's home. Charlie recalled how the four of them would walk three or four miles across fields and unpaved potholed roads in inclement weather to reach their performances. Musicians were fortunate to own an instrument, much less a case to carry it in. The Bowman brothers wrapped their instruments in newspapers and put them under their coats to protect them from the elements. Since there was no radio to advertise their appearances, the brothers had to rely on the local Jonesboro, Tennessee, newspaper, the *Herald and Tribune*. Because this paper was not a daily publication and many households shared it, their concerts often took place before residents read about them. In addition to being good musicians, the boys were good vocalists. On occasion they would rest their instruments and entertain their fans as a barber shop quartet, a talent that was later carried on through the Elbert Bowman family members.

Local fiddle contests became popular, and people urged Charlie to participate in them. Thus, over the next several months he began traveling to fiddle competitions all over the East Tennessee area and neighboring states. In these contests, the fiddler usually played one of three fiddle tunes to display his talent: "East Tennessee Blues," "Cacklin' Hen," and "Money in Both Pockets." Charlie often commented that this latter song required playing a thousand notes a minute. He would ultimately record the song for Columbia Records as part of his "Moonshiner and His Money" music-comedy routine. As Fiddlin' Charlie began participating in these area fiddle contests, he kept a handwritten log that revealed where he entered contests in Tennessee, Georgia, North Carolina, Virginia, and Washington, D.C. Amazingly, he won first prize in twenty-eight of thirty-two events, including Atlanta, Georgia; Bluff City, Tennessee; Bristol, Tennessee; Boones Creek, Tennessee (Roby Chinouth 1st, Charlie 2nd); Boone, North Carolina; Bakersville, North Carolina; Dante, Virginia; Erwin, Tennessee (John Carson 1st, Charlie 2nd); Embreeville, Tennessee; Johnson City, Tennessee; Jonesboro, Tennessee (Cowan Powers 1st, Charlie 2nd); Kingsport, Tennessee; Limestone, Tennessee; Mountain City, Tennessee; Washington College, Tennessee; Washington, D.C.; Wilkesboro, North Carolina; Knoxville, Tennessee; Rome, Georgia (Curley Collins 1st, Charlie 2nd); and Lamar, Tennessee.[3] Charlie recalled the Knoxville fiddler's convention as being a great three-day event located in downtown Market Hall; all three days were packed to capacity.

With Charlie winning an abundance of contests, some participants complained that the judges were partial to him. To remedy this concern, the judges were placed where they could hear the fiddlers but not see them. In spite of this modification, Charlie continued to win; his distinctive fiddle sound could easily be identified without his being seen. Many an old-time fiddle contest concluded with the crowd displeased with the selection of the winners. Such events were not vaudeville shows or popularity contests; the crowd pleasers often did not win. Judges gave no credence to the reaction of the attending spectators, focusing instead on such fiddling qualities as timing (rhythm), clarity (sharpness of the note), tonal quality (smoothness and mellowness), and authenticity (age of the selection).[4] Winning so many contests began to convince Charlie that he was destined to play music professionally. These contests became a means for him to earn a small amount of money while simultaneously displaying his fiddling talents to his ever-growing public. "Fox Hunt Charlie" was starting to make his presence known.

What kind of people were the old-time fiddlers who participated in the local fiddle contests? They were not seasoned professionals by any means. Instead, they were simple hardworking God-fearing people who labored during the day to support their families and played music at night and on weekends for sheer relaxation. Participating in these contests provided a way for them to pick up a small amount of cash, but, more important, it gave them some relief from their daily chores and a refreshing break from the blood, sweat, and tears of daily life. Some carried their fiddles with them, knowing they would probably be called upon to play and maybe even to sing or dance. These fiddlers became heroes to the locals who cheered them as they performed on stage. Country dances were the rage, with many a fiddler returning home exhausted at the end of an all-night dance session.

In the mid-1920s, Charlie and His Brothers were fortunate enough to have been invited to supply their popular brand of music for the political campaign of the Honorable B. Carroll Reece. He was a U.S. representative from the first district of Tennessee who served three separate terms: 1921–31, 1933–47, and 1951–61. He is as well known in Tennessee history as governors Bob and Aft Taylor. People loved the Bowman brothers' old-time string music and would attend political rallies if for no other reason than to hear their music. Mr. Reece particularly favored Charlie and his brothers and beckoned them on numerous occasions to perform for him, thereby establishing a lifelong friendship with the congressman. Charlie composed a song for the legislator that he appropriately named "Reece Rag" and always included it anytime he was performing for him. Apparently, this composition was never recorded.

Pauline and Jennie often accompanied Charlie and His Brothers to these rallies. Fannie's sister, Aunt Vertie, made each of the girls a beautiful orange-colored flowered dress, which they usually wore when they performed together. Once while they were singing at a political rally for Mr. Reece, with Jennie playing the piano, Pauline reached down to pull up her colorful dress and got it caught in her garter. Needless to say, this unintentional gesture created some surprised looks from the crowd, a few seconds of embarrassment for Pauline, and a reserved smile from Jennie.

Mr. Reece died while still in office in 1961. Since he and his wife did not have children, Pauline for years routinely put flowers and an American flag on their graves at Johnson City's Monte Vista Cemetery. This noble gesture was an indication of the warm spot she had in her heart for the couple. Reece's death, one year before Charlie died, prompted the Jonesboro *Herald and Tribune* to comment about him and his association with the Bowman brothers:

> Charlie Bowman, the fiddler, is well remembered by the older people in Washington County, and they will regret to learn that for two years he has been a shut-in at his home in Union City, Georgia, and can get around only in a wheel chair.
>
> One who is acquainted with the famous Bowman Brothers String Band sends us this reminder of the old days:
>
> The death of Honorable B. Carroll Reece brought sad memories to many of us including those of the Bowman Brothers—J. Walter, Charlie, Argil and Elbert—all of whom were born near Gray's Station. When Mr. Reece started to campaign for Congress in the early twenties and had public speaking all over the district, the Bowman Brothers were selected to play on these occasions. It turned out that the band was a good drawing card and there were large audiences for the speakers. Charlie Bowman was the main fiddler and his brother Walter was a good fiddler, Argil played the guitar and Elbert the five-string banjo. Mr. Reece was their good friend and they took pride in playing for him. They also played for various other leading candidates for public office.
>
> Many people will remember the fiddling contests at the Jonesboro Courthouse, and Charlie Bowman was winner at many of these. These old-time fiddlers bemoan the fact that the younger musicians have turned to rock-and-roll and such modern musical innovations and the old-timers long for the day when genuine country music will return to popularity.[5]

It was common in the early days for fiddlers to put rattlesnake rattles inside their fiddles, convinced that these made the fiddle sound crisper and louder. Jasper recalled that Charlie used them briefly during his early days. Some fiddlers would not dare perform or at least compete in a fiddle contest without these rattles. While some old-timers did not think they added much to the sound, they did acknowledge that the rattles had a very practical application as they kept varmints out of their fiddles while in storage. A spider or mouse looking for a place to take up residence and start a family would seek elsewhere when they encountered a fiddle that had the scent of a rattlesnake.

Charlie began spending increasingly more time performing locally with his brothers, and his love for the fiddle was becoming stronger with each passing day. Fannie obviously noticed it, too, but remained home as the faithful obedient wife, tending to the important task of raising her large family and teaching them right from wrong. An example of her training occurred when she sent young Donnie to Lige Adams's store with a live chicken in exchange for some salt, pepper, and sugar, three items she had written on a piece of paper and sent with him. Lige sold things outright or bartered with his customers. When Donnie got there, Lige gave him the needed supplies and told him to put the chicken in a cage at the back of the store. Donnie returned home with both the supplies and the chicken. When Fannie saw what he had done, she escorted her disobedient young son back to Lige's store to return the chicken and apologize to the storekeeper.

An event that helped launch Charlie's professional career occurred in the spring of 1924 when a local businessman and president of the Rotary Club, Bert Pouder, asked him if he would enter a two-day fiddling contest being held in downtown Johnson City. The Pouder family of Johnson City was very influential and involved in several successful businesses, including a combination furniture store and undertaking service. The contest, sponsored by the United Commercial Travelers, was being scheduled at the Deluxe Theatre. This stately entertainment center had been built just four years earlier and designed mainly for stage

The Deluxe Theatre fiddlers contest in downtown Johnson City, circa 1924 (Charlie, ninth from left). Jennie Bowman Cain Collection.

plays and vaudeville shows. Over the years, a parade of well-known country and western stars routinely entertained on its stage. Since this theater was an imposing place for Charlie, he told Mr. Pouder that he didn't think he was talented enough to enter the contest, a humble response considering the number of fiddle contests he had previously won. Unlike the other competition venues, this one was in a large theater and was somewhat formal; the contestants were required to wear suits, unlike the bib overalls to which he was accustomed.

Mr. Pouder offered the young fiddler five dollars to compete in the contest scheduled for the following afternoon. He informed Charlie that, although he had not heard him play personally, his friends spoke highly of him as being the best fiddler in East Tennessee. Those flattering words combined with the prize money were all the encouragement Charlie needed to convince him to participate in the event. He took the money he received from Mr. Pouder and purchased a new pair of shoes at a downtown store. Charlie likely had second thoughts about entering the contest. As he walked up and down Main Street he saw large signs advertising the event with Georgia's state champion fiddler, Fiddlin' John Carson, being there as a performer rather than a competitor. After finding out that Cowan Powers was in the competition also, Charlie made a not-so-humble response to him, "Mr. Powers, the way I see it, one of us will get first and the other one second." His prophetic words became reality when Cowan Powers took the fifty-dollar first prize and Charlie won the twenty-five-dollar second prize.[6] Receiving a total of thirty dollars for standing on a big stage and doing what he loved to do best made Charlie begin thinking about using his fiddle to acquire even more money. With all this attention and the prospect of making money, he continued to entertain the thought that possibly it was meant for him to play this kind of music professionally.

More employment opportunities came along for the Bowman brothers when they were called upon to perform at the Watauga Swimming Pool in Johnson City. Charlie and His Brothers began routinely playing music at this unlikely venue when the management decided to combine music and dancing with swimming to boost the attendance at the pool. People came to hear the music even if they had no intention of swimming. The local *Johnson City Chronicle* advertised these appearances in a unique way by getting their readers to read the classified ads in their newspapers. They routinely awarded two people a pair of free tickets to the swimming establishment by burying their names inside the classified ads. For example, under the heading "Houses for Sale," a typical ad would read "Mr. John Doe of 123 Anywhere Street has two tickets to the Watauga Swimming Pool at the Chronicle Office." Readers needed to closely examine all the ads to see if their name appeared. The winners were rewarded with a chance to hear Charlie Bowman and His Brothers play old-time Appalachian style music.[7]

In mid-1924, another financial opportunity literally came knocking at Charlie's door when a Mr. Hess from the Aeolian Vocalion Company visited him at his Gray Station home to discuss a potential recording contract with their Red Label series. It is not known if the offer included the Bowman brothers. For reasons not known, Charlie declined the lucrative invitation, which he would later proclaim was the biggest and dumbest mistake of his life. Mr. Hess drove to nearby Morristown, Tennessee, and promptly signed seventy-three-year-old veteran fiddler Uncle Am Stuart, who, according to an old magazine of that era, "smokes cigarettes, drinks corn 'likker', likes the girls and plays a wicked fiddle." Like most fiddlers, he could not read music and played by ear. At the occasion of this visit, Uncle Am was a district manager for a local burglarproof lock company.[8] Having been born before the Civil War and knowing all the fiddle tunes from that era, the veteran fiddler was well known all over the area for playing his music at local dances. Charlie would later become friends with Uncle Am and tour with him when he occasionally played with the Hill Billies. Tony Alderman, an original member of the Hill Billies, remembered when Uncle Am would come on stage at the end of a show and ask the audience if they knew of someone who loved their kind of music but was too sick or poor to attend the show. If anyone identified such a person, Uncle Am would hand over all the money he earned that night to give to that person, displaying the generosity of this great fiddler. Tony called him a polished southern gentleman. Stuart recorded several songs for Vocalion in New York on June 12, 1924: "Grey Eagle," "Cumberland Gap," "Leather Britches," "Sally Goodin," "Billy in the Lowground," "Rye-Straw," "Forky Deer," "Old Liza Jane," "Dixie," "Old Granny Rattle-Trap," "Sourwood Mountain," "George Boker," and "Waggoner."[9] While Charlie missed an opportunity with Vocalion Records, more prospects would come later.

In an interview of Ernie Hodges, another accomplished musician, by country music historian Dr. Charles Wolfe, the fiddler was asked if Uncle Am Stuart influenced Charlie Bowman's style of fiddling:

> Charlie never mentioned him [Uncle Am] in that respect to me. One fiddler playing with another is likely to pick up a few things. That's how they learn it. But Charlie couldn't be described as a student of Uncle Am. Charlie was very musical, and he heard other fiddlers and he never had any special heroes among them.

Ernie also commented about how serious Uncle Am always was and how the others would play practical jokes on him:

> All I got from him (Uncle Am) was through Charlie Bowman. Charlie played with him. He told me he was a right testy old fellow. The boys

were all great on playing tricks after the show. So one night, Charlie told me, they all went out having a good time. Some of them had imbibed a little too much. Anyway one came back, and Uncle Am had gone to bed. Uncle Am was absolutely terrified of snakes, especially rattlesnakes, so one of the boys came in and found a stuffed rattlesnake downstairs. It was a good idea, so he, Uncle Am hadn't quite gone to bed—he slipped it under his bed and lay the cover down on it. They said they almost had to leave town when Uncle Am pulled that cover back and found that stuffed rattlesnake in there. They never would tell him who it was because they were afraid he'd kill him.[10]

Uncle Am mailed a photograph to Charlie just days before the senior fiddler died on March 17, 1926. Charlie wrote these words on the back of the photo: "Here is Uncle Am, his son's wife and grandchild. I received this picture from Uncle Am the day before he died. Take care of it." He gave the picture to Fannie for safekeeping, which shows how important Uncle Am was to Charlie. The family honored this request.

"Leather Britches," one of Uncle Am's fiddle tunes, is a special favorite of old-time musicians. While one version of the song does indeed involve leather pants, in the South the term refers to beans. Leather britches afforded mountain people a unique way to eat tasty green beans throughout the year. As soon as the beans were mature, they were strung together with a large sewing needle and thread. Then they were placed in the sun to dry for several days, after which they were hung in the barn for further drying. It was important that the beans not touch anything, so as to dry properly and not rot. Once they were completely dry, they were put in a cloth or paper sack and stored until winter. When the family wanted some green beans, a string of them was washed and soaked overnight. The beans were then removed from the string and cooked the way any fresh green beans would be prepared, with a little salt, pepper, and fatback. Leather britches tasted as good as garden fresh green beans; some would argue that they were even better. Experienced fiddlers are attracted to this song because of the rolling arpeggios, which offer bowing and fingering challenges.

Sometimes opportunities present themselves through unusual circumstances. Fiddlin' Arthur Smith from Mars Hill, North Carolina, was a great legendary fiddler who was almost ten years younger than Charlie. On one occasion, Charlie and His Brothers and Arthur Smith and his group were performing in nearby Erwin, Tennessee, on the same night but at separate venues. It is unusual that two fiddle concerts were scheduled on the same night in a town as diminutive as Erwin. The weather was so inclement that night that both concerts were at risk of being canceled, so Charlie and Arthur decided to combine their shows. Perhaps they reasoned that two well-known fiddlers would overcome any bad

Uncle Am Stuart and his daughter-in-law and grandson. Pauline
Bowman Huggans Collection.

weather concerns in East Tennessee. Their reasoning was correct; the show was
well attended.

The Upper East Tennessee area was fast becoming blessed with many good
old-time musicians, and one did not have to venture very far to find some of the
best traditional Appalachian music in existence. Charlie routinely played music
with some of these musicians, including Dudley Vance, John Dykes, and Robert
Houston Blizard. Robert's young son, Ralph, remembered Charlie routinely coming to their house and playing music for hours on the porch with his father. The
young lad would listen intently, and while he was forbidden to play his father's
fiddle at first, Ralph disobeyed and learned to play it anyway, later showing his
dad just how good a fiddler he had become. Ralph credits Charlie Bowman
with influencing his style of old-time long bow fiddling. Ralph, founder of the

Traditional Appalachian Musical Heritage Association (TAMHA), would later go on to win many state and national awards, including the 2002 North American Fiddler's Hall of Fame, the 2002 National Heritage Fellowship Award, and the 2003 Tennessee Governor's Award in the Arts.

The way fiddlers bow largely distinguishes them from their peers, some having a very individualized style. Learning to bow correctly is an important element in the technique. Fiddlers tend to be labeled as "short bow" or "long bow" artists. The terms has nothing to do with the length of the bow but rather how much of it is used before the fiddler reverses direction. Short bow, or "jiggy bow," fiddlers mostly use syncopated up and down motions as they fiddle, while long bow fiddlers routinely take the bow from one end to the other before reversing it. Obviously, all fiddlers use a degree of both as they fiddle. Examples of well-known long bow fiddlers include Eck Robertson, Fiddlin' Arthur Smith, and bluegrass fiddler Kenny Baker.

As 1924 ended, Bob Taylor's prophetic words about a fiddler's instrument being his bride, with the honeymoon lasting forever, were starting to be fulfilled for Tennessee Charlie. He was about to make the most important decision of his life, a resolve that would take him out of the Upper East Tennessee area and onto stages all across the country. The Hill Billies were soon coming to town with one top priority in mind: to recruit Fiddlin' Charlie Bowman into their band.

Chapter 4

A HILLBILLY HILL BILLIE

In the spring of 1924 an event took place in Galax, Virginia, that would have a dramatic influence on Charlie Bowman's musical career in just over a year. This occurred at about the same time as the fiddle contest at the Deluxe Theatre in Johnson City. Alonzo Elvis Alderman, better known as "Tony," looked out his window while cutting a customer's hair in his downtown barbershop and saw a man walking down the street carrying a guitar. After finishing with the customer, the barber dashed down the street, located the chap, and introduced himself. The guitar-toting person was Joe Hopkins, a railroad express agent from White Top Gap, Virginia. Since business was sluggish at the barbershop at that very instant, Tony asked Joe to wait until he could run home and fetch his fiddle. Alderman had previously switched from French horn to fiddle after his father had purchased one and brought it home. Ernest "Pop" Stoneman, a family friend, and future legend in his own right, taught the young fellow to play it.

When Tony returned to his shop, the two began playing music together. Shortly thereafter, Joe's brother, Al, came by for a shave and made the event a trio. Unknown to these young men at the time, a soon-to-be famous string band was in the making. The three-person group quickly grew to four when clawhammer banjo player and local storekeeper John Rector from Fines, Virginia, heard about the threesome and decided to make it a quartet. Al assumed the role of lead singer, piano player, and leader of the group. An important musical assemblage that would long be remembered in the annals of time was established that day in the vicinity of Tony Alderman's barbershop, but surprisingly it would be another seven months before their newly formed band acquired a name.[1]

John Rector proved to be a valuable asset to the foursome. He had impressive credentials, having previously played with Henry Whitter and James Sutphin in the Virginia Breakdowners, with whom he had earlier made some records in New York City. When John, anxious to make a return trip to New York, asked the boys if they wanted to go back with him to perform and record for Victor Records, they unanimously responded in the affirmative. This was a bold move for them, as it meant leaving their secular jobs and being away from their families for long periods to travel and play music professionally. Nevertheless, the four musicians went to New York in the summer of 1924 in Al Hopkins's 1921 Model T Ford, traveling for three days over less than desirable roadways.[2]

When these aspiring musicians arrived in the Big Apple, they met with some surprises as soon as they entered the studio to record the predetermined six songs they had selected. Clifford Cairns, Victor's A&R man, would not allow them to use their own instruments; instead, they were required to play Victor studio instruments that were attached to a single large recording horn used to magnify the sound. Many years later, Tony recalled this session:

> We played in front of a big horn, banjo ten feet back in the corner. I was
> fiddling like mad on a fiddle with a horn on it, which I couldn't hear.
> John Rector couldn't hear me either, and no one could hear the guitar.
> Nobody could hear anybody else, to tell the truth. Victor played the
> record back to us and my father could have done better on his Edison.
> No reflection on Victor, it was us. So we went home a little sad and
> ashamed that we had not done better.[3]

Tony showed humility in his comments because, truthfully, the fault of the session was in Victor's recording techniques, which were not yet developed to an acceptable standard. The boys left New York realizing the ordeal had been a dismal failure; no records from this session were produced. However, a second recording opportunity materialized shortly.

In early January 1925 the four young gentlemen were invited back to New York City, this time to record for Okeh Records. They were assured that this record company had the latest state-of-the-art sound recording equipment and that the problems they experienced previously with Victor Records would not be a recurring concern. This time, John Rector drove them to New York City in his new 1925 Dodge. In spite of the group riding in a new automobile, the trip was challenging for them. The weather was so cold they wrapped hot bricks in news-papers and sat on them to help keep warm, a trick often used by country people to keep their beds warm at night. On the way, they stopped by to see the Hopkins's brothers' father, who lived in Washington, D.C. The elder Hopkins made a com-ment that would soon figure into the naming of their band. He laughingly asked them, "What d'you hillbillies think you'll do up there?"[4] When the group arrived at the Okeh Records New York studio on January 15, 1925, legendary music pio-neer Ralph Peer, who had not yet made the switch from Okeh to Victor Records, met them. They recorded six songs: "Old Joe Clark," "Silly Bill," "Cripple Creek," "Whoa! Mule," "Sally Ann," and "Old Time Cinda."[5] These were the days of the ten-inch breakable 78-rpm records, played on a machine with a needle that was not much better than a nail. Unlike with the previous recording session, they were allowed to use their own instruments. Tony remembered a humorous event from this second session:

> The microphones we were using were composed of graphite elements and if you stomped your foot very hard the crystals would mesh and a $200 microphone would be ruined. Now heck, us country boy's couldn't play our music without tappin' our foot to the rhythm, so they finally put rubber pads under our feet so that we wouldn't ruin the mikes.[6]

The young musicians were quite satisfied with the way they sounded on this second session. At the conclusion of it, Ralph Peer asked Al the name of his group and was astounded to learn that they did not have one, even with their increasing popularity. Ralph explained to him that they needed a name to put on the record labels. Al's classic response to Mr. Peer was that they were nothing but a bunch of hillbillies from North Carolina and Virginia, and that he could just call them anything. Taking a clue from Al's reply, Ralph immediately turned to his secretary, Madge, and told her to call the group "The Hill Billies." Al recalled that she wrote down the name in shorthand.[7] Al could have suggested that they be called Al Hopkins and His Hill Billies since he was the leader of the group, but he chose not to. It is quite possible that had the elder Mr. Hopkins not said what he did when the boys stopped by to see him, Al would not have answered the way he did, and Ralph would have consequently named them something else. It is interesting that he called them the "Hill Billies" and not the "Hillbillies." While the word "hillbilly" was not new, using it to define a kind of musical genre was unique. Reportedly, when Earnest "Pop" Stoneman heard about their new group designation, he laughed until tears came to his eyes and told them that they had a name that nobody could top.

The boys readily accepted the "Hill Billies" to define their musical genre even though many people distanced themselves from this word, considering a hillbilly to be a crude, uneducated person, depicted by such images as Li'l Abner, Ma and Pa Kettle, Lum and Abner, Tennessee Ernie Ford, Cousin Minnie Pearle, Rod Brasfield, Snuffy Smith, Homer and Jethro, *Hee Haw, The Andy Griffith Show,* and *The Beverly Hillbillies.* The word "hillbilly" was first coined in April 1900 when the *New York Journal* ran an article on "Hill Billies" with this description: "a free and untrammeled white citizen . . . who lives in the hills, has no means to speak of, dresses as he can, talks as he pleases, drinks whiskey when he gets it, and fires off his revolver as the fancy takes him."[8] Al's band looked like hillbillies, acted like hillbillies, sang like hillbillies, and played their music like hillbillies—because they were hillbillies and quite proud of it. The word "hillbilly" means mountain man, and mountain men they were. The name proved so successful that other bands began copying it. Consequently, the Hill Billies hired a

Washington lawyer to incorporate the name "Al Hopkins's Original Hill Billies Inc" but failed to secure legal rights to the name. Thus, other bands continued using the name: the Blue Ridge Hillbillies, the Lonesome Valley Hill Billies, the Beverly Hillbillies, the Kentucky Hillbillies, the North Carolina Hill Billies, and the Southern Hill Billies. Tony Alderman once confided that they really were not attempting to stop use of the word; they just felt proud that they were the first to coin it and were truly the original Hill Billies.

Charlie first met the Hill Billies in 1924 when Al and his group drove to the Bowman log house in Gray Station. By this time another brother, John Hopkins, was playing ukulele with the group. A fourth brother, Elmer Hopkins, occasionally played harmonica for the band but never recorded with them. They had come to participate in Johnson City's second fiddle contest, an event won by Dedrick Harris. The Hill Billies' extensive touring made them quite well known. They became aware of Charlie's particular style of fiddling, as well as the numerous fiddle contests he had won. Not seeing the fiddler at the contest, they decided to visit him at his house and talk to him about the possibility of becoming a member of their group. The men pulled up in the front yard of the log house, and Charlie invited them inside. Al said that his father lived in Washington, D.C., and that they all could stay with him at no cost until they could get on their feet financially. He also confided that he eventually wanted his group to go to New

Mountain City Fiddlers Convention, May 1925. *Left to right:* John Hopkins, Al Hopkins, Tony Alderman, John Rector, Uncle Am Stuart, and Fiddlin' John Carson. Jennie Bowman Cain Collection.

A HILLBILLY HILL BILLIE

York and make some more records. Al shared with Charlie his belief that they could all make a decent living doing what they all loved best, playing old-time Appalachian style music. The hillbilly brand of music was catching on by 1924, due largely to the likes of Fiddlin' John Carson and Uncle Am Stuart.

While Al's invitation to travel and make money on the road certainly enticed Charlie, he told him that he really wasn't interested. Since he was thirty-five years old with a wife and seven children still living at home, he reasoned that playing in this band would mean being on the road too much. Al persistently tried to convince the fiddler to join them, but, when he recognized he was not succeeding, he herded the group back to their car and departed. Little did Charlie know then that this would not be the last of the Hill Billies. They made good on their promise by journeying to Washington, D.C., and living with Mr. and Mrs. Hopkins.

Friday and Saturday, May 8 and 9, 1925, would prove to be the turning point in the life of Fiddlin' Charlie Bowman. Those were the dates that the now famous inaugural Mountain City Fiddlers Convention was held in Johnson County near the North Carolina line, about fifty miles from Johnson City. This event, sponsored by the local Ku Klux Klan, began as an effort to raise money for a local farmer who had fallen on difficult times.[9] To give some perspective of the occasion, when Cumberland Plateau resident Uncle Jimmy Thompson rode into Nashville on November 28, 1925, to fiddle on WSM's ("We Shield Millions") very first Grand Ole Opry radio broadcast, he had no idea he would be ushering in a country music tradition. Likewise, when Charlie Bowman arrived in Mountain City on May 8, 1925, to participate in this premier fiddlers convention, he had no idea he was destined to become a pioneer in the world of old-time Appalachian

Mountain City Fiddlers Convention, May 1925. Charlie Bowman *(kneeling, second from left)* and Argil *(third from left)*. Jennie Bowman Cain Collection.

style country music. The Mountain City event occurred a full six months before Nashville's Grand Ole Opry went on the air. Family members cannot explain why Elbert and Walter did not attend the convention; only Charlie and Argil made the trip that day.

Every old-time musician who ever was or hoped to be was in attendance. While there had been other fiddler conventions with good attendance, the Mountain City extravaganza brought all the old-time musicians together into one location. A famous photograph of thirty well-known performers is a "who's who" of old-time musicians. In addition to Charlie and Argil, others included Edgar Hickam, Demp Harris, Eva Ashley Moore, Ralph Story, B. K. "Bertie" Jenkins, Walt Bacon, Roby Chinouth, Lonnie Durham, the Hopkins brothers (Al, John, and Joe), Uncle Am Stuart, John Rector, G. B Grayson, Clarence "Tom" Ashley, the Powers family (Cowan, Charlie, Ada, Carrie Belle, and Orpha Lou), John Carson, Roe Greene, Sam Dykes, Dudley Vance, Smokey Davis, Dedrick Harris, and Waits Wiseman.[10]

Charlie once estimated that hundreds of musicians were there, "so many you couldn't stir them with a stick." After the high school auditorium was filled to capacity almost collapsing the floor, the grammar school auditorium and courthouse were opened. Still, some people had to be turned away. Music lovers were all over the grounds, standing on cars and sitting in windows and anywhere else they could hear and get a glimpse of the musicians. Considering this was 1925, prize money of sixty dollars was quite impressive, with a twenty-dollar gold piece going to the winner and another forty dollars split among the others. Dudley Vance of Bluff City won first prize with the song "Twinkle Little Star," Charlie won second with "Sally Ann," and Uncle Am Stuart won third. Another winner was G. B. Grayson, who played "Cumberland Gap."[11]

The Buster Brown Shoe Company was a sponsor of the Mountain City event. Its leading salesman, Mr. N. C. Parsons, presented Charlie with a unique enterprising opportunity.[12] He had seen him buck dance and approached him about doing a movie commercial for his company, which Charlie graciously accepted. Jennie Bowman had two photographs in her scrapbook. One showed the Buster Brown representatives standing alongside an old Model A Ford and the other revealed Charlie's feet buck dancing in a pair of Buster Brown shoes. She penned these words on the back of the photograph:

> Back before sound pictures, the Buster Brown Shoe Company paid
> Charlie to do a buck dance wearing Buster Brown shoes. It was shown
> on theatre screens. The advertisement said you could treat Buster Brown
> Shoes as rough as you can and they will take the punishment. This is a
> picture of Charlie's feet doing a buck dance.[13]

Buster Brown Shoe Company representatives, sponsor of the 1925 Mountain City Fiddlers Convention. The man is believed to be Mr. N. C. Parsons. Jennie Bowman Cain Collection.

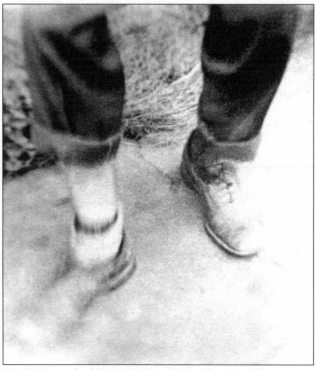

Charlie Bowman buck dancing in Buster Brown shoes. Jennie Bowman Cain Collection.

This venture was about two years before the first sound pictures. Until then, Charlie had previously been recognized for his hands through his fiddle. Now he was being acknowledged for his feet through his rugged Buster Brown shoes. The Appalachian-mountain buck dance, as performed by European-Americans, generally begins with a stamp, followed by a forward heel brush and a toe slap with the free foot. The dancer's posture is straighter than the Appalachian clogger's but more relaxed than the English and Irish step dancer's. Buck dancing is usually done without a partner.[14]

To say the 1925 Mountain City Fiddlers Convention was a great success is an understatement, as affirmed in an excerpt from the May 12, 1925, edition of the Bristol, Tennessee, *Herald Courier:*

> The fiddlers' convention that was staged . . . at this place last Friday night, and continuing through Saturday night was a decided success. Some of the most noted fiddlers for many miles around were present. John Carson, the famous old-time fiddler of Atlanta was here, also A.G. Stuart of Morristown, brother of the noted preacher; George Stuart, the Group from Galax, VA; the Powers family of Dungannon, Va., Bowman brothers of Johnson City, Tenn., Johnson brothers of Boone, N.C. and others from sections in North Carolina, Virginia and Tennessee.
>
> The contestants in the various string bands were awarded liberal cash prizes . . . [Winners included] the Powers family and the Group of Galax, Va., and the Bowman brothers of Johnson City and the Johnson brothers, of N.C.
>
> Everybody was well pleased with the splendid manner in which the various performers acquitted themselves in their respective parts, especially that rendered by Mr. Carson as many of his records have been heard in various parts of the United States.[15]

During this convention, Charlie encountered the Hill Billies a second time. It is quite possible that the fiddler's main motive for attending was the hope of meeting the Hill Billies again and possibly becoming one of them. Since Al had not yet found a suitable second fiddler for his band, he again extended his invitation to Charlie. This time the East Tennessean enthusiastically accepted the offer but insisted that he would have to wait a couple of months until after the birth of his and Fannie's eighth child, Hansel. The expectant father reasoned that this would give him enough time to break the news to his pregnant wife and attempt to convince her that he was making the correct decision for the family.

Why would Charlie refuse Al Hopkins's request in 1924 yet eagerly accept his offer only a year later? What happened to change his mind in twelve months? Being thirty-six years old, Charlie might have reasoned that while he was in his prime as a musician, time was marching on. Elbert, Walter, and Argil had absolutely no interest in going on the road with him; they were content to perform close to home so they could be with their respective families. Had Alfred been interested in his brother's music, he could have become their agent. He was definitely capable, with his maturity and strong business sense. Charlie was now obviously torn between two options—making money touring or remaining at home with his ever-growing family. His logic was likely that he could better provide for them financially by performing professionally rather than staying in Gray Station and working odd jobs. Since he had barely traveled outside the local East Tennessee area, this new venture would also afford him an opportunity to see the rest of the country.

Charlie had to weigh the fact that he was leaving behind a thirty-nine-year-old wife and eight relatively young children. By this time, Elmer and Joe were married with families of their own; the remaining eight children, however, ranged from a newborn to fourteen years of age. Perhaps he reasoned that his two oldest daughters, Pauline and Jennie, were now mature enough to assist with the chores around the log house. Also, his sister's boy, Hobart Hale and his wife, Pearl, who lived just down the hill from their house, would be available when needed. Additionally, Charlie was keenly aware that he could rely on his six brothers and sisters and their spouses to offer assistance to his wife and children. His rationale apparently convinced him that he was doing the proper thing. Even with Charlie on the road, his family continued to grow with Melba and Jean, the last two children, who came along within five years of their father's initial departure. When the champion fiddler joined the Hill Billies in 1925, he did not likely predict just how successful his career would be or that he would be touring for twenty-two years as a part of other bands or as a leader of his own.

Winning second place at the Mountain City Fiddlers Convention with so many well-known and talented fiddlers competing against him convinced Charlie that he had sufficient talent to make a significant amount of money playing the kind of music he and his fans loved. Joining the Hill Billies seemed to provide the vehicle for accomplishing that dream. It was appropriate that Charlie won second place playing the fiddle tune "Sally Ann":

> Going to the wedding, Sally Ann,
> Going to the wedding, Sally Ann,
> Sift that meal and save your bran,
> I'm going home with Sally Ann.
>
> *Chorus:*
> I'm gonna marry you Sal, Sal,
> I'm gonna marry you Sally Ann.[16]

Charlie's fiddle might just as well have been named Sally Ann. Without fully recognizing it, he was choosing it over Fannie Mae. While he loved them both, by his very actions he was overtly making a choice of one over the other. He would soon "divorce" Fannie Mae, his bride of fourteen years, and "marry" his fiddle. Regardless of Charlie's rationale to travel with the Hill Billies, his doing so would cost him significantly within the next ten years. The price tag for being away from his family for extended periods of time would prove to be more expensive than he perceived. It is likely that Charlie began to travel with the Hill Billies in July or August of 1925, just weeks after Hansel was born. According to a 1926 *Radio Digest*, the "marriage" between Charlie and the Hill Billies went smoothly because "they all talked the same language, played the same tunes and no rehearsals were needed to break in the new trouper."[17]

With Tony Alderman as a good fiddler and a top-notch comedian, why would Al want to hire Charlie? Why would he need two fiddlers, as he certainly had no intention of getting rid of Tony? The Hill Billies had become famous primarily because of their showmanship, which is not to say they were not good musicians—they were. Their primary focus, however, was on their comedy routines, singing, and zany outfits. A shrewd businessman, Al wanted to retain the showmanship aspect that had brought the band to fame, but he also wanted them to be the best instrumental string band in the country. Twin fiddles offered two distinct advantages for the band. First, they provided amplification, which was often a problem. Second, they gave fullness of sound, with one fiddler playing the melody and the other playing the harmony. Charlie fit this bill twofold because, while he too liked to tell jokes, dress up in zany outfits, and do some crazy things on stage, there was a serious side of him that made him want to play his fiddle, getting everything out of it that he could. With Fiddlin' Charlie Bowman on board, the Hill Billies were even more compelling and prepared to dive into the fierce competition of vaudeville.

Charlie's decision to tour with Al and the boys paid off immediately when the band began playing music for four or five hours on WRC, a radio station in Washington D.C. Baskets of mail, numerous telegrams, and many long distance phone calls poured in to the station, placing the boys in high demand. Al once made a bold statement over the air that there was not a single old-time tune that his band could not play, and he further challenged the listeners to submit their requests. Subsequently, people invited them to play music for their organizations. This unanticipated popularity caused them to start touring around the local area, at both indoor and outdoor venues.

As Charlie had predicted, the hillbillies began to receive income that far exceeded anything they had earned before. They made as much as thirty to forty-five dollars a night in the days when eight dollars per week was considered a

The Hill Billies. *Left to right:* Tony Alderman, John Hopkins, Charlie Bowman, and Al Hopkins. Jennie Bowman Cain Collection.

decent salary. The admission price to one of their performances ranged from twenty-five to fifty cents, and they frequently filled large auditoriums and open-air theaters.[18] Typical of the publicity the Hill Billies were getting is illustrated in a January 10, 1926, letter addressed to WRC from two appreciative listeners in Mt. Sterling, Ohio:

> Dear Sirs . . . In appreciation of our reception of your program given
> by Charlie Bowman and the Hill Billies, we filled out the enclosed card
> and upon reading the enclosed clippings from the *Ohio State Journal*
> of Columbus this morning decided to enclose them as they express our
> sentiments thoroughly. We are looking forward to their return. . . . Very
> truly yours . . . Dr. & Mrs. D. Starr.[19]

Tennessee Charlie must have been flattered that the letter writer singled him out, implying that he was leader of the band. Further, a lengthy critique in a Columbus, Ohio, newspaper showed approval of the group's style of music and particular esteem for their new trouper:

> There have been fiddling contests held all over the country. Some of
> the champions chosen we have been able to hear and we didn't care

particularly for them because we didn't like the brand of music they had to offer. We have also heard many old-time fiddlers broadcasting from stations all over the country, and always turned to something that interests us more.

It remained for WRC at Washington to come out Saturday evening with an organization that could hold us from the beginning to the end of the program, and the entertainment offered by the Hill Billies from that station takes front rank as to interest and worth.

These Hill Billies, as they wished to be called, came from the mountain regions of our southern states with a collection of old-time melodies, some of which have never been written down but have been passed on from fiddler to fiddler through the generations. At least one of the musicians was a real champion, if that has anything to do with it for he had won twenty-eight out of thirty-two contests in which he had participated. He called himself Fiddling Charlie Bowman, champion of East Tennessee, and if he is only a sectional champ, we'd like very much to hear the state prize fiddler. The latter must be really good.

The repertoire consisted of orchestral numbers, fiddlers, and banjos; a quartet, and banjo and violin as well as vocal solos. Their first number was "Goin' Down the Road Feeling Bad" with a vocal refrain. They repeated with "Oh, Miss Lisa, Po Gal" and if anyone cared to roll back the rugs it would have been possible to have a real shindig, for the time to their music was just about the catchiest we have heard lately.

Then Fiddlin' Charlie came to bat with two violin solos, descriptive numbers, that for sheer picturesqueness were hard to beat. The first was "Cacklin' Hen," and Charlie had the cackle there just as natural as life. His next was "The Fox Chase" with a few descriptive remarks to round out the listener's picture. He put in on the violin the baying of hounds hot on the trail, hounds that were running hard and away from the hunter. Incidentally, the fiddler had a lot of "stuff" that could be used in some of our present day violinists in high-class dance bands.

The quartet sang a song that had some of the "dirtiest swipes" in it that it is possible to get in any quartet song, and when they came to "Carry Me Back to Ole Virginny," they left out all suggestion of 'barber-shop.' The voices didn't blend so well, but they knew how to sing just the same.

We haven't mentioned the banjo player who was ever bit as hot as the rest in the solos he played. It was far and away the best program of its kind we have ever listened to, and we don't expect to hear another like it until the Hill Billies come back to some broadcasting stations.[20]

While not actively involved in the music of his four younger brothers, Alfred Bowman retained some items in his personal collection from their performance days. One was a March 26, 1926, *Radio Digest Illustrated* magazine, a weekly ten-cent publication listing all the radio stations and their programming. It featured the Hill Billies in an article titled "Hill Billies Capture WRC, Boys from Blue Ridge Mountains Take Washington With Guitars, Fiddles, and Banjos; Open New Line of American Airs." This magazine played a major role in bringing the Hill Billies into national prominence. The group was lauded for its music and more:

> A few weeks ago, Radio Station WRC at Washington, D.C. broadcast a concert by an organization called "The Hill Billies." The response was astonishing. Letters and post cards arrived from the mountains of Tennessee, from the hills of Kentucky and the Carolinas and the Blue Ridge counties of Maryland and Virginia. Phone calls, local and long distance, demanded favorite numbers, and repeats, and what not. A voice with a distinct Georgia drawl asked that they play "Long Eared Mule" and added the significant remark, "You all can't fool me, ah know where them boys come from. They's Hill Billies for suah. They ain't nobody kin play that music 'thout they is bawn in the hills and brung up thar." And he was right. The Hill Billies are really boys from the ranges that skirt the east coast states. They are six keen-eyed, ruddy-cheeked youths who have captured the rhythms of the hills, and who, with fiddles and other stringed instruments, present the classics of the country entertainments.
>
> They can pull the innards from an automobile, build a radio set or grace a drawing room. They can sing a Negro spiritual to suit the longest-faced deacon, or they can turn it into a "can't-keep-still-your-foot" country-dance. They can wield a double-bit ax or pick a pianissimo. Al rumbles a deep base lead in "Get Away Jordan." And jumps to a Tyrolean yodel in "Sleep, Baby, Sleep." If John gets tired of singing baritone in the quartet, he just grabs Elmer's second tenor part, and Elmer can shift to baritone or get out the race. Bowman and Alderman present a stunt in which each bows the other's fiddle and fingers his own.[21]

Fiddlin' Charlie could play fifteen standard and some not-so-conventional instruments, such as brooms, saws, washtubs, and thick balloons, to the delight of his fans. His music has been described as "real corn on the cob, shuck your own" fiddle music. A 1926 *Washington Times* newspaper article reported, "He can pull music out of anything from a one-string banjo to an underfeed furnace."[22] The 1926 *Radio Digest* article further declared:

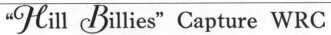

Radio Digest Illustrated, March 6, 1926. Alfred Bowman Collection.

Charlie plays any ding-busted stringed instrument that is or can be.
. . . He does mean things with a banjo, a guitar is more easy meal to his
grist, while the fiddle—he actually makes a fiddle sit up and bark . . .
imitates two houn' dogs chasing a red fox through the Tennessee hills . . .
fiddles his way through a barnyard selection, introducing the cacklings
of the foul from gobbler to bantam hen.[23]

Since the skilled fiddler had won numerous competitions over the years, radio
station WRC began using his expertise and management skills to coordinate its
own fiddle contests. One such event was featured in the *Washington Times* article

titled "Hill Billy Fiddler Is to Aid in Contest" and offers some insight to the class of music being played in 1926:

> Fiddlin' Charlie Bowman, champion old-time fiddler of most of the territory between the Blue Ridge Mountains and the Mississippi River, is to volunteer his expert advice and management to the old time fiddlers' contest radio station WRC will stage next Tuesday evening.
>
> Charlie Bowman is the bright particular fiddling star of the now famous Hill Billies of Tennessee—the itinerant group of young men who have been singing and fiddling and "guitaring" their way to fame in this section of the country during the past few months.
>
> Some months ago, when Tennessee was much on the front pages and Tennessee doings were causing rifts in friendships as well as discussions among the learned and the eloquent throughout the world [a reference to the Scopes Monkey Trial], attention was called to the fact that the nearest to a simon-pure American was the typical Tennessean of the mountain district.
>
> And Fiddlin' Charlie is all of that. Straight as an arrow, just a bit more than 30 years of age and the father of eight children, his whole family history is written in the rocks and trails and roadways around Johnson City, Tennessee.
>
> The contest takes places so far as the date is now set—next Tuesday evening.
>
> The tentative rules for the contest as far as the suggestions of Charlie Bowman go are very simple: The identity of each fiddler will be made known to the radio audience by number. Each fiddler may have an accompanist if he so desires and can provide. The accompanist may play the piano, banjo, mouth organ, or any musical instrument. Each fiddler pays his own expenses.[24]

While it is not known how many return visits the Hill Billies made to the Mountain City Fiddlers Convention, it is acknowledged, however, that they attended the 1926 event. This is based on information contained in a 1960 record collector publication on the subject of Tony Alderman:

> A very versatile man was he in many respects, in 1926 he built a small radio station and set it up on one occasion in the lobby of a hotel in Mountain City, Tennessee during a fiddler's convention there and at least 100 artists did some broadcasting over it. They were kept busy till after 3 o'clock in the morning filling requests called in over the

telephone. He also built a loud speaker for the show for ballyhoo pur-
poses and was also a good photographer.[25]

Within a few years, Jennie Bowman would enter this convention, competing
with one of the Powers Family girls. Jennie won a five-pound box of Whitman
chocolates after playing "Ragged Annie" on her fiddle.

True to his word, at least initially, Charlie returned to his Gray Station home
to see his family. On each trip, people from all over East Tennessee gave him
a hero's welcome, making him a celebrity of sorts. The log house became so
crowded that many people spilled into the yard. Such outpouring of fan support,
while encouraging to Charlie, robbed his family and him of quality time together.
With fame and fortune coming his way, Fiddlin' Charlie Bowman was beginning to look, act, and feel like a celebrity. The Hill Billies' performance schedules
became so hectic at times that he was not able to return home as frequently as he
would have liked and as often as he promised Fannie that he would.

The group made several publicity photographs promoting the comedic
aspect of their shows. In one of these pictures, Charlie is playing a mouth harp
and wearing a coat and tie (a rarity for him), while the others are decked out in
bib overalls. It should be noted that their humor went far beyond the written
script, which often appeared to be corny and not very funny. They made people
roll in laughter by the clever combination of the jokes they told, the zany outfits
they wore, the way they acted, the expressions on their faces, their body language,
their vocal inflections, the timing of their monologues, and their keen interac-

The Hill Billies comedy routine. *Left to right:* Tony Alderman, John Hopkins, and Charlie
Bowman. Jennie Bowman Cain Collection.

A HILLBILLY HILL BILLIE

The Hill Billies playing off stage. *Left to right:* Tony Alderman, Charlie Bowman, Al Hopkins, and John Hopkins. Jennie Bowman Cain Collection.

tion with each other. Most acts involved a comedian and a straight man, and they would frequently depart from their script, purposely or inadvertently, and ad-lib their lines. Comedy became a major part of Charlie's performances, especially as he approached his senior years.

The Hill Billies were faced with a quandary when they first began singing together. While most bands typically have a baritone, tenor, bass, and lead singer, all vocalists in the Hill Billies were baritones. Because most of them had a rather wide vocal range, however, they were able to remedy the problem by having Joe sing tenor, Elmer sing baritone, Al sing the lead, and Charlie sing bass. If one of them was absent, the others simply switched parts to compensate for the missing singer.

Saturday, February 19, 1927, was a momentous night for the Hill Billies when they accomplished something of which few string bands can boast. They were invited to perform at a banquet for the White House Correspondents' Association at the Mayflower Hotel in Washington, D.C. The main attendee was the president of the United States, Calvin Coolidge. After their performance, they received a thank-you letter with this letterhead: "Press Room, The White House, Washington." Signed by John Lambert, the president of the association, it was addressed to "Mr. Al Hopkins, Manager, 'The Hill Billies,' Washington, D.C." It said,

Dear Mr. Hopkins:

May I take this opportunity to express the profound appreciation of the White House Correspondents' Association for the splendid entertainment you and the "Hill Billies" so kindly provided at the banquet at the Mayflower Hotel Saturday night.

The novelty of the offering was commented on generally, and it may please you to know that President Coolidge, Speaker Longworth, Senator Reed, of Missouri, and other honor guests made special references to the act in expressing their pleasure at having been present.

The correspondents "covering" the White House and the President are much indebted to you and your colleagues.[26]

Reminiscent of a song, "Them Hill-Billies Are Mountain Williams Now," recorded by another group, the Hoosier Hot Shots, those Washington, D.C., politicians may have received something that night they hadn't seen before. They were likely more accustomed to being entertained by a gathering of upscale "Mountain Williams," but on that night they received a heavy dose of entertainment from a bunch of "Hill Billies," and they apparently loved it.

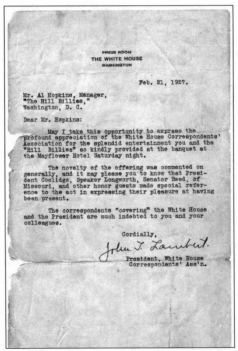

Letter to Al Hopkins from John Lambert, president of the White House Correspondents' Association. Charlie Bowman Collection.

Tony Alderman *(left)* and Charlie Bowman *(right)* bow each other's fiddles while fingering their own. Jennie Bowman Cain Collection.

The role of Charlie's and Tony's fiddling varied, depending primarily on the songs they played. Some tunes were unmistakably meant for one of them, while others were more appropriate for both. During any given concert, a combination of songs featured only Tony on some, Charlie on others, and both as co-fiddlers on the majority. Their twin fiddling was more complementary than competing; each had a role and assumed it to perfection. In a classic photo from that era, the two musicians added new meaning to the term "co-fiddler" when Charlie would stand behind Tony, and each fiddler would bow his own fiddle while simultaneously fingering the other's fiddle. This achievement demanded some precise coordinated timing on the part of both individuals.

In 1927, Ralph Peer switched from Okeh Records to the Victor Recording Company and brought a team from his new company to Bristol, Tennessee, to record some local artists. This was two years after Charlie began touring with the Hill Billies. The Bristol Sessions, as they later became known, have long since been recognized as a major influence in the shaping of country music. Recordings were made of such performers as the Carter Family, Jimmie Rodgers, Earnest Stoneman, Henry Whittier, the Tenneva Ramblers, Uncle Eck Dunford, and several others. As he had done for Okeh Records, Ralph sought talent from the southern Appalachian region for commercial musical records. Since Charlie was on the road performing with the Hill Billies at this particular time, he was unable to participate in the sessions. Had he still been living in Gray Station, it is likely that he would have been included. He would, however, within a year participate in Columbia Records' Johnson City Sessions.

Between mid-1926 and late 1928, the Hill Billies' northeast itinerary included New York City. On four different trips they recorded for jointly owned Brunswick and Vocalion Records. Artist and repertoire man Jimmy O'Keefe orchestrated these efforts. Also, during these visits, they performed on some of the biggest theater stages in the Big Apple, including Broadway. Although there are no known logs of their travels, a few newspaper ads confirmed that they performed for the Keith-Albee Vaudeville Theatre Circuit ("The Great Artists of the World Exclusively"). According to Charlie's oldest daughter, Pauline, while the boys were playing over radio station WRC in Washington, D.C., Mr. Albee heard them and liked their music. Ironically, he had a distaste for radio and rarely listened to it, but on that particular night, he was tuned in when he overheard the Hill Billies' broadcast. He was so captivated with their music that he made a personal trip to the nation's capital to sign them up for some vaudeville shows. This circuit later merged into the Keith-Albee-Orpheum vaudeville circuit and even later into the Radio-Keith-Orpheum Corporation, becoming known as RKO.

A theater flyer for Sunday, April 11, 1926, shows the Hill Billies as part of a nine-act bill:

> 1- "The Last Word in Versatility, Alma Neilson assisted by Dan B. Ely and Dave Rice and The Frivolity Five, This Act Teaming In Entertainment Value;" 2- The Beau Brummel Entertainers, Ed Healy and Allen Cross, Showing the Smartest Style In Song, Exclusive Material Including Almost Everything From Opera To Jazz;" 3- "Special Novelty Attraction, The Popular Novelty Attraction, The Hill Billies, The Music of Hills, Blue Ridge Mountains, Va. To Georgia;" 4- "Extra Added Attraction, Eye and Ear Entertainment, Presented by George Weist and Ray Stanton with Gladys Gerrish and a Company of Broadway Players, Titled 'Rhyme and Reason;' 5- "Added Novelty Feature, The Dainty Terpsichorean Demonstrator, Virginia Bacon of the Wayburn Studies of Stage Dancing, Inc. Entertaining Delightfully and to Master the Charleston;" 6- "The Zellias Sisters, Aerial elegance;" 7- "Gautier's Animated Toyshop;" 8- "Lew Murdock and Mildred May in 'Foot Loose;' and 9- "Harry Jans and Harold Whale, Known as 'Two Good Boys Gone Wrong.'" The theatre featured two shows daily "at reduced prices" at 2:15 and 8:15 with a Sunday Matinee at 3:15. This show consisted of all vaudeville acts on stage with no movies shown.[27]

Another advertisement for Tuesday and Wednesday, July 17 and 18, 1928, at the Elkins Theatre in Elkins, West Virginia, shows the Hill Billies as the headliners:

They Are Coming In Person, The Original Hill Billies with Al Hopkins and His Buckle Busters, Brunswick recording artists and the full troupe of WRC and WJZ radio stars, Most Popular Entertainers.

Two Performances Each Night, First Show At 7 P.M., Second Show At 9 P.M. Great News—Great Entertainment—No Other Act Like It, A Positive Sensation.

Featuring Charlie Bowman, Champion Fiddler Of The South. Elvis Alderman That Funny Comedian And Fiddling Fool With Spark Plug, The 16 Year Old Wonder, Double Show In One With Regular Picture Program, One Hour Of Music, Fun And Comedy By The Hill Billies.

Presenting Al And John Hopkins, The Two Popular Entertainers In Old And New Songs, Frank P. Wilson, King Of The Steel Guitar, This Show Comes Direct To Elkins From The Ritz Theatre, Clarksburg [West Virginia]. Don't Miss It! Best Production Offered In Elkins.

After the first performance of the Hill Billies, we will present to you a moving picture 'Danger Beware'. Columbia Pictures presents 'Stolen Pleasures' featuring Helen Chadwick and Dorothy Revier. A drama of foolish wives and husbands. What would you do if you found your wife in the arms of another man? Who would be to blame, your wife, the other man, or you? Ask yourself this question and then see the powerful dramatic sermon against jealousy and stolen pleasures. It's the story of the foolish husbands and wives of the world.

Also A Two-Reel Comedy, Admission: Children 25 cents—Adults 50 cents, Watch For Casey Jones Following This Program.[28]

The Hill Billies performed in Johnson City at least on one occasion, based on a Thursday, September, 1927, *Johnson City Staff-News* clipping titled "Personnel of Hill Billies Is Given; Play Here Friday":

When the Hill Billies under the direction and management of Al Hopkins appear at the Capital Theatre Friday evening in a concert, the personnel of the stars of the organization will be:

Al Hopkins, manager, pianist, who hails from Mitchell County, North Carolina but who has been a resident of Washington D.C. for the past twenty years.

"Fiddlin' Charlie" Bowman, born and reared in Washington County near Johnson City, one of the best known "fiddlers" in the country.

Elvis Alderman, "Willie Green," champion hand-saw player of the south.

Frank Williams, better known as "Dad" Williams, who is recognized as the leading novelty fiddler of he south. He is a North Carolinian.

Frank [Wilson], another of the Tar Heels, is a whiz of a steel guitar player.

This notable organization, which has been playing big time vaudeville, doing radio broadcasts and making records for leading phonograph companies, will give their full concert at the Capital Friday evening. On Tuesday night, they charmed the banquet guests at the Motorcade Dinner at the John Sevier [Hotel] and many were heard to express their intentions of attending the concert Friday evening in order to hear them again.[29]

Vaudeville survived from 1875 until about 1933. The word "vaudeville" comes from the French phrases "val de Vire," meaning "valley of the river Vire," and "voix de ville," interpreted as "voices of the town." The relatively healthy vaudeville that Charlie knew in 1925 was quite different from the more anemic version he would experience six years later when he began traveling with H. M. Barnes' Blue Ridge Ramblers. Some of the best-known vaudeville circuits were the Keith-Albee, Orpheum, Pantages, Palace, Paramount, Loews, and Hammerstein. The theaters produced a vaudeville bill, scheduling between eight and ten acts per show. This medium was an extension of the medicine and minstrel shows from the early 1800s, which consisted of a three-part program: songs and jokes, skits and specialty acts, and a dramatic presentation. The shows consisted mostly of specialty acts that included songs and jokes, the number and length varying from theater to theater. A wide variety of performers ranged from musicians, singers, dancers, carnival acts, comedians, animal acts, magicians, mimes, acrobats, and even escape artists.

To attract a large audience, the theater would feature some well-known first-class acts as top billing. The type of audiences attending would fluctuate widely between matinee and evening performances. A Saturday afternoon might bring in schoolchildren, mandating the theater to make sure the entertainment was not boring for this age group. On the other hand, the evening crowd would be mostly adults with dissimilar entertainment tastes. None of the performers preferred to be the closing act, as many patrons would leave early to get ahead of the exiting traffic. Instead, they preferred the next to the last prime time slot. At about the same time the Hill Billies were playing in vaudeville, the media had become a two-way conductor, bringing Tin Pan Alley music into the South and old-time southern music into the densely populated industrialized North and Midwest.[30]

Vaudeville, at least initially, was successful for three primary reasons: the performances were family oriented, tickets were reasonably priced, and the variety on stage suited the tastes of nearly everyone present. Those who did not like a particular act had only to sit patiently for a few minutes until something else replaced it.[31] The Hill Billies/Buckle Busters were important cogs in the vaudeville machinery as it approached its waning days.

Chapter 5

RECORDING IN THE BIG APPLE

On April 30 and May 1, 1926, the Hill Billies were in New York City recording eight songs (four 78-rpm records), not for Okeh Records, as they had done in early 1925, but for the jointly owned Brunswick and Vocalion labels.[1] Brunswick started selling records in 1920, with Vocalion following suit in 1921. The two labels remained separate and independently owned until 1924 when Brunswick acquired Vocalion. Initially, the company issued records on both labels. Since the band's songs could potentially be released on either (or in a few instances both), the company chose to employ two different names for the group. Once again, poor Al had to come up with yet another name for his now famous band. This time he simply chose "Al Hopkins and His Buckle Busters," identifying himself as the leader, something he had elected not to do before. Consequently, each time the record company released songs, they used "The Hill Billies" for Vocalion and "Al Hopkins and His Buckle Busters" for Brunswick.

Charlie was obviously captivated with the name Buckle Busters; later in his career he formed a band of his own called "Charlie Bowman and His Buckle Busters." When asked the significance of the term, the entertainer explained that a "buckle buster" was a situation so hilarious that it would cause people to bend over in laughter and bust their belt buckles. The boys had no concern over which label or name was used because they were selling records, busting buckles, and earning an abundance of revenue. Their records sold for seventy-five cents each, a relatively hefty amount of money considering the times. As previously noted, whenever the Hill Billies arrived in New York City for a recording session, they received a bonus contract for appearances on Broadway and other theater stages. Things were going well for these hardy mountaineers.

On the six songs the Hill Billies recorded for the joint labels, Charlie sang and played fiddle or banjo. Interestingly, three of these songs are the same as those recorded at the early 1925 Okeh sessions before Charlie joined the group: "Old Joe Clark," "Silly Bill," and "Cripple Creek." Even the other three songs, "Whoa! Mule," "Sally Ann," and "Old Time Cinda" (shortened to "Cinda"), were rerecorded at future sessions.[2] With such a large repertoire of songs, why would

the group rerecord these six songs? When listening to the six Brunswick/Vocalion selections and the six Okeh ones, it is obvious why Al wanted duel fiddlers in his band. The blend of their music resulted in a louder, fuller, and more robust sound, illustrating that Al Hopkins knew what he was doing when he brought the Gray Station fiddler into his group in 1925.

Two things are unique about the May 1, 1926, session. Only two songs, "The Hickman Rag" and "Possum up a Gum-Stump, Cooney in the Hollow," were recorded that day; strangely, both record labels show Charlie Bowman as the artist, with no mention of the Hill Billies. The former song's label lists "Charlie Bowman, Fiddler, with Piano, Guitar and Ukulele," while the latter shows "Charlie Bowman, Vocal Refrain by Al Hopkins, Fiddler, with Guitar." Why they recorded only two songs that day and why Charlie was the main artist on the labels remains a mystery.

Vocalion records listing Charlie Bowman as the artist. Bob Cox Collection.

Charlie and Al teamed up to record "Donkey on the Railroad Track" about a stubborn donkey sitting on a CC&O railroad track refusing to move for an oncoming train. Al was the narrator, with Charlie in a duel role of imitating both the train and the donkey on his fiddle:

> Jim McCasey on the locomotive leaving Erwin on the CC&O Railroad, John Sifford, engineer, calling his flagman . . . [whistle]. The flagman gives John the highball signal and answers with two short blasts like this . . . [whistle]. The train leaving the yard . . . [engine]. Just outside the yard a road crossing, John pulls the whistle cord something like this . . . [whistle/engine]. Getting up a little bit of steam now going toward Poplar. Just a little further down the road another road crossing . . . [engine/whistle/engine]. John looking out ahead of course discovered some form of livestock on the track but he couldn't tell what it was so he blew the whistle to scare it off . . . [whistle]. Whatever it was, it wouldn't get off so John said I don't want to kill it so I will give it one more chance

... [whistle]. So it wouldn't get off, and of course, the train approaching nearer and nearer [engine]. So by this time, John discovered that it's a good-looking mule, and he hated to kill him so I'll give you one more chance ... [whistle/engine]. The mule wouldn't get off so John said I'll throw the fog into the sun of a gun, and I will knock you off. So this is the way he hit him ... [thump]. And the mule just laughed at John something like this ... [sound of the mule braying after being bumped by the train].[3]

"Mississippi Sawyer" is one of the most widely known fiddle tunes in America. It is named for the uprooted trees, called "sawyers," that would threaten river traffic in the raging floodwaters of the Mississippi River. The rollicking melodies of Charlie's fiddle and John Hopkins's ukulele in unison mimic the tossing and turning of the monstrous logs as they treacherously and haphazardly migrated downstream in the mighty Mississippi River.[4]

"Old Joe Clark" is yet another well-known fiddle tune that crossed the boundaries of three genres: old-time, bluegrass, and country music. The song's title is derived from a veteran of the War of 1812. The tune may have first originated as a children's song with whimsical and crude lyrics:

> Wished I had a nickel, Wished I had a dime,
> Wished I had a pretty girl to kiss and call her mine.
>
> I will not marry an old maid, I'll tell you the reason why,
> Her neck is so long and stringy, I'm afraid she'll never die.
>
> *Chorus:*
> Fare thee well, Old Joe Clark, Fare thee well, I say,
> Fare thee well, Old Joe Clark, I'm a goin' a way.[5]

Record sales from the Hill Billies' first recordings did remarkably well, prompting the group to be invited back to the record studios in New York City October 21–23, 1926, for yet another session. The increasing popularity of their music is evidenced in the fact that they recorded twenty songs in their second session, as compared to only eight in the first. These popular string band performers were definitely on a roll.

Charlie wrote the instrumental tune "East Tennessee Blues" a few years before he began touring with the Hill Billies, winning several fiddle contests with it. While the Hill Billies were preparing for a recording session in New York City, Charlie played the lively tune for Al, who apparently had never heard it. The bandleader agreed to include it in the forthcoming session. Al asked Charlie the name of the song but was told that he had never named it. Perhaps the Tennessee fiddler figured that if Al could have a band with no name, he could certainly

Identical versions of "East Tennessee Blues" with different band names. Bob Cox Collection.

do likewise with a fiddle tune. After listening to the song, Al suggested the title "East Tennessee Blues." Charlie would later say that he wasn't so sure the name fit the melody because it really wasn't a blues song, but he agreed to settle for that title because, after all, Mr. Hopkins was the boss.[6] Al liked the timing of the song. Years later, Ed Kahn (a folk music historian from California), wrote Charlie a letter saying that he thought this was one of the best fiddle tunes he'd ever heard. Obviously, he was not alone; "East Tennessee Blues" remains one of the most popular numbers in America. It was eventually recorded on both Vocalion and Brunswick labels. The flip side of the Vocalion record is "Governor Alf Taylor's Fox Chase," and the reverse side of the Brunswick one is "Round Town Gals."

As mentioned previously, Charlie's dad was likely acquainted with Bob and Alf Taylor because he lived so close to them. The classic tune "Governor Alf Taylor's Fox Chase" was supposed to have taken place on Buffalo Mountain. Only two people perform on the record: Al delivers the narration and Charlie imitates the barking hounds chasing a fox. Each time the dogs run out of hearing range, Al instructs Charlie to play a tune:

> Governor Alf Taylor of Tennessee and his sons, Alf, Nat, Dave, and Blaine, own a kennel of foxhounds, from fifty to one hundred famous dogs. So Uncle Alf and his boys and their good old friend, Ben Jenkins, with his dog, Old Zeke, and Uncle Alf's old hound, Limber, went up on Buffalo Mountain to try out the dogs, especially Old Zeke, to see if he could run a fox. In case the dogs didn't start anything, Uncle Alf took his fiddle along so as to amuse himself and the boys if the dogs happened not to start a fox, but in case they did when they went out of hearing, Uncle Alf furnished a little music all along to entertain the boys himself. So now we go with a tune, a little music, and then we will turn old Limber loose, the best foxhound that ever went in the woods [fiddle

selection]. All right boys, we're are going to turn Old Limber loose now, and we will see what he will do [sound of dog on fiddle].[7]

The song concludes with the boys turning Old Zeke loose to join Old Limber. After going out of hearing range, the two dogs came back with Old Limber catching a red fox and Old Zeke seizing a rabbit.

Dr. Bob Taylor, a grandson of Alf Taylor, related in a 2005 letter to the author a little-known and unique story about Old Limber and his grandfather's bid for governorship of Tennessee:

> Thank you for introducing me to the remarkable music of your great-uncle Charlie Bowman.
>
> I learn from it that my grandfather, Alf Taylor, and Charlie Bowman are quaintly yoked by "Old Limber," the storied Tennessee foxhound. Our forbears collaborated in spreading Limber's little legend.
>
> In 1920, Tennessee Democrats were the majority party, but they were divided on issues, menaced by a national Republican tide and burdened by an unpopular tax that infuriated the farmers.
>
> As Alf Taylor saw it, his chief obstacle to winning the governorship was his age. He was seventy-two years old. His stratagem for assailing the age issue was predictable. He would construct a myth.
>
> The myth would revolve about Old Limber, an aging Walker hound from his sons' substantial pack. Old Limber was approximately age six at the time.
>
> His name was further accentuated by the Old Limber Quartet (often spelled "Quartette"), comprised of three sons (Nat, Alf, Jr., and Dave) and their friend Bob Wardrep.
>
> The Old Limber myth differed from telling to telling, year to year. It was studded with superlatives, digressions, and humorous exaggerations.
>
> Alf Taylor believed that Limber was "the greatest dog that ever lived." His sons' dogs pursued "the finest runners on American soil."
>
> The tall tale would be told from political platforms and before service clubs. It was sometimes coupled with the promotion of Henry Ford's doomed bid to lease dams and purchase nitrate plants in the Muscle Shoals area, a project Taylor believed would deliver cheap power and fertilizer to Tennesseans.

In 1922 a stenographer from a Memphis newspaper, the *Commercial Appeal*, recorded perhaps the only complete printed version of the myth. According to Bob,

> It was set in or near Carter County, although Old Limber's hunting territory also touched other East Tennessee counties, especially Washington.

When the other dogs "heard and recognized the voice of Old Limber it took two men to hold each dog. [Laughter.]" Old Limber led the pack of thirty-two Walker hounds during the last three hours of the chase, which culminated in Happy Valley (Carter County).

Alf indicated that, in the past and in a manner of speaking, he had followed the pack on foot and boasted that he "could break down any boy (of his seven surviving sons) I have behind this pack of Walker dogs after a red fox and have done it a hundred times in the Appalachian Mountains. So get it out of your heads that I am too old to be governor of Tennessee."

Alf Taylor was elected governor in 1920, assisted perhaps by the Old Limber myth.

Bob said that Alf and the Old Limber Quartet went to New York in 1924 and made a record for the Victor label, possibly being an abbreviated version of their campaign routine:

> The Center for Popular Music, Middle Tennessee State University, has an original. On it, the former governor, employing his gift and taste for vivid detail, introduces the Quartet.
>
> He declares that the spirituals they would sing ("Pharaoh's Army Got Drownded" and "Brother Noah Built an Ark") were learned from hearing the master of the hounds (probably an African American named Ace Harding) around the foxhunt campfires. He only refers to Limber and does not recount the hunt story.
>
> Apparently, the composing talents of your great-uncle Charlie Bowman, of Washington County, then embellished the Old Limber myth by setting it to fiddle music.
>
> It thus appears that music was as much a part of the Old Limber myth as the hounds themselves. Music, Alf Taylor, and Limber himself were given immediacy and durability by the recording devices, which by the mid-1920s were obviously attracting southern performers.[8]

The Hill Billies recorded two songs that at first glance would appear to be identical. However, the tune "Cacklin' Hen," recorded on session 2, is quite dissimilar from "Cluck Old Hen," from session 3:

> Cacklin' Hen
> Old hen cackled, cackled in the barn;
> Ain't laid an egg, walked mighty proud;
> Old hen cackled, cackled in the corn;
> Old hen cackled, cackled in the lot;
> Last time she cackled, cackled in the pot.

Cluck Old Hen
My old hen is a good old hen;
She lays eggs for the railroad men;
Sometimes eight, sometimes ten;
That's enough eggs for the railroad men.[9]

On May 12–14, 16–17, 21, 1927, the Hill Billies went to New York City for their third Brunswick/Vocalion session, recording a total of twenty-six songs. This would be the final time Charlie would appear on records with the group and the first time his brother Elbert would join them. Since Elbert was a fine guitarist and banjo player, it is possible that Al invited him to join them. While the younger brother might have desired to record and tour with the Hill Billies, his wife and four little boys very likely contributed to the six-day brevity of Elbert's involvement with them. Charlie performed on nineteen of the twenty-six songs, alternating as fiddler, banjoist, and vocalist. Elbert played guitar with the group on eighteen selections, producing the steel effect on one of Charlie's most popular compositions, "The Nine Pound Hammer." Al Hopkins sang lead with the rest of the group echoing key phrases (shown in parentheses):

"Nine Pound Hammer" record label and that of the flip side, "CC&O No. 558." Bob Cox Collection.

Nine pound hammer, (nine pound hammer),
Just a little too heavy, (little too heavy),
Baby for my size, (baby for my size), baby for my size.

Chorus:
Roll on buddy, (roll on buddy),
Don't you roll so slow, (roll so slow),
Baby how can I roll, (baby how can I roll),
When the wheels won't go.

I'm going on a mountain, (going on a mountain),
To see my baby, (to see my baby),

And I ain't coming back, (ain't coming back),
No I ain't coming back.

Chorus:
Now roll on buddy, (roll on buddy),
Don't you roll so slow, (roll so slow),
How can I roll, (how can I roll),
When the wheels won't go.[10]

Charlie Bowman is credited for writing the words to this song from a melody that he heard from some black railroad workers in East Tennessee. The fine print on the record label reads, "Hammer and Steel Effects by Elbert Bowman." In later years, Elbert remembered this session by associating it with another historical event that occurred that same year—Charles Lindbergh's nonstop solo flight across the Atlantic Ocean. He related how the record producers did not actually employ a nine-pound hammer and a rail to make the steel sound. Instead, Elbert simulated the sound at the end of each verse by striking his banjo hoop with a small metal rod. He was pleasantly surprised that the record company saw fit to include his name on the record label.[11] Historian Archie Green gave some supplementary insight into the origin of the well-known song:

> Bowman credited bandleader Al Hopkins, a gifted country piano player and creative musician, with arranging the piece for the six performers involved. In addition to these musicians, another band member, Walter "Spark Plug" Hughes from Cranberry, North Carolina, was present and performed without his name being entered in the New York session's ledger sheets. Hughes, when only ten or eleven years old, had begun to entertain professionally with an older fiddler and balladeer, Clarence Greene. While the Hill Billies (Buckle Busters) were appearing at a Spruce Pine (Mitchell County, North Carolina) fair, the band "adopted" the young musician—too little to spark the girls—and took him on the road. Hughes' memory of the song's birth was that the boys had "fixed that number up right in the hotel room—the Knickerbocker Hotel."[12]

Few icons in American history have evoked more sentiment than the romantic coal-fired steam locomotive affectionately known as the "Iron Horse." Between 1829 and the mid-1960s, this magnificent hunk of metal laboriously chugged along the vast countryside, belching large plumes of black smoke from its haughty stack and blowing its unique mournful and melodic steam whistle. Indeed, this ancient relic of yesteryear appeared to possess human qualities of frailty and persistence. Around the end of the nineteenth century, railroad tracks began appearing all across the southern Appalachian mountains of East Tennessee and neighboring states, bringing with it high expectations of fiscal growth.

Three railroads figured prominently in this mountainous region: the Southern Railway (formerly the East Tennessee, Virginia & Georgia Railroad), the ETWNC (East Tennessee & Western North Carolina Railroad, known as "Tweetsie"), and the CC&O (Carolina, Clinchfield and Ohio Railroad). The latter rail system eventually spanned 277 miles over the rugged terrain of four mountain ranges, crossing through five states: South Carolina, North Carolina, Tennessee, Virginia, and Kentucky. The CC&O, home based in Erwin, Tennessee, for years made daily excursions between Spartanburg, South Carolina, and Elkhorn City, Kentucky. While the railroad's glory days might have ridden off into the sunset, its legend has been well preserved in myriad songs involving high-speed locomotives, brave engineers, colorful outlaws, homesick lovers, runaway trains, vagabond hoboes, political campaigns, funeral processions, and disastrous wrecks. In the late 1920s, the marriage between the railroad and old-time music was consummated when Vernon Dalhart, a pioneer of the early recording industry, sold a million copies of his song "The Wreck of the Old 97."

The railroad played a significant role in Charlie's family history since his father worked as a brakeman on the East Tennessee, Virginia & Georgia Railroad, once almost losing his life while switching cars. The rail line connected Gray Station with the rest of the world sometime after the turn of the twentieth century, thereby allowing merchandise to be transported in and out of the community and providing passenger service for nearby Johnson City.

The flip side of "The Nine Pound Hammer" was "CC&O No. 558," regarding a local train engineer, J. Fred Leonard, better known as Fogless Bill. While many trains traversed through Gray Station, no train engineer is as well known as Leonard. Local residents knew when he was at the throttle because of his distinctive train whistle, described as sounding somewhere between a steamboat and a foghorn. Because of the Bowman family's earlier railroad connection, Charlie became acquainted with Fogless and his family, as well as other railroad engineers in the Erwin vicinity. The late Tom Hodge of the *Johnson City Press* once quoted in his column an Erwin, Tennessee, resident's observation regarding the renowned train engineer:

> He was a rather large man, bespeckled, with a gold tooth or two, handsome rugged features, dressed in big overalls, blue chambray shirt, a red bandana handkerchief tied loosely around his neck, a slouch hat pulled down over his brow and smoking a crooked stemmed pipe. The pipe was filled with Granger Roughcut tobacco.[13]

A scene that played out numerous times in East Tennessee in the early 1920s involved Fogless Bill directing his CC&O steam-driven locomotive north from Erwin into Gray Station. As the trainman maneuvered his bulky engine into the depot, he frequently observed his fiddling buddy standing near the station where he was taking a music lesson from the engineer. Each time J. Fred sounded his unmistakable whistle, Charlie bowed his melodious fiddle in unison, in effect playing a fiddle and train whistle duet with the legendary engineer. Charlie soon composed "CC&O No. 558," which was recorded by the Hill Billies on Brunswick Records on May 16, 1927:

> Down in Tennessee among the flowers and the hills,
> Lives an engineer and his name is Fogless Bill,
> You can tell him by his whistle every time that he blows,
> The musical engineer on the CC&O.
>
> He opened up the throttle and he's never late,
> There never is a passenger who has to wait,
> He's hard on the fireman who shoves in the coal,
> To keep up the steam that makes the drivers roll.
>
> *Chorus:* Fogless Bill sitting at the throttle,
> Fogless Bill on the CC&O,
> Fogless Bill sitting at the throttle,
> Fogless Bill on the CC&O.[14]

Another Charlie Bowman composition, "Emery's Fast Ride," is reminiscent of "The Wreck of the Old 97," involving Erwin CC&O train engineer Emery Slagle. According to the lyrics, he was traveling between Erwin and Spartanburg, South Carolina, at speeds approaching ninety miles an hour. The song dialogue is between the courageous Emery and his apprehensive fireman. Apparently, this song was never recorded:

> Emery left Erwin about nine o'clock.
> He was going to Spartanburg without a single stop.
> Emery says we'll make it if it's in our power.
> He may have to put her up to ninety miles an hour.
> The fireman says to Emery, It's an awful thing.
> To try and make her fly and she has no wings.
> Emery says to his fireman, you shovel in some coal.
> I'll stick my head out the window and watch the drivers roll.
>
> *Chorus #1:*
> I'll watch the drivers roll, watch the drivers roll.
> Stick my head out the window, watch the drivers roll.
>
> The locomotive got to speeding, doing its very best.
> Started for Spartanburg, expecting no rest.
> As they climbed up the mountain the speed was very high.
> The foreman said to Emery, I'm not ready to die.

Then he fell to his knees, said Lord have mercy on my soul.
The only way I'll stop him is to quit shoveling coal.
I'll quit shoveling coal, I'll quit shoveling coal.
The only way I'll stop him, is to quit shoveling coal.

Chorus #2:
Don't quit shoveling coal, don't quit shoveling coal.
I got my head out the window, watch them drivers roll.

They run into Spartanburg, the fireman smiled and said.
We've made it all right, but I thought we'd all be dead.
The fast ride we have had will always be in my mind.
An engineer like Emery Slagle is hard to find.
Is very hard to find, is very hard to find.
An engineer like Emery, is very hard to find.[15]

Charlie's "My Railroad Shack" deals with a young chap lamenting over the loss of a "good gal" who left him the previous week. He was sitting in his little railroad shack anxiously waiting for her return. Every time he hears the train whistle, he runs up the track hoping to see his sweetheart on board:

It's late evening, I'm watching for the train to come in.
My good gal left me way last week.
The way I'm worried it's a sin.
She told me she was leaving.
Didn't say when she' coming back.
She left me all alone, I'm all by myself, in my little railroad shack.

Chorus #1:
When I hear a train whistle, I go running up the track.
I go and meet all the trains thinking maybe she coming back.
If she's been on these trains, she kept goin' down the line.
It keeps me so blue till I could die, but I laugh just to keep from cryin'.

As I was walking, walking up the railroad track.
Each cross tie seemed to say, she'll soon be comin' back.
She wrote me a letter, said she was through with me.
She'd fell in love with another man in Johnson City, Tennessee.

I wrote her a letter while sitting in a railroad shack.
Wondering all the time what I could do to get my gal to come back.
I told her I loved her, I wasn't telling her no lies.
Without her here, I had no friends but the rails and the old cross ties.

She wrote another letter, said she's coming back home soon.
I met every train that runs at night also morning and noon.

I kept this up for days and as sure as I'm alive.

Old 47 train came creeping in, brought my baby to my surprise.

Chorus #2:

And now I'm not worried cause I got my baby back.

We're both settled down once again, in our little old railroad shack.

No more cross tie walking and now my mind don't roam.

Cause I got my baby back home.[16]

The entire compilation of songs the Hill Billies recorded for Brunswick and Vocalion offers the listener a sense of their wide versatility. Their songs ranged from slow to upbeat and serious to comedic. One moment they are imitating a couple of fox hounds in "Governor Alf Taylor's Fox Chase" or a stubborn animal in "Donkey on the Railroad Track." The next, Al is singing solo with backup from Carson Robison, who whistles and plays guitar in "Down the Old Meadow Lane." Often the boys would lay down their instruments and sing a cappella, such as in "Echoes of the Chimes," and shortly thereafter all of them would engage in a rollicking comedy routine like "Ride That Mule," where each musician would try to ride the animal only to be swiftly tossed. Charlie's more serious side can be heard in the very beautiful "Kitty Waltz"; his speed is obvious in the lively "Mississippi Sawyer." At the appropriate time, the musicians would slow things down and harmonize the very haunting and tear-jerking "Sweet Bunch of Daisies." Their song repertoire was so extensive that they could comfortably entertain a crowd for hours without repeating a tune.

Because of the many recording sessions and performances affiliated with the vaudeville circuit, Charlie became acquainted with many notables of that era, not the least of whom was early pioneer recording star Vernon Dalhart. The fiddler recollected sitting in the recording studio while Dalhart recorded. Vernon played a harmonica (or mouth-harp, as Charlie referred to it). On occasion, Carson Robison, would join him and play guitar and sing with him.[17] The seriousness of Vernon Dalhart's work is illustrated in this quotation:

> Charlie Bowman, a country fiddler from Columbia in the twenties,
> told Jim Walsh he knew Dalhart very well and met him in New York on
> one of his recording sessions and on several occasions later. He was a
> very nice person to talk to, and was a very good mouth-harp player and
> singer. He was very serious about his recording work along with Carson
> Robinson. Vernon was high tempered. He would fly off the handle if he
> made a mistake while making a recording, but only got mad at himself.[18]

Vernon Dalhart (1883–1948), whose real name was Marion Try Slaughter, was arguably the most popular recording artist in America during the first couple of years of the electric era. Amazingly, he recorded over five thousand songs between 1916 and 1939, working at some point for nearly every record company in the country and known by about one hundred pseudonyms. Charlie was such a positive person that he had a way of making something negative sound positive. A case in point is what he had to say about Vernon Dalhart, that he "only got mad at himself."

Another example of Charlie's overall positive attitude concerns Fiddlin' John Carson. On the negative side, Charlie really did not think the pioneer was that good of a fiddler. John performed much of his life fiddling by himself and without any accompaniment. Charlie would often remark about how the well-known performer would take his fiddle and make a hit with an audience anywhere, anytime with his on-stage hilarity. He called John Carson a great, great man, implying that he was a greater entertainer than a fiddler.

After three years of touring and recording with the Hill Billies, Charlie's tenure with them came to an abrupt halt in middle to late 1928. Why did this versatile fiddler leave the security of the popular Hill Billies? Were they not still making an abundance of money, having loads of fun, and traveling all over the east performing in numerous vaudeville theaters? Weren't they as popular as ever? In truth, their road performances were getting further and further apart, not because people were tiring of them but because of Al's slackness in scheduling show dates for the band. Although their leader had always worked diligently to line up work for his band, he seemed to be growing weary of so much traveling and performing. In addition, Al appeared to have other interests competing for his time. Living in New York City was expensive, and less money was coming in from the shows. Charlie remembered being called to New York City by Al on one occasion only to arrive with not a single engagement lined up for the band. Perhaps by now Charlie was also getting weary of their vagabond lifestyle. Possibly he wanted to get back to his wife and family in Gray Station. An analysis of Charlie's "Southern Blues" might offer some insight into why he left the Hill Billies:

> I'm a lonesome man, just got in your town.
> And I don't know why I ever started running round.
> People don't seem to like me, since they think I'm very lowdown.
> I have no friends here in this northern town.
> Don't know any one, haven't got a friend around.
> Because I'm a stranger, everybody seems to dog me around.
>
> *Chorus #1:*
> I'm going back south, that's where I ought to be.
> I'm going back south, that's where I want to be.
> Back to Johnson City, best town in Tennessee.
>
> I wonder how some people can treat a poor drifter so.
> I wonder how some people can treat a poor stranger so.

They ought to remember they gonna reap what they sow.
I love Johnson City but I thought I'd do some running round.
For a long long time, I've been going from town to town.
Seems I can't find friends, every body turns me down.

What would my good gal say? If she knew I'se way up here?
I love her so much, to me she is so dear.
Maybe she'd say nothing, maybe she don't really care.
I'm going to leave here, I guess I'd better not roam.
I'm going to leave here, I feel so much alone.
I love Tennessee, Johnson City is my home.

Chorus #2:
So I'm going back south if I wear out all my shoes.
I'm going back south where I'll get all the latest news.
There I know I'll be welcome, and I won't have the southern blues.
So I'm heading back south, that's where I ought to be.
I'm going back south, that's were I want to be.
Back to Johnson City, best town in Tennessee.[19]

For whatever his reasons, Charlie concluded his association with the Hill Billies and returned to his family in the log house in Gray Station. Not content with returning to one fiddler, Al moved quickly to replace his former fiddler because of some scheduled performances and another Vocalion/Brunswick recording session lined up for December 20 and 21. A grateful Ed Belcher from West Virginia became "Tenn-O-See" Charlie's replacement. Unlike the two previous recording sessions when they recorded twenty and twenty-six songs respectively, the December date would be their final one, yielding but ten songs.[20]

By leaving the Hill Billies, Charlie missed out on a prestigious event. The group achieved another significant accomplishment. Warner Brothers contacted them to make a five-minute Vitaphone film short for the 1929 Al Jolson movie, "The Singing Fool," the first "all-talkie" movie to be made by Hollywood. This movie company used the Vitaphone sound-on-disc system, which was codeveloped by Bell Telephone Laboratories and Western Electric to produce many movie short subjects in the 1920s to complement their main feature movies. The quality was inconsistent, often evoking unintentional laughter from the audience. During the short, the Hill Billies performed three songs in what appeared to be an old log cabin. This film, lost for many years, now resides in the Library of Congress and is available for public viewing. Initially, the film was missing the sound track, but it was later located and added to the film.[21]

The Hill Billies remained strong after Charlie's departure, continuing for another five years. However, tragedy struck in October 1932 when Al Hopkins lost his life in a grinding head-on car collision in Washington, D.C. His untimely death signaled the beginning of the end for the Hill Billies. They stayed together for about another year, performing shortly prior to their demise at the Willard Hotel on November 20, 1933, before the Wisconsin Society of Washington, D.C.[22] The group soon disbanded of necessity because Al was the glue that held them together. As their leader, lead vocalist, piano player, business manager, song arranger, and tour scheduler, his roles were essential for their intactness. The other band members either could not or would not step up to the plate and assume Al's hefty leadership post, thus bringing to an end one of the most popular and colorful string bands of all time. Tony Alderman continued playing music as leader of his own bands until his death in November 1983.

Charlie would reminisce years later about the greatness of Al Hopkins, how efficient he was as a manager and how much respect he had for his former boss. The Hill Billies, who had consisted of the likes of Al Hopkins, John Hopkins, Joe Hopkins, Elmer Hopkins, John Rector, Tony Alderman, Charlie Bowman, Elbert Bowman, Fred Roe, Henry Roe, Jack Reedy, Frank "Dad" Williams, Walter "Sparky" Hughes, Uncle Am Stuart (who died while working with the group), James O'Keefe (piano), Fran Trappe, and Ed Belcher were now only a memory. However, history would be kind and not forget them. Perhaps their greatest contribution was to establish the string band as an integral part of old-time country music.[23]

When Charlie arrived back in Gray Station in mid-1928 following his tenure with the Hill Billies, some people thought his musical career had come to a finale; Fannie, however, knew otherwise. Familiar with how much he loved his fiddle, she was certain he would soon be seeking new opportunities for touring and performing. In reality, Charlie's career was not ending, just changing directions. Within fifteen months after leaving the Hill Billies, he recorded on a new label with a new group. Instead of Brunswick/Vocalion Records with the Hill Billies, this time he recorded with Columbia Records, joined by his brothers and using the name Charlie Bowman and His Brothers. It wasn't the end of his book; it was just the closing of another illustrious chapter.

Chapter 6

"UNCLE FUZZ" COMES TO TOWN

After returning home from touring with the Hill Billies, Charlie initially found another outlet for his music when he, his three brothers, and several local string musicians convened each Saturday night in downtown Johnson City along the east side of Fountain Square to play music. The group leaned against the windows of the storefronts, putting one foot behind them, while they played their instruments. These spontaneous meetings were a precursor to what is known today as jam sessions. Anyone who wanted to play could join in with the group. These Saturday night meetings attracted massive crowds of spectators and musicians from all over East Tennessee. The big drawing card was their hometown hero and vaudeville star, Fiddlin' Charlie Bowman. The popular entertainer quickly located a co-fiddler in the person of David Bowman (no known relationship to the family), who would fiddle on such tunes as "Virginia Waltz," "Missouri Waltz," and "The Blue Danube Waltz." David later commented that Charlie was known for the unique little "wiggle" in his wrist when he bowed his fiddle.

After coming off the road, Charlie returned to working odd jobs, including house painting and carpentry work. He was also employed a short while at the Gray Station rock quarry along with his stepson, Joe Ferguson. Jasper remembered when he and some of his relatives would routinely haul drinking water in one-gallon glass jugs from Lige Adams's store to the quarry for Charlie and Joe.

Then one day Tennessee Charlie spotted an attention-grabbing ad in the local newspaper:

> Can You Sing or Dance Old-Time Music? Musicians of Unusual Ability—Small Dance Combinations—Singers—Novelty Players, Etc. Are Invited To call on Mr. Walker or Mr. Brown of the Columbia Phonograph Company at 334 East Main Street, Johnson City, on Saturday, October 13th, 1928—9 AM to 5 PM. This is an actual try-out for the purpose of making Columbia Records. You may write in advance to F. B. Walker, Care of John Sevier Hotel, Johnson City, or call without appointment at address and on date mentioned above.[1]

Frank Buckley Walker, head of the Columbia Record Company's "hillbilly" recordings division, submitted this advertisement. The executive was to Columbia Records what Ralph Peer was to Victor, and Art Satherley to American Records. Peer had pioneered the idea of taking a mobile recording unit into areas where the musicians lived rather than bringing them to a location such as New York City that was out of their comfort zone. In the seven years between 1925 and 1932, Walker scheduled several recording sessions in Atlanta (1925–32), New Orleans (1925–27), Memphis (1928), Johnson City (1928–29) and Dallas (1927–29).[2] He once related to Mike Seeger during an interview:

> We built it [the recording visit] up in advance—getting the word
> around that at a certain time of the year we were going to be there, and
> these people would show up sometimes from eight or nine hundred
> miles away. How they got there, I'll never know and how they got back
> I'll never know. This was natural. Life in the country, particularly in the
> early days, was a lonesome life. Farmers would often talk to themselves
> and to the horses and stock . . . and the sound of the railroad train, that
> lonesome whistle has a powerful emotional impact.[3]

Walker and Satherley were piggybacking off Peer's successful moneymaking idea, but the Columbia executive took it to a higher level. During his thirteen years with Columbia Records (1919–32), Frank developed a successful three-fold business approach that included improving recording techniques, finding unique ways of attracting new talent, and focusing on better ways to market his products. He was once quoted as saying that he would do whatever it took to find new talent, even if he had to ride a horse into the mountainous backwoods to find real people with real country flavor.[4] Walker quickly noted that many old-time musicians played their instruments unaccompanied, and as good as they were, sometimes their listeners were less than enchanted about their sound until they started playing with a string band. Frank's home base was in Atlanta, a convenient in-between place for his mobile recording trips. He made two jaunts to Johnson City, one on October 16, 1928, and the other on February 20, 1929, each time staying at the convenient downtown John Sevier Hotel. He acquired the unusual habit of not shaving during these visits, so that it was not long before he attained a fuzzy five o'clock shadow, earning him the nickname of "Uncle Fuzz."[5] Perhaps he surmised that by not shaving he would look like a hillbilly and could relate better to the musicians he was recording. He became so well known by his nickname that he even received mail at the John Sevier Hotel addressed to "Uncle Fuzz."

On his first trip in 1928, Mr. Walker procured a makeshift studio in the Brading-Marshall Lumber Company's business office on the east end of Main Street in downtown Johnson City (located diagonally opposite the historical

First Christian Church). He scheduled auditions for Saturday, October 13. Those who successfully passed were scheduled for a recording session the next week. Hopeful amateur musicians from all over the area brought their fiddles, banjos, guitars, and voices to Johnson City to display their talents for the recording executive. These became known as the Johnson City Sessions.

Participants in the 1928 project included the Shell Creek Quartet, the Grant Brothers, the Roane County Ramblers, Renus Rich and Carl Bradshaw, Clarence Greene, the Wise Brothers, Ira Yates, Uncle Nick Decker, the Proximity String Quartet, Hardin and Grindstaff, the Greensboro Boys Quartet, Richard Harold, Charlie Bowman and His Brothers, the Bowman Sisters, Bill and Belle Reed, the Reed Children, the Reed Family, the Hodgers Brothers, the Hodgers Quartet, Bailey Briscoe, Robert Hoke and Vernal Vest, McVay and Johnson, Earl Shirkey and Roy Harper, George Roark, the Ed Helton Singers, the Garland Brothers and Grindstaff, Dewey Golden and His Kentucky Buzzards, the Holiness Singers, Frank Shelton and the McCartt Brothers/Patterson.[6]

The 1929 assemblage consisted of Blalock and Yates, Jack Jackson, George Wade and Grancum Braswell, the Roane County Ramblers, Wyatt and Brandon, Roy Harvey and Leonard Copeland, the Spindale Quartet, the Queen Trio, Earl Shirkey and Roy Harper, the Moatsville String Ticklers, the Weaver Brothers, Byrd Moore and His Hot Shots, the Bateman Sacred Quartet, Fred Richards, Clarence Ashley, the Bentley Boys, Charlie Bowman and His Brothers, Fran Trappe, Eph Woodie and the Henpecked Husbands, Ira and Eugene Yates, and Ellis Williams.[7] While the Bowman Sisters surprisingly did not participate in the 1929 session, they were later extended a personal invitation to record at Columbia's New York studios.

Charlie envisioned this audition as an immense opportunity for the Bowman family. He and his three brothers, Elbert, Walter, and Argil, along with his two oldest daughters, seventeen-year-old Pauline and sixteen-year-old Jennie, showed up for the Saturday audition and were subsequently scheduled to record on Tuesday, October 16, 1928. Charlie Bowman and His Brothers chose "Roll on Buddy" and "Gonna Raise the Rukus Tonight," whereas the Bowman Sisters selected "My Old Kentucky Home" and "Swanee River." "Roll on Buddy," recorded by Charlie Bowman and His Brothers, was a companion song to his former hit song "The Nine Pound Hammer," which had been recorded earlier with the Hill Billies. He wrote the words to "Roll on Buddy" in his own handwriting and gave it to Frank Walker at this session. It has a chorus and a fiddle interlude between four verses. It begins,

> I'm going to the east Cairo,
> I'm going to the east Cairo,
> I'm going to the east, I'm going to the west,
> I'm going to the land I love best.

Chorus
Roll on buddy roll on,
Roll on my buddy roll on,
You wouldn't roll so slow if you knew what I know,
Roll on my buddy roll on.[8]

While Charlie is credited with writing this song, most versions start with "I'm going to the east pay road, I'm going to the east pay road." Charlie's original copy reads, "I'm going to the east Cairo, I'm going to the east Cairo." It is believed that he was referring to the city of Cairo (pronounced "Kay-row"), located in southern Illinois at the junction of the Ohio and Mississippi Rivers. An old song, "Goin' Down to Cairo," from late summer 1858, tells about an early frost that destroyed the corn and tobacco crops in that region. Since crops south of the river were not been damaged, planters from this region sent a portion of their crops upriver to Cairo. The song recounts the merriment from the trips the

Columbia Records songs recorded by Charlie Bowman and His Brothers for Frank Walker. Bob Cox Collection.

thousands of people made to this city to get their needed food supplies.[9] Of note, Charlie mentions Fannie Mae in the final verse as "a good woman."

The second song, "Gonna Raise the Ruckus Tonight," was an old pre–Civil War song that reflects a bitter yet humorous view of slavery and social conditions in the South, as sung by generations of both black and white singers. The word "ruckus," meaning a disturbance, is pronounced as if it were spelled "ruekus." A couple of versions exist with slightly different wording. After recording both songs, Charlie was convinced that Frank liked what he heard based on his body language and the big smile on his face. These were the only songs Charlie Bowman and His Brothers recorded that day. With the vaudeville entertainer's reputation as a renowned fiddler and performer, it is surprising that Uncle Fuzz limited the session to just two songs. Charlie was accustomed to recording more songs when he was with the Hill Billies. Perhaps Frank Walker wanted to obtain a sampling of all the local talent, fully expecting a follow-up visit to Johnson City.

Jennie Bowman has been described by her siblings as having a natural-born talent like her father. With a pretty face and a bubbling personality, she was undeniably the most talented of Charlie and Fannie's children. She could sing, yodel, and play several instruments, including the piano, fiddle, and later the accordion. Her siblings also possessed varying degrees of talent. Jasper played the mandolin and guitar and joined numerous bluegrass bands over the years. Howard was an outstanding singer and guitar player who occasionally performed locally. Donnie could not sing or play an instrument, but he was an expert dancer. Pauline sang and played the ukulele and harmonica. Jean specialized in dancing, wearing thin the family's living room carpet. Lester, the least talented musically, did not play any instrument, dance, or sing, but he was the best business-minded person of the family.

At the time of the first Johnson City Session, neither Jennie nor Pauline had much experience in performing. Consequently, when it was time for them to record in front of a microphone, they became timid and nervous. Frank Walker had a knack for making people feel comfortable in these situations; his secret was to talk to them about things they could relate to so as to quickly get their minds off recording. Soon he had the two young ladies sufficiently calmed down and ready to record their two songs. Not only was Uncle Fuzz responsible for recording Charlie Bowman and His Brothers, the Bowman Sisters, and several local people, he was also instrumental in recording Bessie Smith, Gid Tanner and the Skillet Lickers, Charlie Poole, and Vernon Dalhart, to name just a few. Later, he moved to MGM Records, where he signed Hank Williams Sr. to a contract. Fred Rose was responsible for Hank switching to the new label after being turned down by Paul Cohen at Decca.[10]

Several country music historians regard Jennie and Pauline as the first sisters to make a country record. In an attempt to verify this claim, Staley Cain, husband of Jennie, once sent a letter to the John Edwards Memorial Foundation at the Folklore and Mythology Center at the University of California in Los Angeles to verify this assertion. On October 20, 1972, he received a response:

> Dear Mr. Cain: The Bowman Sisters may well have been the first sisters group to record for the hillbilly market. The Wisdom Sisters recorded in 1926, but I'm not sure whether they were really "hillbillies," although their records were issued in Columbia's Old Time Tunes series . . . Sincerely . . . Anne Cohen.[11]

Uncle Fuzz made a return visit to Johnson City on February 20, 1929. Pauline remembered this session being held in the 200 block of West Main Street, just down the street from the now defunct West Side School. As before, Walker had his traveling recording equipment with him. As previously noted, Charlie Bowman and His Brothers showed up to record without the Bowman Sisters. Perhaps the girls could not attend or maybe one of them was sick. Their absence was certainly not because their first record did not sell well. In fact, they would be invited to New York City within eight months to cut another record for Columbia. Charlie Bowman and His Brothers recorded two more songs for Frank Walker: "Moonshiner and His Money" and "Forky Dear." The first song was a comedy routine with dialogue between Charlie and Frank Wilson, a good friend of the Bowman brothers who had formerly played slide guitar for the Hill Billies. This song's format was used by countless old-time string bands, interspersing comedy dialogue with musical selections using the words "let's have a little tune."

On this selection, Frank Wilson encounters Charlie and his brothers sitting around a moonshine still guzzling 'tater brandy. The boys cordially offer their guest a quart of the potent home brew, which he promptly and audibly consumes. While Walter Bowman's voice can be heard briefly at the beginning of the song, Elbert and Argil do not say anything on the record. Charlie invites Wilson to grab a guitar hanging on a branch of a nearby tree and to join them in an instrumental ditty called "Money in Both Pockets." After the song concludes, Frank comments that, while the selection is good, it really does not fit his pocket, meaning that he is financially strapped. Charlie instantly offers another instrumental tune aptly titled "Boys, My Money's All Gone," which satisfies all five musicians.[12]

The opposite side of the record was an instrumental jig called "Forky Dear." The Columbia Records personnel apparently did not know the correct title of this tune; they spelled it "Forky Dear" rather than "Forky Deer," "Forked Deer," or "Forkey Deer," as it was alternately spelled. In reality, a "Forked Deer" is a two-point buck considered prime venison. Charlie would later compose another moonshine song titled "Tennessee Moonshine Song":

Down in Tennessee where the tall corn grows.
We get up in the morning when the rooster crows.
Down there everybody has a good time.
We save our money make our own moonshine.
We take our corn to an old water mill.
The miller grinds it he grinds it with a will
We take the meal up a holler run it through a still.
Then we drink corn licker and get our fill.

We all gather over on the hill.
Start the old fiddle and our feet won't be still.
We dance awhile then someone will cry.
Pass around the bottle my throat is getting dry.
The bottle was empty to their surprise.
They looked at one another making big eyes.
I said wait I'll wet your lip.
I'll go down Ford Creek and get a little nip.

Come down and see us any old time.
We can get a drink of good moonshine.
We've always got it good and handy.
Pure old corn and good apple brandy.
We make it out of corn and out of rye.
There another kind we wanna try.
We wanna try a batch out of Irish tater.
Always try a batch out of punkin later.

Chorus:
If you want a snort you're feeling kinder weak.
Come and see me down on Ford Creek.
I'll give you a drink then you can eat.
My corn is made right it can't be beat.[13]

As previously noted, Columbia executives invited Jennie, Pauline, and Charlie to record two additional songs. By then, the Fannie and Charlie Bowman family had just moved from Gray Station to Bristol, Tennessee. This time, instead of Frank Walker coming to Johnson City, the Bowmans were invited to the New York City recording studios on October 23, 1929. Columbia must have been impressed by the sales of their first record to finance their trip's expenses. It is not known if the Bowman brothers were also invited to this session; they did not participate in the recordings. When the three of them arrived in New York, the girls were stunned at the enormity of the city, which was very different from the rolling farmlands they were accustomed to in Gray Station. Charlie was famil-iar with Manhattan because of his vaudeville tours with the Hill Billies. Upon arrival, they went to the Columbia Building, which was then the second tallest building in New York City (the Empire State Building was the tallest). Pauline remembered that the ride up the Columbia building elevator nearly scared her to death. After finishing the session, she was too frightened to return to the ground floor. She finally mustered enough courage to glance below; she said the people on the ground looked like dots and the cars appeared as toys. After she settled down, Columbia recorded two more takes by the sisters, "Railroad Take Me Back" and "Old Lonesome Blues." For the recording session, Charlie wrote the words to the former song on the back of some stationery from the Hotel Lockerby, Indianapolis, Indiana. The composition opens with Charlie imitating on his fiddle the train's mournful steam whistle, followed by its leisurely chugging from the station. The person depicted in the song is leaving his lover behind but hopes to return soon to her. He admonishes her to remain faithful to him during his uncertain absence. After six verses and two whistle interludes, the recording

Columbia Records songs recorded by the Bowman Sisters. Bob Cox Collection.

"UNCLE FUZZ" COMES TO TOWN

concludes with a Doppler-effect sound of the train fading into the distance. The latter song was a four-verse blues ditty containing lyrics seemingly inappropriate for seventeen- and eighteen-year-old girls.

Again, it is surprising that Columbia Records recorded only two cuts by the Bowman Sisters while they were in New York City; these Tennesseans had made a long trip just for two songs. In any event, Charlie accompanied them on his fiddle on "Railroad Take Me Back," and Fran Trappe, a blind accordion player (who later figured into the family's musical history), provided back up on "Old Lonesome Blues." The Bowman Sisters' records are difficult to locate today. However, during the 1970s Rounder Records issued "Old Lonesome Blues" as part of an album they titled *Banjo Pickin' Girl: Women in Early Country Music* (#1029).[14] Dr. Charles Wolfe remarked about the Bowman Sisters on the occasion of Pauline's death in December 2003: "The Bowman Sisters were in many ways the Boswell Sisters of country music, and with the close, precise harmonies and jazzy swinging, were trying to take country to places it was just not ready to go. They were a generation before their time, and its a shame history hasn't treated them more kindly."[15]

After this New York session, Charlie Bowman did not make any additional records. The Bowman Sisters, however, received one additional opportunity two and a half years later for a new label. While Charlie's recording days were over, the entertainer's career was anything but finished. He would continue his trailblazing efforts in the old-time country music field.

Chapter 7

WOPI: OVER THE AIR ON THE STATE LINE

An event that occurred at precisely 6:30 P.M. on June 15, 1929, provided Charlie Bowman with yet another opportunity to play his old-time music. Radio station WOPI ("Watch Our Popularity Increase") in Bristol, Tennessee, known as the "Voice of the Appalachians," went on the air that evening at 1,500 kilocycles, with 100 watts and 199.9 meters, claiming to bring "the news while it is news." The person responsible for the vision and energy behind this new station was Mr. W. A. Wilson. WOPI immediately began to live up to its name by transmitting live Appalachian and other musical acts over the airways. An advertisement for the station boasted: "For a station of its size, WOPI enjoys a list of live talent permanently attached to its studios that is capable of competing with nationally known radio entertainers."[1] Bristol has the unique distinction of having its main downtown thoroughfare, State Street, split right down the middle between Tennessee and Virginia. Patrons could shop in either state simply by walking across the street.

WOPI provided a distinct advantage for Charlie: he could drive thirty miles to Bristol, play his music over the airways, and then return to his family in Gray Station. This was approximately one year after he returned from his tour with the Hill Billies. While employment at WOPI was a far cry from the money he made performing on the road, it provided an outlet for his music while allowing him to stay at home and be a father to his family. Family members remembered that Charlie was one of the first, if not *the* first, performer to broadcast on this new station. Jasper recalled that the local Eads Coffee Company sponsored his program.

In the fall of 1929, Charlie made a bold decision. He moved his ever-growing family from the old log house in Gray Station to a contemporary two-story rented dwelling on Locust Street in Bristol, Tennessee, just a short distance from the downtown WOPI studios. This choice had one negative consequence: Charlie and Fannie were now paying rent on the new place in addition to making a house payment on their old residence. His actions seemed to indicate that he intended for his association with WOPI to be a lasting one. By this time, there were nine children living at home, with their last child, Jean, due to arrive within a year.

Charlie opted to keep his log house for a while should it become necessary for them to return to the country. This turned out to be a wise decision, as his association with WOPI was short lived, and they returned to their former dwelling around the end of 1930.

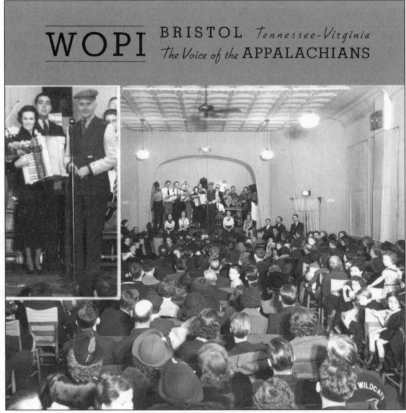

Jennie Bowman Cain and Tennessee Ernie Ford at WOPI. Jennie's husband, Staley, is standing in front of the stage, on the right. Jennie Bowman Cain Collection.

The Bowman family's move to Bristol was similar to the Beverly Hillbillies loading their belongings onto a rickety swaying truck and heading for a mansion in Beverly Hills. Hobart and Pearl Hale, who lived just down the hill from them in Gray Station, looked after their home during their absence, not that there was much to care for. While the new two-story rented residence was certainly no Beverly Hills mansion, it was a vast improvement over their dilapidated country home. The outhouse was actually an inhouse with a new device called a commode. The children were so intrigued by it that they flushed it repeatedly just to watch it function, oblivious to the expense of a water bill. There were no slop jars to keep in the closet or under the bed and no going down a lonely dark narrow path at night to a small, smelly, critter-infested pine shed. There were no kerosene lamps to fill or wicks to trim; they simply flipped a switch and there was light instantaneously. There were no fly bushes to shoo flies from the food table because the windows in the new dwelling contained both screens and glass. The children did not have to carry heavy water jugs from the cistern to the smoke-house for baths because there was no cistern or smokehouse. All they had to do was turn the handles on the water fixture and out came hot and cold running water into their indoor tub.

In need of reliable transportation, Charlie purchased a used car that resembled a green box on four wheels. The children called it "Smokey Stover," after a popular comic strip character who drove a two-wheeled fire truck.[2] Although both Jennie and Pauline learned to drive on the unpaved, potholed roads of Upper East Tennessee, Jennie did most of the navigating.

When the stock market crashed on Black Monday, October 28, Charlie likely wondered if he had done the right thing by moving his family to Bristol. Just six days earlier, Jennie and Pauline had recorded for Columbia Records in New York City, but buying records and tickets to music performances now appeared to be out of the question for most Americans. The curtain on the vaudeville stage slowly began to descend without people even realizing what was happening. Within a few short years, it essentially ceased to exist.

While Charlie's family was living in Bristol, Fran Trappe rented a room in a boardinghouse near them. Fran had played with the Hill Billies on numerous occasions. In fact, he bought Jennie her first accordion and taught her how to play it. Later, the accordion became Jennie's instrument of choice when she began performing in vaudeville. Jennie's scrapbook contains a letter sent November 30, 1930, from a WOPI disk jockey named "Fran" but gives no last name:

> Dear Jen: I got your letter yesterday morning, too late to play your
> tune for you, and I had to rush to Kingsport yesterday afternoon. I was
> certainly tickled pink to hear from you. It sure has been almost a year
> since I saw all of you last, but it seems so much longer than that. . . .
> You know, I saw your dad one night last summer, and it seemed like
> old times for just a few minutes. . . . Talking about old times, I just hap-
> pened to think about the night I tried to do the square dance down
> there in the country. I sure did make a mess out of that, but I had more
> fun than anybody there. Lots of love, Fran.[3]

Not long after Charlie became a regular on WOPI, he met Ernest Jennings Ford, a ten-year-old local boy who hung around the radio station. Within eight years, this talented young man became a full-time announcer for WOPI. Between 1937 and 1939, he left the station to study voice at the Cincinnati Conservatory of Music.[4] Instead of telling people his actual birthplace, Bristol, Tennessee, he claimed that he came from the imaginary town of Bent Fork, Tennessee. Old "Sixteen Tons Ern"—later hailed as "Tennessee Ernie Ford"—got into radio after working at a dry cleaner and a grocery store in Bristol. He once told people that working for WOPI, where he was paid $17.50 a week during the Depression, was one of the easiest things he had ever done. While his earlier songs had a strong hillbilly flavor, he later took advantage of his beautiful baritone voice and sang gospel music almost exclusively. Ernie's hillbilly personification most likely attracted Charlie's family to him. He often joked that he could play the fiddle but not good enough to get a Union card. Ironically, Mr. Ford was featured in Chevrolet radio commercials.

In 1930, WOPI played "Jake Leg Blues" and "Jake Walk Papa." The lyrics of these songs described people suffering from jake leg, a paralysis of the legs and feet and sometimes the wrists. This malady was usually temporary but could be permanent. Spotting persons with jake leg was easy; their foot would literally "slap" the ground as they walked. It was reported that during this time the East Tennessee area had between 500 and 600 documented cases of jake leg. It was caused by a popular legal tonic containing 70 percent alcohol known as Jamaica "Jake" Ginger, which was sold as a remedy for digestive problems and mild upper respiratory infections. The real culprit in the drink was one of the additives, tri-ortho-cresyl-phosphate, an industrial plasticizer used to help mask the strong ginger taste and make the drink more palatable. Based on the number of jake leg cases, Gray Station's residents appeared to have been hit hard with digestive problems and mild upper respiratory infections.

While at WOPI, the Bowman family became good friends with the original Carter Family of A.P. (Alvin Pleasant), Sara, and Maybelle, from Maces Springs, near Hiltons, Virginia. Howard remembered when he, Charlie, Jeannie, and someone known as "old man Nuckles" were invited to eat supper with Sara and A.P. They drove to the Carter residence in an old Hudson automobile. Among the many mouthwatering items Sara served her guests were ham meat, squirrel gravy, cornbread, and biscuits. Howard and Jennie sang for the Carter Family, but the Carter Family did not return the favor during their visit. Just before A.P. died, he asked his daughter, Janette, to keep the Carter Family music tradition alive. She honored her father's request with the help of her brother, Joe. They opened first the Carter Store and later the Carter Fold in Maces Springs to allow old-time musicians the opportunity to perform each Saturday night with buck dancing on a concrete floor in front of the stage. Janette personally screened each act to ensure that it met A.P.'s old-time music criteria. Pauline remembered the Carter Family performing in about 1939 in front of the Jonesboro Court House. She distinctly recalled Sara's autoharp playing. Pauline, Jennie, and Charlie entertained that same night.

Charlie introduced Howard to the entertainment world on August 31, 1929, by allowing him to participate in a show with Charlie, Jennie, and Pauline. Being a good singer and guitar player, he occasionally played with his famous father when they performed locally. On the flyer for this event, the admission was shown to be ten cents for children and twenty cents for adults. It mentioned Bert Bence and his wife, Ted ("the girl who plays the one-string fiddle"), on the same program. Within two years, Bert and Charlie worked together as vaudeville performers with the H. M. Barnes' Blue Ridge Ramblers. Howard later began singing with Jennie at courthouses and other venues in Johnson City, Jonesboro, Elizabethton, and Embreeville.

Charlie's association with WOPI ended in late 1930, and he moved his family back to the log house in Gray Station. This action caused much consternation to his family. The reason for this relocation is unknown, but several factors probably contributed, including the bad local economy caused by the stock market crash. Charlie probably missed being on the road and playing his fiddle professionally before live audiences. Even though his music was being broadcast into the radios of many East Tennesseans, he must have missed the glamour and excitement of live performances in front of his many fans. The move was extremely difficult for the family, since they had become accustomed to the advantages of modern appliances for a little over a year. Now it was time for them to pack their belongings and return to their old lifestyle, with its outhouse, slop jars, kerosene lamps, straw tick mattresses, cistern water, and fly bushes. However, moving back had one positive note: they returned to one house payment.

Since Charlie needed employment, he found work in Kingsport at Tennessee Eastman Company for four to five months. During this time, the Gray Station native purchased a new piano and had it delivered to the living room in the log house. Perhaps Charlie saw this as a consolation prize for his family. Jennie eagerly took to the piano, mastering it to perfection. As for Charlie, what appeared to be a major lull in his musical career would soon change within just a few months with an opportunity to return to Vaudeville.

Chapter 8

THE BLUE RIDGE RAMBLERS

In the fall of 1930, Philadelphian H. M. "Hank" Barnes, leader of a traveling musical road show known as the Blue Ridge Ramblers, arrived in Gray Station to participate in a foxhunt in the East Tennessee hills. This trip afforded him a bonus opportunity—to invite the now well-known Fiddlin' Charlie Bowman to join his itinerant group. Abundantly aware of the Tennessee fiddler's musical talents from his vaudeville travels with the Hill Billies, he was taking direct aim at a contest-winning fiddler who had gained experience with the Hill Billies and WOPI. Mr. Barnes organized the Blue Ridge Ramblers in 1928 to tour all across the East Coast as part of the Loews Metropolitan Theatre Vaudeville

H. M. "Hank" Barnes, leader of the Blue Ridge Ramblers.
Jennie Bowman Cain Collection.

Circuit. Since its establishment, this musical unit had consisted of such talents as Frank E. "Dad" Williams (fiddle), Fred Roe (banjo), Henry Roe (guitar), Jim Smith (fiddle), Harry Brown (mandolin), Lonnie Austin (piano), Frank Wilson (slide guitar), and Jack Reedy (banjo). Later additions to the group would include Bert Bence (with his wife, Ted, and their dog), sisters Madeline and Florence Gray, Bob Cult, Jack Pierce (fiddle), Harry Brown (mandolin), Russell Jones (steel guitar), and Walter "Sparkie" Hughes (guitar). Hank Barnes was analogous to Al Hopkins in that he traveled with the band as their business manager and leader. However, unlike Al, he did not perform with his group or even appear on stage with them; his primary job was scheduling stage appearances.[1]

The Ramblers were recording stars, having cut fourteen records for Brunswick, Supertone (Sears, Roebuck & Company), and Melotone in New York City on January 28–29, 1929. Two songs were British releases, two were released on the Supertone label under the name of the Smoky Mountain Ramblers, and two were issued in Canada on the Melotone label under the name of Le Orchestra Cartier. The fourteen songs were "Golden Slippers," "Old Joe Clark," "Repasz Band March" ("La Marche Mt. Laurier"), "Lineman's Serenade," "Who Broke the Lock on the Henhouse Door?" "Blue Ridge Ramblers' Rag," "Flop Eared

The Blue Ridge Ramblers. *Top row:* Madeline Gray, Bob Cult, Jack Pierce, Charlie Bowman, Sparkie Hughes, Florence Gray; *middle row:* Pauline Bowman, Henry Roe, Dad Williams, Fred Roe, Jennie Bowman; *sitting on floor:* Bert Bence and his dog. Bert was comedian and master of ceremonies. Jennie Bowman Cain Collection.

THE BLUE RIDGE RAMBLERS

Mule," "She'll Be Coming 'Round the Mountain When She Comes," "Goin' Down the Road Feeling Bad," "Honolulu Stomp," "Three O'clock in the Morning," "Echoes of Shenandoah Valley," "Our Director March" ("La Marche De Notre Directeur"), and "Mandolin Rag."[2] This recording session transpired a full year before Charlie, Pauline, and Jennie joined the Ramblers.

Advertising with the slogan "Brunswick Records Play on All Phonographs," the Brunswick Radio Corporation issued its records as part of the series "Songs from Dixie, Old and New." An old 78-rpm record sleeve from that period shows them listed under the heading "Outstanding Records," including songs from five other groups: "Who Broke the Lock on the Hen House Door?" and "She'll Be Comin' 'Round the Mountain," by the Blue Ridge Ramblers; "Carolina Moon" and "I Wish I Had Died in My Cradle," by McFarland and Gardner; "No Hiding Place Down There" and "Dip Me in the Golden Sea," by Frank and James McCravy; "The House at the End of the Lane" and "My Blue Ridge Mountain Home," by Dalhart and Robinson; "Rabbit in the Pea Patch" and "Down in Arkansas," by the Pickard Family; and "Wednesday Night Waltz" and "My Tennessee Mountain Home," by Luther and Robinson.[3]

"Old Joe Clark'" and "Golden Slippers," by H. M. Barnes's Blue Ridge Ramblers. Bob Cox Collection.

During Mr. Barnes's stopover in Gray Station, Charlie introduced the bandleader to Jennie and Pauline, who by this time were eighteen and nineteen years old, respectively. Hank knew of these young ladies from their Columbia Records sessions and desired to hear them sing. After listening to them perform several songs, he extended an invitation for them to join his energetic group. After discussions with the family and among themselves, all three accepted his offer. Being a Rambler meant going into vaudeville, and it meant remaining on the road for extended tours.

Why did Charlie return to the vaudeville tour after an absence of only three years? Perhaps a bigger question is why did he take his two oldest daughters with him? As a forty-one-year-old seasoned veteran with three years of vaudeville experience behind him, Charlie certainly knew what he and his daughters were

The original record sleeve of "She'll Be Comin' 'Round the Mountain When She Comes." Bob Cox Collection.

getting into. Leaving his family behind this time to follow his fiddle was somewhat easier for him than it had been six years earlier. In 1925, Charlie had left behind a thirty-nine-year-old wife and seven relatively young children, ranging in ages of from a few weeks to fourteen years. Now, in 1931, he was leaving a forty-five-year-old spouse and seven relatively young kids, ranging in ages of from six months to seventeen years. Instead of having her two oldest daughters to assist her, Fannie now had to rely heavily on her two oldest sons, Lester and Donnie.

Fannie tearfully watched her two daughters depart from the log house not knowing when, or even if, they would ever return. Thus began more than two years of grueling performances on the Loews Vaudeville Circuit, traveling up and down the eastern states. It is doubtful that the two young ladies really knew what was ahead of them, but the bright lights of some of the biggest stages in the country were calling them.

The first performances for Charlie, Pauline, and Jennie in their new nomadic job were scheduled for January 12 at the Princess Theatre in Mount Hope, West Virginia. For reasons unknown, the Bowman sisters traveled there by bus without their dad. Before boarding, they chose to spend the night in Johnson City with Charlie's sister, Ethel, and her husband, Hugh, who lived close to the downtown bus station. The addition of the three Bowmans to the Ramblers increased the band size to twelve, as Lonnie Austin had left the group by this time. Bert Bence, comedian and master of ceremonies, and his wife, Ted, traveled and performed with the robust group. Two other sisters, Madeline and Florence Gray, soon joined the act, as well as Vincent "Jimmy James" Gamelli. Madeline later married band member Henry Roe. During Charlie, Pauline, and Jennie's tenure with the band, the personnel changed often. Some wanted to play in other groups, others were fatigued with the strain of the road. While Pauline once called Mr. Barnes an "old buzzard" because he was a stern businessman, she said he was actually a true gentleman, very nice to work for, and compassionate of the needs of her and her sister. Charlie later showed these same qualities when he formed his own bands.

Jennie and Pauline soon became so popular that they were given their own act, as the Bowman Sisters, in the shows. Given that the Ramblers were heavily slanted toward the hillbilly sound, the story of two bashful little country girls leaving the rough confines of an old rural log house to sing on the vaudeville stages night after night received much hype in the local newspapers.

On your phonograph maybe you've heard those two little Hillbilly girls—Pauline and Jennie Bowman sing their blues songs of the hills— maybe you've heard their "My Old Kentucky Home," "Old Lonesome Blues," "Swanee River" and "Railroad Take Me Back" and most probably you've liked them too. But you could hardly know that these two back- woods girls—hardy mountaineers[—]were found by an executive of one of the famous recording companies while on a foxhunt some fifteen miles out of Johnson City, Tennessee.

The two girls singing in their corn patch attracted his attention and every endeavor was made to get them to come to New York to make a recording. The natural timidity, the lack of city clothes, the objection of their mother could not overcome so this progressive executive arranged for a traveling studio to come to Johnson City where the girls, who are just sixteen and eighteen years old, met them and after some careful instructions four recordings were made and today are becoming best sellers at every music shop.

The Bowman Sisters with their father, Charles, are this week at the Capital Theatre with the Blue Ridge Ramblers and Saturday night leave from Wheeling to make their first journey to New York to make further records. Their popularity on the air as well as in the theatre this week is only a forerunner of future fame. The Blue Ridge Ramblers are offering as a concluding event to their week's engagement at the Capital Theatre, an Old Fiddlers Contest and Barn Dance Band Convention tonight at 8:15. Many entries assure the contest as the greatest event of its kind ever shown in the valley.[4]

The information in the article was slightly exaggerated: their ages were not quite accurate, and the sisters were reported as having been discovered singing in a cornfield behind their house and overcoming several obstacles to go on tour. Supposedly, they were hardy mountaineers who were timid, didn't have the proper clothes to wear, and whose mother begged them not to go on the road. Obviously, that last impediment was undeniably true.

Newspaper advertisements for the Blue Ridge Ramblers. Jennie Bowman Cain Collection.

A collage of the Bowman Sisters. Jennie Bowman Cain Collection.

A comparison of the Blue Ridge Ramblers and the Hill Billies yields both similarities and contrasts. Undeniably, the Hill Billies intentionally endeavored to look and act like their name—hillbillies with comedy routines that were pure corn. Similarly, the Blue Ridge Ramblers attempted to look and act like hillbillies; pictures of them usually showed them dressed in country garb with the men in overalls. An old-time music magazine described their music:

> The pattern of the Blue Ridge Ramblers performance can be related
> to some by the Hill Billies: many of "lead" instruments are given solos,
> during which most or all of the other players drop out. For instance,
> there is a 3-fiddle chorus in "Golden Slippers"; Austin has several piano
> solos (notably in "Old Joe Clark"), and Wilson takes numerous steel

guitar solos. Vocals are few, and generally raucous chorus efforts by all. The repertoire declares itself in the discography alongside: some traditional fiddle tunes, some minstrel standards, and a couple of standard marches.

The orchestra approach of the band, and probably its composition too, removed most characteristics of regional traditional style and made it a Pan-Southern group foreshadowing, in a sense, such '30s bands as the Prairie Ramblers. The emphasis on soloists hints too at a prefiguration of Western Swing, but though the Blue Ridge Ramblers had ragtime elements in their music, there was little jazzy about them. The piano-oriented "rhythm section" has some similarity to that of Charlie Poole's "Highlanders" big band (in which Lonnie Austin played), and it is possible that Poole's group was to some extent similarly conceived.[5]

The Blue Ridge Ramblers definitely had an unpolished, no-holds-barred sound, with all of them singing the lead melody rather than individualized harmony parts. Their music was very lively and uplifting with an effervescent appealing sound. Whatever they did and however they sang, it all seemed to converge in the final product. Some critics have alleged the group fell through the cracks between pure country music and jazz.

The vaudeville that Charlie knew when he performed with the Hill Billies in 1928 had a slightly different twist by the time the three of them joined the medium in early 1931. Vaudeville was in its waning years trying to survive the Depression and the latest craze—talking pictures. Now instead of scheduling all stage acts, the theaters began interspersing live acts with movies. Mr. Barnes first aligned his Ramblers with the Loews Metropolitan Theatre Circuit, the brainchild of Marcus Loew, who purchased Metro Pictures, Goldwyn Pictures, and Louis B. Mayer Pictures, calling his new endeavor MGM. As the first person to combine live vaudeville acts with motion pictures, he made it possible for people to go to one of his theaters, watch a movie, and be entertained with a live stage show. Of the more than 125 theaters Mr. Loew built during his lifetime, the majority were deluxe, supermodern houses. He was in the process of constructing twenty-four more when he died in 1927.[6] Using a variety of performers, the theaters scheduled two to eight vaudeville acts between each movie. The Ramblers averaged two to three shows per day, but often did more, particularly if another act failed to show or had to be canceled. The Bowman Sisters typically sang two songs per show. The grand finale of the Ramblers' act featured two men and two women square dancing, with Charlie's fiddle taking the lead. After performing at a theater for a few days, the group would pack their few belongings and move to another. This grueling routine occurred night after night for about three years.

Charlie was accustomed to living in the Big Apple, having traveled there with the Hill Billies, but Jennie and Pauline had been there only briefly when they recorded for Columbia Records. One of the first things the two ladies did after arriving was have their individual pictures made by a professional photographer. These portraits were used to advertise the Bowman Sisters on the marquee of the Loews theaters. Pauline informed the photographer that she wanted to look "hillbilly"; Jennie, on the other hand, expressed her desire to appear "sexy." Both got their wish. It is surprising that, unlike their photograph made in front of the log house, neither of them looked very "hillbilly" in their individual pictures, yet they looked quite the part in their group picture with the Ramblers.

When the group traveled in New York City, they would usually stay at Mansfield Hall at Eighth Avenue and 50th Street, near Madison Square Garden. Numerous other performers, including circus acts and special people stayed there also. Charlie and his daughters became acquainted with the tallest man in the world, who slept in two beds. They likewise met the smallest man in the world, Clarence C. "Major Mite" Howerton. He was a nineteen-year-old midget who was twenty-six inches tall and weighed twenty-pounds. Clarence worked at Coney Island's Dreamland Circus and the B&B Circus, and he also appeared in the 1932 film *Free Eats*. Perhaps his most popular role was as a Munchkin (Herald #3) in the popular 1939 film *The Wizard of Oz*.[7] Major Mite and the Bowman Sisters became close friends and strolled throughout Manhattan together, to the surprise and amusement of bystanders. Pauline recalled walking the streets of the massive city without fear of crime. She and Jennie particularly enjoyed strolling up and down trendy Fifth Avenue, where they would gaze at the expensive clothes in the store windows. These fashion shops were very different from anything they had seen at Lige Adams's plaintive country store back home in Gray Station.

As far as is known, three separate diaries were logged on the Blue Ridge Ramblers. The first, maintained by Lonnie Austin, covered their tours from June 1928 through July 1929.[8] The other two journals were kept by Jennie (see appendix B) and Pauline, covering their tours from January 1931 through December 1932. An entry Lonnie made in April 1929, from his Mansfield Hall hotel room while on a four-day tour at Loews Delancy Theatre, displayed his weariness of being in New York City on long stays: "Just sitting here all alone tonite, although I'm playing solitaire. I can't say I'm unhappy for I heard today that we leave for Norfolk in two weeks, and I'll sure be tickled to death because I believe I'm getting a bit tired of N.Y. City. I'm glad we're going away for a while at least."[9] This was just a few months before he quit the Ramblers. Whereas Lonnie's diary was relatively comprehensive, the Bowman Sisters' accounts resembled ledgers, concentrating more on tour dates, cities visited, theaters where they performed, and hotels where they resided. Their diaries did contain occasional brief observations, however. An entry Jennie made in March 1932 during a two-day tour at the Apollo Theatre in Martinsburg, West Virginia, is a typical entry: "Got caught in a blizzard and did not get to the towns we were supposed to play Monday and Tuesday."[10] While on a three-day tour at the Capital Theatre in Shamokin, Pennsylvania, Pauline reported: "Jack [Pierce] and Sparkie [Walter Hughes] left the show. Jack joined the Oklahoma Cowboys later."[11] Despite their dissimilarities, these three diaries collectively displayed the lengthy and grueling aspect of the vaudeville road shows.

On April 22, 1931, the Bowman Sisters recorded three songs for Art Satherley of the American Recording Company (see Appendix A). He was the Frank Walker of Columbia Records and Ralph Peer of Okeh and later Victor Records. It is not known if Charlie participated in this session. One song, "Lonesome Blues," is believed to be a different composition from "Old Lonesome Blues," which they recorded earlier for Columbia Records. For whatever reasons, these three recordings were never released. Perhaps one explanation for this is that an acquisitions jungle began when the American Recording Company was formed in August 1929 by the merger of three small record companies: the Plaza Music Company (Jewel, Domino, Oriole, Banner, and Regal labels), the Pathe Phonograph and Radio Corporation (Pathe, Actuelle, and Perfect labels), and the Cameo Record Corporation (Cameo, Romeo, and Variety labels). In October 1930, Consolidated Film Industries then bought American Recording Company and subsequently purchased Brunswick/Vocalion and Melotone from Warner in December 1931, where they were assigned to the Brunswick Record Corporation side of the business. As if that were not enough, in 1934 Brunswick Record Corporation acquired both Columbia and Okeh Records. The Columbia Broadcasting System (CBS) in turn procured American Recording Company and Brunswick Record Corporation in February 1938. The new organization became known as the Columbia Recording Corporation. At about this same time, Decca obtained the right to pre-1932 Brunswick and Vocalion material.[12] With all these transfers and mergers taking place, perhaps the three American Record Company songs by the Bowman Sisters were never issued because no one could figure out which record company owned them or on which label they should be placed.

During the next few years, the Ramblers toured extensively all over the northeast, eventually appearing in every New England state. A true family historian, Jennie kept copious records of these travels, collecting newspaper clippings, theater flyers, and photographs of their vaudeville travels. An examination of her diary shows that they performed on stage 249 days (almost five days a week) in 1931 and 168 (over three days a week) in 1932, meaning that in the two years they were in vaudeville they performed about four days a week, on average. Adding the travel times to the numbers meant they had left little time left to do much but follow the tour schedule. The Blue Ridge Ramblers brought a unique type of entertainment, "Hillbilly Vaudeville," to the vaudeville scene and it was well received by their ever-growing audience. As important components of the group, Pauline and Jennie were becoming well known for their country blues style of singing.

Charlie received a pleasant surprise when the Blue Ridge Ramblers and the Hill Billies shared the same stage in South Cumberland, Maryland, on March 21, 1932, just seven months before Al's death and approximately a year and a half before the Hill Billies disbanded. It is believed that the Hill Billies switched to the Loews Metropolitan Theatre Vaudeville Circuit in the spring of 1932.

While touring with the Ramblers, Pauline and Jennie missed the mouth-watering southern-style food that their mother fixed each day in Gray Station, particularly breakfast. The transplanted Bowman girls could not get accustomed to the typical northern-style breakfast with eggs, bacon, and fried potatoes, as opposed to eggs, sausage, grits, gravy, homemade biscuits, and cold, salted sliced tomatoes. Consequently, during a five-day tour in Uniontown, Pennsylvania, in February 1931, Charlie requested the manager of a nearby café to surprise his two young offspring by fixing the three of them a full-course southern break-fast like Fannie would have cooked. After the manager agreed, Charlie gave him specific instructions for preparing the meal. The next morning, the young ladies were astonished and blissfully consumed their food. For five fleeting days, they closed their eyes each morning and pretended that they were back at the long wooden table in the log house, eating their mother's country cooking with their siblings. This special time triggered Pauline's homesickness, eventually causing her to make some life-altering changes.

The Ramblers not only entertained on the vaudeville stage for the Loews Circuit, they also appeared on several local radio stations in cities they were touring. Jennie's diary shows that they broadcast on ten outlets:

WWVA (Wheeling, West Virginia, Feb. 22–28, 1931)
WCAU (Philadelphia, Pennsylvania, Mar. 21, 1931)
WPG (Philadelphia, Pennsylvania, Apr. 5, 1931)
WRAW (Reading, Pennsylvania, Apr. 6–8, 1931)
WTIC (Hartford, Connecticut, Aug. 22–29, 1931)
WCSH (Portland, Maine, Sep. 18–24, 1931)
WCAX (Burlington, Vermont, Nov. 30–Dec 6, 1931)
WHP (Harrisburg, Pennsylvania, Jan. 9–15, 1932)
WCOD (Harrisburg, Pennsylvania, Jan. 9–15, 1932)
Unknown (Binghamton, New York, Apr. 28–30, 1932)[13]

Being in vaudeville and performing on some of the leading stages in the Northeast opened up additional opportunities for Jennie and Pauline, including making a toothpaste commercial for Colgate. Company officials had seen their vaudeville act and had decided that these two little hillbilly singers would be an effective drawing card for their product, and they were instructed to appear at the company's New York office at a specified date and time. Since the distance between there and where they were staying was too far to walk, Charlie agreed to transport them. However, when the time came for them to leave, their father failed to honor his commitment. Accordingly, the commercial never became a reality. This was just one of several missed opportunities for the Bowman family.

The Blue Ridge Ramblers took a well-deserved two-and-a-half-month summer break from the road after performing at the Colonial Theatre in Lancaster, Pennsylvania, on May 19, 1931. Charlie, Pauline, and Jennie returned home to Gray Station. Consistent with Charlie's desire to perform with his fiddle and with his ever-growing popularity, he agreed to rejoin his three brothers for some local performances. In July, the group was called on to play music as part of a celebration for the paving of the highway between Johnson City and Kingsport. This project was part of a federal program that began in 1930 for the building of selected main roads between Florida and Michigan. The ceremony, sponsored by the local Chamber of Commerce, included several speeches, a ribbon-cutting ceremony and, naturally, some traditional Appalachian music from Charlie Bowman and His Brothers. Ironically, what started out on a happy note ended in tragedy when an electric storm struck with little warning, causing people to scramble. Two individuals were killed instantly when a bolt of lightning struck the tent under which they had just taken shelter.

The Bowman trio rejoined the Ramblers on August 8 in Amherst, Massachusetts, at the Publix Lauter Theatre. Hank Barnes added a new trouper by the name of Richard Dixon to his entourage. After becoming acquainted with his fellow Ramblers, the newcomer composed a poem that he titled "Impressions." While somewhat humorous, it offers some insights into the actual personalities of the band members:

I joined a show the other day
The people, each one in their way
Impressed me. So in metred verse
I now will try to do my worse.

Bert: He's boss and M.C. too
Our money sticks to him like glue.
A fine big-hearted guy to boot
And always wearing a full-dress suit.

There's Pappy Williams—What a man.
He's always boarding in the can.
They took his knife, his shirts and socks.
And almost had him breaking rocks.

And now here's Ted, Believe me folks.
She certainly can crack those jokes.
She acts as end man in the line
And loses Curley in her spare time.

On stage, Jim ain't allowed to laugh
By orders of his better half.
We're trading him in for a Ford
Because he only plays one chord.

His wife; a singer of great fame
We call her Polly; that's her name.
Has lost her voice; Oh, what a shame.
I wonder if she is to blame.

For Harry, who makes all the noise.
The man who sings without a voice.
He's known to all of us as king.
It is too bad that he can't sing.

You'll find out in this paragraph
The way to cut a drop in half
From Henry. Who gets us to Dutch
Because he always talks too much.

I'll introduce a girl named Flo.
Who dances in this big-time show.
She probably will wed a Duke
And serenade him on her uke.

I've thought and thought since I began
How to put Charlie on the pan.
If Opera you should chance to crave
This gentleman? Will be your slave.

The sweetheart of our show, it seems
Is Jennie. Darling of our Dreams.
It's useless though to love I've found
As long as Ernie is around.

The smallest man in this whole act
Is Spark-Plug. He's a little cracked.
But we all understand the lad
Which really makes it not so bad.

And now the last one on the list.
The one I surely should have missed.
Dick's no one I can recommend
Unless you're ready for the end.

Epilogue: If I have said a word or two
Which someone might believe untrue.
There's one thing left for me to do.
So I apologize to you.[14]

The impact the Blue Ridge Ramblers were having on their audiences can be sensed from a local paper regarding a performance at the Merrimack Square in Lowell, Massachusetts, November 1–3, 1931:

> One of the most enthusiastically received musical groups to appear on a local theatre stage in many days gave a program of hill-billy tunes last evening and yesterday afternoon at Merrimack Square Theatre under the headline, "The Blue Ridge Ramblers."
>
> The name is significant enough of the trend of music played, but the actual playing of the stringed instruments and harmonies, together with the mountain pronunciations in the vocal numbers and the odd, yet intricate dance steps all helped to place the audience in the environment of Kentucky's hills.
>
> Five men and five young, peppy and decidedly attractive girls comprise the troupe. All are dressed as though on their way to husk corn or hunt "b'ar." The presentations consist of several group number, duets and solos. The sisters (Jennie and Pauline) who sing the "blue" numbers are particularly good.
>
> The troupe will end its engagement at the Paige street theatre after the performance this afternoon and evening.[15]

While performing at the famous Steel Pier in Atlantic City, New Jersey, the Bowman Sisters occupied a dressing room at the end of the pier overlooking the Atlantic Ocean. When high tide came in, the waves pounded the pier supports, shaking their quarters to the extent that they felt they were going to plunge into the ocean. Aside from this fear, the Steel Pier was an electrifying place to be, with its lively carnival atmosphere and an array of performances. The circus-like arenas allowed for an assortment of vaudeville acts, minstrel shows, and other performances. Without a doubt, the most unique and famous act at the Steel Pier, and the one remembered most indelibly by Pauline, was the "High Diving Horses," which performed there for forty-nine consecutive years. Several times each day, a trained horse and its daring female rider leaped from a sixty-foot tower into a pool of water. An advertisement declared that the riders broke an average of only one bone per year. While no injury statistics were provided for the horses, the popular act was eventually canceled after protests from animal rights activists.

Another Steel Pier act consisted of a young boy, his father, and a gentleman known as "Uncle Will." The youngster began performing with the Will Mastin

Trio at the age of four, soon becoming the indisputable star of the show with his tap dancing, singing, and mimic. His name was Sammy Davis Jr.[16] Pauline recalled that he came to her dressing room to hear her play the ukulele and harmonica. Sammy became so fascinated with her harmonica playing that she not only gave him one but also taught him to play it. After Sammy achieved proficiency on the instrument, he and Pauline played a duet, with him sitting on top of her dresser or, as often as not, on her lap.

On January 5, 1932, Pauline and Rambler band member Vincent "Jimmy James" Gamelli eloped, after a courtship of five months. The two were afraid to tell Charlie about their nuptial plans, so they sneaked off between engagements in Charleston, West Virginia, and Brunswick, Maryland. The couple exchanged vows in a Methodist Church parsonage in Frederick, Maryland, which was less than twenty miles away. They waited until after the Brunswick engagements to tell Charlie that they had become husband and wife. Pauline recalled that her father "pulled him a good one," meaning that he threw a temper tantrum. The news of Pauline's marriage greatly disturbed Fannie, especially since she had not met the young entertainer, who had played with several small bands before joining the Ramblers. His talents included songwriting; playing banjo, guitar, and trombone; as well as doing comedy in the show.

A collage of Jimmy James. *Left:* Pauline Bowman and Jimmy James; *right:* Charlie Bowman and Jimmy James. Pauline Bowman Huggans Collection.

Jimmy's parents had emigrated from Sicily, and Pauline liked Jimmy's mother, who cooked an abundance of delicious Italian food. After enjoying Ma Gamelli's cooking over a period of several months, Pauline determined to cook her a delicious East Tennessee country-style dinner. With permission from her mother-in-law, she took over her kitchen and made pork chops, mashed potatoes, gravy, and homemade biscuits. Since there was absolutely nothing Italian about the meal, Pauline was anxious as she escorted her mother-in-law to the table. Mrs. Gamelli took her seat and began eating without saying a word, remaining expressionless for several minutes. Pauline feared that she did not find her hillbilly cooking palatable. Suddenly, the Italian lady looked up at the nervous cook, grinned sheepishly, and exclaimed in a loud voice, "I like! I like!"

While the Ramblers were performing in Huntington, Pennsylvania, on January 21, 1932, a local newspaper carried an article titled "The Hill Billies Are Here in Person":

A distinct novelty in the way of stage attractions promised all who go to the Grand Theatre tonight. This is the appearance of the famous Blue Ridge Ramblers, appearing at seven thirty and nine thirty P.M. in connection with Claudette Colbert in the Paramount super picture "Secret of a Secretary."

Dramatizing the lives and customs of the primitive mountain folk of the Blue Ridge has long been a favorite subject of American novelists, but rarely is the public given an opportunity to see them in person and observe their unique customs at close range.

The Blue Ridge Ramblers consist of twelve young men and girls, who have won wide recognition by reason of their programs broadcasted from important stations of all parts of the country, especially in the rendition of old mountaineer melodies which have never been written in manuscript, but handed down from generation to generation. This part of their program should be of special interest to those appreciating new and unusual entertainment.

It is a happy combination of old and new mountain music. In addition to their radio engagements, the Blue Ridge Ramblers have played successful Vaudeville engagements at leading theatres, both East and West. They come to the Grand Theatre direct from Harrisburg. They are also known as recording artists, having successfully recorded a good many records.[17]

With so many performances by the Ramblers, it would be reasonable to assume that Fannie attended some of them. However, based on her daughters' two diaries and family members' memories, she was present at only one, at the Paramount

Theatre on February 8–10, 1932, in nearby Bristol. It is not known how many of her children accompanied her, but it is known that Pauline introduced Jimmy to Fannie at this performance. While Fannie's reaction to the show is undocumented, it is predictable. After all, it was H. M. Barnes who convinced her husband and her two oldest daughters to leave their family and go on the road.

In addition to maintaining diaries, Pauline and Jennie also kept autograph books to collect comments from vaudeville performers with whom they performed. These compilations were similar to today's typical high school annuals. An example of one entry, dated April 10, 1932, is to Pauline and Jimmy James from vaudeville organist Dusty Rhodes:

> Dear Pauline and Jimmy. Two swell kids. I love to work with you and hope someday we will work together again. From a real trooper. Best wishes and lots of luck. Your Pal, Dusty Rhodes.[18]

Other performers who signed their autograph books include the Roberts Sisters, Bob DePeron (of the DePeron Trio), Georgia Goodner (Junior Frolics), Teddie Goodner, Walter "Sparky" Hughes, Bertha Tyner (Yodler), Smiley Boy Burnette (Gene Autry's future cowboy sidekick), Texas Daisy (WSM), Bill Robinson, and Bert and Ted Bence.[19]

Jennie collected photographs of other entertainers with whom she shared the stage. These included Dave Vines (a single Vaudeville act); Duke Dewey and his wife, Eileen Bradfield (known as the Dixieland Rubes); Florence and Madeline Gray (two redheads from Connecticut known as the Gray Sisters); Dick Hart's Tennessee Ramblers; the Hoosier Hot Shots (American Record Corporation, Perfect Label); the Arizona Ranch Girls (Ard Sisters: Lorene, Dinky, Ione, Polly, Clarine); the Texas Rangers (Jack Pierce, Red, Shad, Esther); Renfro Valley Folks (Slim Miller); Wilbur Hall (a comedian who played several instruments including a tire pump); Max Felix; and the Hickory Nuts.[20] A few of these people had previously been with the Ramblers. Attrition among groups was quite high in those days, as the work required dedication and constant travel on the vaudeville circuit.

On May 11, 1932, the Blue Ridge Ramblers began traveling upstate New York, as part of the Smalley Time Circuit, beginning with the Community Theatre in Catskill, New York. It is not known if the Loews Metropolitan Theatre Circuit dropped the Ramblers or vice versa, but Pauline recalled it was Mr. Barnes who made the decision to switch to the Smalley Time Circuit. They performed in twenty-one New York cities over the next two months, then their tour turned southward. The clientele of this new circuit was more affluent, and many of their performances were held at expensive resorts instead of theater stages. Switching to the Smalley Time Circuit had one noteworthy advantage, or disadvantage: radio broadcasts were not a part of their new contract.

Within two months, Pauline returned home after learning of the impending death of her half-brother, Elmer Ferguson, the elder son of Fannie and her first husband, Jake Ferguson. She caught a bus at Franklin, Massachusetts, but arrived too late to see Elmer alive. At only twenty-nine, he had died of lung disease after years of working in the zinc mines of Embreeville, Tennessee, near Erwin. This trip home eventually caused Pauline to make a life-changing decision.

Chapter 9

CHARLIE'S VARIETY FIVE

Between early 1931 and late 1934, the Bowman family took numerous reprieves from their Blue Ridge Rambler vaudeville tours to return home to their family in Gray Station. As with all such previous trips, people flocked to see their hometown heroes, continuing to seize quality time from the family. However, this was show business, and the Bowmans had become celebrities. Their many East Tennessee fans wanted to see them perform the same routines that had made them famous. It was during one such trip that Charlie called on two of his fellow Ramblers, Frank "Dad" Williams and Walter "Spark Plug" Hughes, to join him, Jennie, and Pauline to form a stage act. Since they could not perform in the official capacity as the Blue Ridge Ramblers, they chose an alternate name, the Variety Five, with Charlie as manager, master of ceremonies, and fiddler. This was his second experience as a bandleader, having been the leader of his brothers' band, but it would not be his last. The Variety Five allowed Charlie, Jennie, and Pauline to continue performing during those slack times when they were not booked with the Ramblers. Jimmy James, however, did not participate in these performances.

On December 28, 1931, these five musicians were contacted by the local Majestic Theatre in downtown Johnson City to be a part of their annual "New Year's Follies" variety stage show. All five agreed to do the midnight show in spite of their being on leave for only four days and scheduled to begin a three-day engagement on January 1 in Bridgeton, New Jersey. That night the theater was filled to capacity. The *Johnson City Chronicle* wrote about the performances in an article titled "Artists Usher in New Year at the Majestic: Superior Talent Combined in Midnight Vaudeville Program at Theater":

> An Enthusiastic audience that crammed the Majestic Theatre to capacity, cheered, applauded and repeatedly encored the various acts and numbers that composed the exceptionally entertaining "New Year's Follies" presented at the Majestic on New Year's Eve. Full credit for the success of the big event should go to George Gookin, stage manager and musical director of the Majestic, who produced the big show, which was presented in detail by Carroll King, Majestic master of ceremonies.

The show carried a New Year's theme and culminated with the tottering passage of "Old Man Depression, Mr. 1932," and the appearance of the snappy, peppy, dainty "Miss Prosperity, Miss 1933," at the stroke of twelve o'clock. This feature was appropriately staged and was highly acclaimed by the audience, which was composed not only of hundreds of Johnson Citians, but scores and scores of visitors from neighboring cities and towns.

The show proper can honestly be termed "big time" vaudeville. This outstanding individual and group hit was registered by the "Variety Five," an aggregation of three men and two young ladies who could have held the stage indefinitely but who were arbitrarily limited to one encore on each number, on account of the length of the program. They are all experienced professionals who know how to sell their number and how to get the most out of them. This act would and has gone over big in the leading vaudeville theaters of the country. The members of the "Variety Five" are Charlie Bowman, manager and specialty violinist; his two daughters, Pauline and Jennie Bowman, harmony singers; Frank (Dad) Williams, champion novelty fiddler; and (Spark Plug) Hughes, the wizard of the guitar. This act, which has been on tour among the leading broadcasting stations and over the choicest vaudeville circuits, happens to be a Johnson City act, as this is the home of Charlie Bowman and his daughters. Being home for Christmas, they were available for the big special show and kindly consented to appear.

What was probably the outstanding personal triumph was registered by Charles Ryburn, of Erwin. This young man, a highly talented pupil of Ned Wayburn, is now conducting a dancing school at Erwin. His offering, in addition to the lead tap on the opening ensemble was an amazing acrobatic dance in which he went through twist, bends, nip-ups and splits that one ordinarily associates only with the finest feminine acrobatic dancers or a freakish contortionist. Rayburn scored heavily. He also received indirect credit through the success of dainty little Miss Virginia Lee Stillman, one of his pupils. She was Miss 1933 and then came back and rendered a tap dance, perfect in rhythm and routine and most creditable to such a little miss.

Howard Mattox, of Erwin, proved to have a delightfully toned tenor voice and charmed the audience with his solos, interjecting as an interlude of lovely ballads into the program. Another pleasing intre-act was the dance routine of Miss Dorothy Starr, who appeared in entrancingly beautiful wardrobe and presented a willowy, rhythmic dance that brought resounding volleys of applause.

Another lovely little lady who registered heavily with the audience was Miss Mary Bradley of Elizabethton. Miss Bradley appeared on one of the contest programs some time ago and her dance act went over so big that she was called back by special request to appear on the New Year's program. This accomplished, graceful and shapely little lady again registered heavily and had to take several special bows.

The comedy hit of the evening was scored by the "Hi-Brown Hot-chas from Harlem," namely Miss Mary McCarren and Mr. Herbert Hull. Working in blackface and hi-brown makeup, this talented team put over comedy gags, dance duos and vocal solos to the intense delight and repeated applause of the audience. The broken rhythm of Hull's solo, with break-ins by the stage band, made a novelty that registered heavily, while Miss McCarren in her role of the abused sweetie, kept her partner busy. Their team dancing and Hull's singing were outstanding.

Full credit must be given to "Gookin's Gangsters," as the Majestic stage band is known. These young men had a strenuous evening, accompanying so many different and diversified acts, but they did it in an accomplished and professional manner.

Especial credit and thanks for materially adding to the pleasure of the program goes to the Marquerite Hyatt School of the Dance. Through the courtesy of Miss Hyatt, an exceptionally clever dance unit of five "Hyat-tites" was furnished the Majestic and this ensemble was one of the bright-est spots on the program. These clever and talented ladies, even of whom is an advanced student at the Hyatt school were: Misses Nellie Gray, Eva Montgomery, Dorothy Starr, Lena Crowley and Julie Maxwell. At the con-clusion of the program, the audience—delighted with the entire show, demonstrated a reluctance to let the curtains close and gave a surprisingly heavy amount of finale applause. It was one of the best shows offered at the Majestic in several years, not excluding all-professional companies.[1]

In the following excerpt from an undated *Johnson City Chronicle* article, Charlie Bowman and his Variety Five are again identified with the implication that they were playing routinely as a group:

The next act was strictly professional, being Charles Bowman and his famous "Variety Five." Versatile artists, every one, they gave twenty min-utes of rapid-fire entertainment. Frank "Dad" Williams played the violin in every conceivable way, letting the tempo down for a minute and keeping the audience in an uproar of applause. Charlie Bowman, him-self acted as master of ceremonies for the act, did comedy bits, played the violin and kept things pepped up all the time. Walter "Spark Plug"

Hughes proved a versatile guitar artist, worked in vocal and instrumental numbers, helped out in the ensemble and kept both his guitar and voice effectively busy. Pauline Bowman, charming harmonica player, proved to be a harmony singer as well and the duets she sang with her sister Jennie, and the trios with Jennie and "Spark Plug," were delightful. Jennie, likewise, doubled doing ukulele numbers as her specialty. And then Dad Williams, did his stuff, and how! He played the violin in every conceivable posture, rendering "Pop, Goes the Weasel" in so many different positions and variations as to have the audience in hysterics. He also did a novel organ imitation and fiddled all through the different acts. The "Variety Five" was a whole show in itself and it is no wonder they have been so successful on stage and radio.[2]

New Year's Eve 1935 on the Majestic Theatre stage was a memorable occasion for the Bowman family. Not only were Charlie, Jennie, and Pauline welcomed home by their many local fans, but also joining them on stage were the Bowman brothers—Elbert, Walter, and Argil. A January 2 article in the *Johnson City Chronicle*, "Majestic New Year's Frolic Plays to Crowd," describes the evening:

> More than two hundred patrons were turned away from the Majestic Theatre at the gala midnight frolic on New Year's Eve, the management finding it necessary to close the doors and stop selling tickets when it was found that every seat and every available bit of standing room had been occupied. It was a record-breaking attendance and every one of the patrons thoroughly enjoyed the big two and one-half hour show, which was delightful in every phase.
>
> Starting with short subjects at 11:30 p.m., the vaudeville program came on at 11:55 and after greeting "Miss 1935," swung into forty-five minutes of fast moving variety. Then followed the big feature picture "Forsaking All Others" starring Joan Crawford, Clark Gable and Robert Montgomery, and nearly everyone stayed through this delicious modern story of romance and comedy. It was a great show and although the audience was not dismissed until two o'clock Tuesday morning, everyone was bright-eyed and happy when they left the theatre.
>
> Every act on the program was good, in its particular realm of entertainment activity of course there were some outstanding, such as the Bowman Family who were welcomed back here after an absence of two years during which time they have been broadcasting and playing leading vaudeville theatres.
>
> In the order of their appearance the acts were as follows—each being capably supported by the Majestic Stage band.

1. "Father Time" by Bill Toohey singing "Auld Lang Syne" just at midnight. As the clock struck twelve, "Miss 1935" deliciously portrayed by little Miss Jean Carter, came on the stage to the strains of "Happy Days Are Here Again" and wished everybody a "Happy New Year." Little Miss 1935 enjoyed every bit of the entertainment in her honor and stayed until the finale.

2. Here appeared for the first time on the program, the popular "Dancing Darlings" from the Reese Holloway School of the Dance, six graceful, pretty, evenly sized and beautifully costumed young ladies, presenting a modern dance routine. They were the Misses Norma Bailey, Louise Connor, Irene Steppe, Marion Harrower, Jane White and Reese Holloway.

3. "The Three Musketeers" of song were next seen and heard, each doing a favorite selection in rapid-fire order. These young men were Bill Toohey, Jim Ferguson and Jim Toohey.

4. The Dancing Trio, Miss Reese Holloway, Jane White and Kermit Jennings here offered a beautifully graceful continental stage dance.

5. Here came a high-light, welcoming back a popular "Crooning' Troubadour" who had been absent from the Majestic stage for nearly two years; Walter "Sparkie" Hughes, who with his tinkling guitar, offered a group of delightful songs.

6. Miss Reese Holloway here did her "Hot Harlem" solo dance to a big applause.

7. Contrasting next came Miss Jane White whose lovely voice delightfully entertained with a couple of numbers.

8. Not to be outdone by the young ladies, a couple of boys from the Bowery, come on here and did their theme dance. Jim Toohey and Kermit Jennings and they certainly surprised their friends with their rhythm work.

9. Making a sort of competition affair out it, the Holloway Ensemble came on next to outdo the boys and made a tie of it with their modern buck dancing.

10. Introduced here as a special feature, a novelty buck gracefully done by pretty Miss Katherine Seitzer.

11. Right back came the team of hoofers, but this time with a graceful feminine addition to the team, Miss Reese Holloway, and trio did "Flashes of Broadway" in fine fettle.

12. At this point a special announcement was made welcoming back home that ever-popular family of radio and vaudeville entertainers, the Bowman Family, headed by Charlie Bowman in person. Charlie

presented the various members of his family, his brothers, the Bowman Brothers, offering yodeling and crooning numbers. Charlie, himself, of course, starred and the audience could not get enough of him, but the lateness of the hour and the long feature yet to be shown, forced the management to bring on the finale at this point; the last number being led by the Holloway Ensemble.[3]

Interestingly, Charlie was frequently referred to as a "specialty violinist" instead of a "specialty fiddler." He was known everywhere as Fiddlin' Charlie Bowman, not Violinist Charlie Bowman. Some musicians tend to be identified as "fiddlers" and others as "violinists." These two terms are often used interchangeably, but is there a difference between them? If a person were to enter a music store and ask the clerk for a fiddle and a violin, the employee would sell the customer two identical instruments. This suggests that the difference between the two items lies not in the instrument but in the person who plays it and the technique used, perhaps with a few minor adjustments to the instrument itself. Some people define a fiddle as a violin played as a folk instrument. Another definition is that while a violin has four strings tuned a fourth apart and played with a bow or plucked, a fiddle can be played with smoothness one moment and lightning fast the next, referred to by fiddlers as pyrotechnics. *Fiddler Magazine* offers this humorous definition: "A fiddle is a violin with attitude."

The violinist's repertoire consists mostly of operatic and classical music from the masters: sonatas, suites, and concertos. The musician's performance is multi-faceted: playing without flaw, demonstrating an understanding of each piece, the era it represents, and the musical objective for the number. Most violinists play their music as a member in an orchestra. They typically sit together on stage and position their violins firmly against their chins. They dress formally and read sheet music secured to music stands. They alternately maintain eye contact with their music and the conductor, who synchronizes all the musicians into one desired product. The audience, also formally dressed, sits relatively motionless and expresses its approval with thunderous applause at appropriate times.

On the other hand, the fiddler's range consists of ballads, hoedowns, jigs, reels, waltzes, blues, flings, and hornpipes. Like favorite jokes, the tunes have been passed down over time. Some players make minor changes and pass them on to others, a tradition unheard of in the violinist's camp. Fiddlers often play as a member of a small band such as old-time, bluegrass, Cajun, western swing, and country. In an old-time string band, the fiddler, dressed in casual garb, usually plays acoustical music by ear in an informal setting. With fiddle against shoulder, the musician takes the lead as if a conductor and stands instead of sits. The equally casually dressed members of the audience express their approval not with thunderous applause but by clapping to the beat, singing along, tapping their toes and dancing. The fiddler appears to be in a trance, playing effortlessly and incessantly with little sign of tiring, stringing melody notes together like a skilled knitter and improvising along the way, rarely playing a tune the same way twice. It is as if the performer takes a song and breathe life into it with creative improvisation.

Inside of one of Charlie's fiddles that he later gave to Jennie were five words: "Stradivarius Model, Made in Germany." More than a few persons have picked up an old fiddle and become overly excited after seeing the name Stradivarius imprinted inside it. The general population associates the name with a violin, not with a fiddle. However, during the early part of the twentieth century, the imitation Stradivarius model was produced in mass quantity in Europe and exported to the United States, where demand was heavy. Most of them were sold for under fifteen dollars, which included the case and a bow.

Charlie, Jennie, Pauline, and Jimmy officially left the Blue Ridge Ramblers just before Christmas 1934. Quite possibly, after six years, Mr. Barnes also decided to call it quits; the once popular act had apparently run its course. This gave Jimmy the opportunity to make the switch from hillbilly to big band music. He had grown tired of playing hillbilly music and wanted to be in an orchestra where he could play the trombone instead of the guitar and banjo. Pauline traveled with her husband as he began seeking employment in a big band orchestra. Between 1935 and 1937, Jimmy James played in several groups as a trombonist before joining the Sid Applegate Orchestra for a short stint.

In 1937, Jimmy began touring with piano player and bandleader Frankie Carle, who was just rising to fame. The pianist would later adopt as his theme song the beautiful "Sunrise Serenade." Jimmy and Pauline began touring with the Carle band around the New England states, although Pauline was not an official part of the show. It was, however, during this time that Jimmy told Frankie Carl about his wife singing country blues songs with her sister as part of the Blue Ridge Ramblers on the vaudeville stage. Frankie was so impressed that one night while they were playing near Albany, New York, at Club Edgewood, he told Pauline that he wanted her to be on the program that night; this was the only notice she received. The thought of fulfilling his request frightened her, but she knew she had to do it because Frankie was her husband's boss. The song the bandleader chose for Pauline was "A Good Man Is Hard to Find (You Always Get the Other Kind)," having been recorded by notables Bessie Smith, Fats Waller, and Eddie Condon. Although Pauline was, by this time, a seasoned veteran, singing without Jennie in a different musical genre, and in front of a big-band audience for an up-and-coming bandleader, was far different. When it came time for Pauline to sing, Frankie introduced her to the audience and accompanied her on the piano while she sang. Once she began everything was fine, and the audience responded positively to her debut with Frankie Carle.

The local Springfield, Massachusetts, newspaper printed an article on Friday, June 14, 1940, about newcomer "Smiling" Frankie Carle and his new dance orchestra:

> Smiling Frankie Carle, dance wizard of the keys, and his recently organized orchestra will make its last appearance of this season at the Butterfly ballroom tomorrow night. During the summer, the ballroom will be decorated and several alterations made in preparation for the fall opening.
>
> The new dance band under direction of Mr. Carle who is widely known as a pianist, radio artist and composer includes musicians of prominence in the field of dance music. Director Carle's orchestra first appeared about a month ago playing for a large crowd of dancers at the Butterfly. Since that time, the band has gained high favor with the public and has appeared nightly in dance spots throughout New England.
>
> The boys wear smart uniforms and the band carries an amplifying system. The music they offer is modern in every way but tempered always to the desires of any given group. The versatile players have done much radio work and have learned what the public wants. Mr. Carle, former featured pianist with McEnelly's Orchestra and Mal Hallett's Band, has gone into several states in an effort to get together a perfect musical organization. The reception accorded his band to date makes its success assured.[4]

After 1932 vaudeville was on its way out, but it did not die a natural death; it was massacred in part by the very performers who had made it successful. Radio was fast becoming a competitive media, the Great Depression had taken money from people's pocketbooks, and the era of talking movies had securely replaced the days of the silent pictures.[5] While vaudeville would linger for a while, struggling on life support, it would eventually become comatose and finally succumb. Some argue that the medium never really died but instead moved to Nashville, where it established new life.

Jennie's last entry to her diary for the Ramblers era was for Jonesboro, Tennessee, on December 30, 1932. She either stopped keeping records or quit performing with the Ramblers. Her scrapbook seems to indicate that, at that time, they went from a two-year relatively continuous tour that began in early 1931 to a two-year sporadic one that began in early 1933. During this time, Jennie met the man who would sweep her off her feet and into the bonds of matrimony. She had been dating a local Gray Station fellow for years, but they had never married.

Meanwhile, Staley Cain had attended one of the Rambler shows, where he saw his future bride performing on stage. He was so taken by her overflowing beauty and musical talent that, after courting her for only two weeks, he asked her to marry him. Jennie promptly accepted his proposal, and they were married before a justice of the peace in the Jonesboro Court House.

At the end of their tour, the Ramblers personnel were notified of performance dates by telegram. Following is a telegram sent to Jennie from H. M. Barnes on October 14, 1933:

> PHILADELPHIA PENN, MISS JENNIE BOWMAN= CARE CHARLIE BOWMAN
> FORDTOWN TENNESSEE= OPENING THURSDAY NEXT WEEK WANT YOU TO
> LEAVE MONDAY OR TUESDAY BY BUS FARE TO JOHNSON CITY TO COME
> ON ANSWER BY WESTERN UNION AS SOON AS YOU GET THIS IF YOU CAN
> LEAVE MONDAY OR TUESDAY FOR PHILADELPHIA= H M BARNES.[6]

The second telegram was delivered three days later on October 17, 1933:

> PHILADELPHIA PENN, MISS JENNIE BOWMAN= 221 HAMILTON WILL
> CALL AS JOHNSON CITY TENN= ON ACCOUNT OF WAITING SO LATE TO
> HEAR FROM YOU AND PAULINE HAVE PUT OFF OPENING UNTIL TWO
> WEEKS BE READY TO COME THEN SHOW IS SURELY OPENING BY THEN
> AM DEPENDING ON YOU PAULINE WILL LET YOU KNOW TWO OR THREE
> DAYS BEFORE YOU ARE TO LEAVE= H M BARNES.[7]

It is doubtful that Jennie received this last communication for two reasons. First, she and Staley were still on their honeymoon after having been married only four days. Second, the first telegram was incorrectly addressed to Fordtown, Tennessee, while the second one was addressed to 221 Hamilton Avenue in Johnson City, the residence of Walter Bowman. Neither was correct. Jennie and Staley had lived with Walter for a brief time while waiting to move into a new house just down the block from him. Whether these factors delayed the opening for Mr. Barnes is not known, but these telegrams implied that Hank Barnes was losing control over the Ramblers. Within a couple months, Hank Barnes would pull the plug on his Blue Ridge Ramblers.

Chapter 10

CHARLIE'S BLUE RIDGE MUSIC MAKERS

When January 1935 rolled around, none of the Bowman family members suspected the momentous changes that would take place within twelve months, the first being the death of Charlie's beloved mother, Nancy, in February. Grandma Bowman's closing years were plagued with increasing health problems, resulting from her ongoing bout with diabetes. By this time, most of her children were grown and living elsewhere, although someone stayed with her essentially full time, as her children and their spouses took turns caring for her. Nancy's problems had become notably worse since Thanksgiving Day of the prior year when the whole family was there for a holiday dinner. Family members noticed a grisly sore that had developed on one of her toes. Insulin had been available to the public since 1923, so it is assumed that she was taking the medication. Two area doctors, Dr. Isenberg and Dr. McCollum, routinely treated her to the best of available technology. Apparently, amputation was not opted for, as her legs had almost decayed by the time she passed away. Nancy's children watched over her bed day and night during her final days. Knowing her precarious situation, she called Alfred to her bedside just before she died and made him promise that he would keep an eye on her children after she was gone. In effect, Grandma Bowman was asking her oldest son to continue watching out for the family, just as he had done in the thirty years that she had been a widow. Her children in 1935 ranged in age from thirty-eight to fifty-four. Her death occurred around seven o'clock in the morning on February 22, 1935, just two weeks shy of her seventy-ninth birthday. Elbert and his family were living in the old home place at the time and remained there for an additional five years.

When Charlie came home to Gray Station after his vaudeville tour with the Ramblers, he continued to play music wherever he could find an audience. Several family members remembered when he performed at the annual Gray Station Fair along with his brothers or anyone else he could round up, including his Variety Five. The fair, which continues to this day, was a much anticipated and exhilarating event for people all across the Upper East Tennessee area.

In the fall of 1935, Charlie made a bold decision to return to the lifestyle to which he had become accustomed; it would mark the third time he would leave his family. By then, Fannie Mae was forty-nine years old with progeny whose ages ranged from five to twenty-four. By this time, several of their children had moved out of the log house. Fannie was most likely anguished but not overly surprised by Charlie's abrupt decision, based on his previous track record and knowing his craving to play his fiddle and perform. Since opportunity seemed to abound in the larger cities, Charlie initially set out for Louisville, Kentucky, just long enough to form his own group, the Blue Ridge Music Makers, and begin broadcasting over radio station WHAS.[1] In October 1935, the group moved to Atlanta, where over the next few years Charlie and his Music Makers broadcasted over three area radio stations: WSB ("Welcome South Brother"), WSGT, and WAGA. They stayed with WSB, which featured eight separate acts, until May 1936. The station manager, Lamdin Kay, and Charlie immediately became personal friends. Many years later, the East Tennessee fiddler spoke highly of Lamdin Kay, calling him "a great great man."

The Blue Ridge Music Makers. *Standing, left to right:* Hal Armstrong, Charlie Bowman, Walter Hughes; *sitting:* "Rhythm" (name unknown) and "Pep" (Clara Louise George). Jennie Bowman Cain Collection.

CHARLIE'S BLUE RIDGE MUSIC MAKERS

Advertisements for the Blue Ridge Music Makers. Jennie Bowman Cain Collection.

While some of the performers were not especially dependable, occasionally missing either the starting time or not showing up at all, Charlie was a model performer, always appearing at the radio station well in advance of the scheduled airtime. He took pride in the fact that he made his job a top priority and never missed a broadcast without a valid excuse. For this reason, he and Lamdin Kay got along quite amicably. The Blue Ridge Music Makers, billed as "a fast moving stage show," took the station by storm and instantly scored heavily with their listening audience. They were referred to as a "spirited group that makes hot mountain music" and, as a result, earned much airtime on WSB. These entertainers were heard Monday, Wednesday, and Friday at 6:30 A.M. on "Sunrise Serenade," Tuesdays at 4:15 P.M., Thursdays at 4:30 P.M., and Saturdays at 12:45 P.M. They operated under the management of the Georgia Artist's Bureau for personal appearances.[2]

"Pep and Rhythm"—"Those Happy Harmony Songsters"—earned great success when the group broadcast over WHAS in Louisville. Pep (Clara Louise George) was only thirteen years old, but she could dance, sing, and play a ukulele like any veteran of vaudeville. Charlie was billed as "Master of Ceremonies, Trick Fiddler and Dancer, Wizard Banjo Picker and Guitar Soloist—The Man of Many Instruments." He also carried with him the reputation of being a vaudeville performer with the Hill Billies and the Blue Ridge Ramblers. Walter "Spark Plug" Hughes, billed as "A Hot Guitarist" and "The Singing Guitarist," teamed up with Rhythm (real name unknown) to form one of the hottest guitar teams on the air. Another member of the group was Ferril "Red" Lambert, an ace banjo player and buck and wing dancer.[3]

While Charlie was promoting his new southern band, another major painful event occurred in his life in 1935; he and Fannie Mae separated. They later divorced. This surprised no one. His being away from home for extensive periods of time over ten years had an enormous price tag; payday came soon after he went to Louisville. Leaving his family a third time was more than their marriage could endure. Charlie's actions further suggested that he cared more for his fiddle and his career than he did for his family. Some would argue that his and Fannie's separation really began in 1925 when Charlie began touring with the Hill Billies and was confirmed again in 1931 when he, Jennie, and Pauline went with the Blue Ridge Ramblers. Now, he had left Gray Station a third time but was going in a different direction—north temporarily, then south and eventually west.

Before Grandma Bowman died a few months preceding the official separation of Charlie and Fannie, she saw the ominous dark storm clouds that hovered over their faltering marriage. Being a family-oriented person, she was no doubt aggrieved by it. Bob Taylor's words were now reaching fulfillment in the life of the East Tennessee fiddler: "No ordinary mortal ever felt the raptures of a fiddler; the fiddle is his bride, and the honeymoon lasts forever."[4] Charlie arranged a song, "Is This Goodbye Forever?" that seemed to address the conflict raging between the couple:

> Do you really mean to say goodbye?
> I have no chance to make amends.
> You say your love for me has vanished.
> Do you really mean this is the end?
> How come you say that we are through?
> You said I was the only one for you.
> You promised that you would always be mine.
> And forever be faithful and true.
>
> If we part it will cause me heartaches.
> But I will always love you.
> I can never get you off my mind.
> Regardless of what you do.
> Please promise me you will come back.
> And we can be lovers again.

And if you do I'll be a happy boy.
It will take away my sorrow and pain.

What have I done to you my darling?
Tell me and I'll make things right.
Until I find out I'll only worry.
About you day and night.
If we do part I will always be yearning.
And I know that I will almost die.
Tell me sweet girl that you'll change your mind.
So we won't have to say goodbye.

It seems you really made up your mind.
But why I guess I'll never know.
I see you mean it, you seem sincere.
It hurts me to let you go.
My thoughts and dreams will be about you.
To forget will be a hard thing to do.
If there's nothing I can do allow me to say.
That I've been true to you.

Chorus: Now why are you proving false to me?
I would not be false no never.
Is what you're going to say to me.
Mean this is goodbye forever?

Last Chorus: I learned to love you but I have lost.
I can't forget you darling no never.
With tear dimmed eyes I will clasp your hand.
Knowing this is goodbye forever.[5]

Chapter 11

CHARLIE'S SOUTHERN MOUNTAINEERS

Charlie left WSB in May 1936 for another Atlanta radio station, WGST. It was there he organized a group that he dubbed Charlie Bowman and His Southern Mountaineers, consisting of three ladies identified as the Calico Kids (piano and vocal), Hal Armstrong (accordion), Don Naylor (mandolin), himself (fiddle), and Curly Hicks (guitar). The seven-member group was heard on Columbia Broadcasting System, WGST, for the Frigidaire Program.[1] As was characteristic then, they shared the same microphone, requiring each one to move in close to it, do his or her part, and then quickly shift away so the next person could be featured. The popular bluegrass gospel band, Doyle Lawson and Quicksilver, later revived this technique. The *Atlanta Georgian* offered its impressions of the Southern Mountaineers: "Those who like hillbilly music tell me that the Southern Mountaineers, heard over WGST at 6 A.M. every day from Monday through Friday, are absolutely among the best. Charles Bowman, leader of the group is widely known."[2]

The group's name was soon shortened to Charlie Bowman and His Southerners after their leader made some personnel changes. Instead of the Calico Kids and Don Naylor, the group acquired Ernie Hodges (fiddler) and Charlotte LeFever (vocalist). Charlie began incorporating an increasing amount of hillbilly comedy into their routines. This was the beginning of a lifelong friendship between him and Ernie Hodges, who became known as the "Stradivari of the Appalachians." The newly hired fiddler became an accomplished fiddler/violinist, having studied for nine years at the Leffingwell Violin School in Atlanta.[3] A serious lung and heart problem later forced him to give up his concert violinist aspirations, turning instead to being a co-owner of Painter and Hodges Fiddle Shop, specialists in fine music instrument repairing. The versatile musician began selling repaired stringed instruments, teaching music lessons, and even raising chickens and farming, which he considered to be the good life. To the delight and amazement of his audiences, Hodges could be a polished violinist one minute and an old-time country fiddler the next. While the fiddle was his instrument of choice, he could play the banjo with equal mastery, even playing classical music on it. Ernie Hodges became an incalculable addition to the Southerners.[4]

The Southern Mountaineers. *Left to right:* Hal Armstrong, Don Naylor, the Calico Kids, Charlie Bowman, and Curly Hicks. Jennie Bowman Cain Collection.

The Southerners. *Left to right:* Ernie Hodges, Hal Armstrong, Curly Hicks, Charlotte LeFever, and Charlie Bowman. Jennie Bowman Cain Collection.

While broadcasting over WGST, Charlie met many local performers such as the Blue Ridge Hillbillies, better known as the Blue Sky Boys: Earl (guitar) and Bill (mandolin) Bollick and a fiddle player named Homer "Pappy" Sherrill (later associated with the South Carolina group, the Hired Hands, that included the legendary DeWitt "Snuffy" Jenkins). The Blue Sky Boys had previously been regulars on an Asheville, North Carolina, radio station sponsored by JFG Coffee, founded by J. F. Goodson. To appease their sponsor, they changed their broadcast names from Earl, Bill, and Homer (from an acronym of EBH) to John, Frank, and George (to an acronym of JFG). They arrived in Atlanta in 1936 and began broadcasting over WGST.[5] While with the station, the trio presented Charlie with an autographed copy of their *Songs and Poems* book with a handwritten note on the cover: "presented to our good friend and pal Chas. Bowman."[6]

In 1936, another profitable prospect came available to Charlie when he and four other musicians were called upon to lobby for the benefits of a proposed 15-mil tax limitation for the state of Georgia. To promote this amendment, the local newspapers featured the comic strip "The Rhyme Family." The Georgia State Real Estate Taxpayers Association decided to carry the cartoon a step further by creating a live "family" imitation of the strip's characters to deliver musical performances all across the state of Georgia. Since the Rhyme Family was portrayed as hillbilly characters, Charlie and four additional musicians fit the bill perfectly and were hired to fill these roles. The group consisted of Dug Dalton (banjo) from Middlesboro, Kentucky; Charlie Bowman (banjo); Ernie Hodges (fiddle) from Corbin, Kentucky; Red Anderson (guitar); and his young son, Raymond (mandolin) from Litchfield, Kentucky.[7] The project required an ugly woman, but since Dug was so pretty, Charlie agreed to dress up as an unattractive woman, fitting right in with his hillbilly and comedy characterizations. The campaign promoters proceeded to print "Rhyme Money," whose real value was redeemed by voting for the amendment. The currency bills contained a poem:

> There was a widow in Macon,
> Whom high taxes had overtaken.
> When her kids went to eat,
> They did without meat,
> Cause Ma couldn't bring home the bacon.[8]

The other side of the bill contained a second poem:

> Taxes on this and taxes on that,
> But please don't tax my big yellow cat.
> My farm's mortgage bound,
> My feet on the ground,
> High tax had got me down flat.[9]

The Rhyme family in an advertisement for the Georgia Real Estate Taxpayers Association 15-mil amendment. *Left to right:* Dug Dalton, Charlie Bowman, Ernie Hodges, Red Anderson, and Raymond Anderson. Jennie Bowman Cain Collection.

Charlie left Atlanta in 1937 and began traveling, working odd jobs and performing all over Alabama, Louisiana, east Texas, parts of Oklahoma, and Arkansas. He drove to Bakersfield, California, where he was temporarily employed in the oil fields as a well drill helper. In this capacity, he was required to assist with the replacement of pumps and tubing after the wells erupted. Charlie next moved to Los Angeles for about a month, playing music with various local groups as he traveled from town to town. Soon, the southern gentleman began feeling the pull of the Deep South.

Chapter 12

THE DWIGHT BUTCHER GANG

On August 1, 1937, another *Journal*-owned station, WAGA, went on the air, joining WSB, WGST, and WATL. Before the newspaper acquired the station's license,
WAGA had been broadcasting as WTFI from studios in nearby Athens, Georgia. The *Journal* brought the station to Atlanta so listeners could hear programs
offered by both of NBC's networks—the "Red Network," which was devoted to
entertainment, and the "Blue Network," which was culturally oriented. Until the
Journal sold the station in 1940, it featured the same hillbilly acts that were heard
on WSB. The popular "Cross Roads Follies" performers, for example, would
present their program on WSB and then dash across town to do another show
on WAGA.[1] During this time, Charlie switched again from being the leader of
his own bands to being a member of someone else's. He united with a musical
entourage known as Dwight Butcher's WAGA Radio Gang. The performers were
Dwight Butcher (leader), Ernie Hodges (fiddle, banjo), Jim Britt (guitar), Charlie
Bowman (fiddler, comedy), Melissa Ann Butcher (ukulele, daughter of Dwight
and Charlotte), "Coon" Langley (comedian), Riley Puckett (guitar), and Charlotte
Butcher (guitar, wife of Dwight). The handsome bandleader from Oakdale, Tennessee, was known to have a soft, pleasing drawl and friendly manner, standing
well over six feet tall with a commanding appearance. Dwight later worked in
Hollywood, New York, and Kansas City before joining the Renfro Valley Barn
Dance in Kentucky, where he became a master of ceremonies every Saturday
night.[2] Riley Puckett was a blind guitarist who had been a part of the highly
successful north Georgia band Gid Tanner and the Skillet Lickers. Charlie often
bragged on Riley's guitar playing and vocalizations; he lived only a short distance
from Puckett near Atlanta.

While Charlie was furthering his memorable career in the Atlanta area, Jennie
Bowman Cain was not sitting on the sideline; instead, she continued singing,
yodeling and playing her accordion, mostly in the Upper East Tennessee area.
She chose to sing with several bands in Georgia and neighboring states that were
conducive to her and Staley's time constraints. In September of 1937, she toured
with Owen Bennett and the Barnyard Frolics, a group similar to the Blue Ridge

Dwight Butcher's WAGA Radio Gang. *Left to right:* Ernie Hodges, Jim Britt, Charlie Bowman, Melissa Ann Butcher, Dwight Butcher, Coon Langley, Riley Puckett, and Charlotte Butcher. Charlie Bowman Collection.

Ramblers in that there were fourteen people—eight men and six women. They entertained on September 22 at the Ritz Theatre in Barnesville, Georgia, and the next day performed two shows at the Langdale Theatre in Langdale, Alabama. That same day, they traveled two miles to Shawmut, Alabama, where they performed at the Shawmut Theatre.

Jennie switched groups to Billy Floyd's Whiteway Revels (four men and six women) at the Chicopee Gymnasium in Chicopee, Georgia. September 27 found them at the Family Theatre in Lagrange, Georgia, with a new name, Billy Floyd's Melody Lane Girls, this time with six women and one man (Fiddlin' Charlie Bowman). Then Jennie changed bands again, this time to the Swamp Stompers, who performed at a Junior High School in Brookhaven, Georgia. and a gymnasium in Chicopee, Georgia. November 15–24, 1937, found them in Gadsden, Alabama, before a live audience at a skating rink, broadcasting twice daily over WJBY. They left Gadsden and returned to Atlanta, where they performed at the Ike Ison Club on Roswell Road for a "Big Apple Dance."[3]

Jennie was offered a rare opportunity to star in the Western film *Yodelin' Boy from Pine Ridge*, starring the popular singing cowboy Gene Autry along with his comic sidekick, Smiley Burnette. The plot involved a pretty cattle rancher who was being troubled by a gang of cattle rustlers. Jennie's good looks coupled with her beautiful yodeling voice made her a natural choice for the film. Possibly, Smiley Burnette, having worked with her in vaudeville, influenced her selection. Jennie had to decline the lucrative offer because she was pregnant with her first child, James Franklin Cain.

Pauline had essentially stopped performing by this time, being content to follow her artistic husband as he toured with the Frankie Carle Orchestra. However, she never forgot her mother and siblings while she was on the road. Occasionally, she would return home to visit them, generally without Jimmy because of his hectic work timetable. She dropped in unannounced early one morning while Fannie was cooking breakfast. Observing the wrinkled face of her fifty-one-year-old hard-working mother with several children still living at home was more than Pauline could bear. She realized just how much she missed them. Consequently, she couldn't bring herself to return to her Italian husband in Massachusetts. Pauline struggled with what to do. As painful as it was for her, she realized that she had to remain with her family. Hesitantly, Pauline phoned Jimmy to tell him of her difficult decision.

Not about to surrender his pretty young wife, Jimmy immediately drove to Johnson City, where he resided for a period of time to see if he could persuade Pauline to go back with him. He rented a house close to Fannie's and lived there for several weeks. Eventually, he had to return to his job, performing with the Frankie Carle Orchestra. Jimmy realized that the bond between Pauline, her family, and her East Tennessee mountains was simply too strong for him to break. He reluctantly returned to his home in Massachusetts, knowing full well that he had lost his spouse. The young musicians' five-year marriage ended in a uncontested divorce, and their love for each other did not die. The estranged couple corresponded frequently, but Jimmy eventually remarried and raised a family. While vaudeville had briefly taken the shy young girl out of the country, it was her family and her Tennessee mountains that brought her home. Pauline was now at peace with herself, because she knew absolutely that she had made the proper choice. In spite of his hurt, Jimmy James was aware of it also.

Jimmy's stint with big band music was relatively short lived. Within a few years, he transformed his trombone into an instrument of comedy. He also created his own hillbilly musical group, the Hickory Nuts, and began broadcasting over WMMN, West Virginia. Later, he moved to Chicago, where he performed over WLS ("World's Largest Store"—Sears & Roebuck). The station was best known for its "National Barn Dance," running from 1924 until about 1957 and blending non-high-brow music, comedy, and country skits. This time, Jimmy teamed up with Ted Moore ("Otto") and Holly Swenson ("Cousin Tilford") to form a hilarious trio known as the Virginia Hams. The 250-pound Ted is best remembered in his "Little Genevieve" role, appearing as a crybaby dressed in a ruffled baby dress and bonnet.[4] Jimmy was living proof of what Charlie always knew—once a hillbilly, always a hillbilly. Pauline never forgot Jimmy. Many years later, she remarked in a choked-up voice just how good a man Jimmy James really was. She truly knew that "A Good Man Is Hard to Find," and she had certainly found a good one, only to give him up. At Pauline's ninetieth birthday party, she asked family members if anyone could possibly locate Jimmy so she could talk to him over the phone one final time before she departed this life. Attempts to find him failed, as most assumed he was probably deceased. Ironically, Jimmy James died in January 2004, just one month after Pauline passed away in December 2003.

Around 1937, Jennie Cain returned to WOPI in Bristol, performing as part of a group known as the Merrymakers. A local advertisement said that without the Merrymakers the Saturday Night Jamboree would lose much of its appeal. Jennie identified the group only by their first names: Harry, Clyde, Jennie, Jack, and Sleepy.[5] A young Tennessee Ernie Ford, who hung around the station in 1929, was now one of its full-time announcers. People teased him by referring to him as Tennessee Ernie Chevrolet. He kept his listeners in stitches with his keen hillbilly wit, always talking about his hometown, Bent Fork, Tennessee. Probably his most remembered line was that the population there never changed in all the years because every time a new baby was born, someone moved out of town. While Ernie was announcing over WOPI, the station used the local fire department for commercials. A city insurance company presponsored announcements of all the fires that occurred inside the city limits of Bristol. When the city fire whistle sounded, people from all over town heard it and immediately turned their radios to WOPI to find out the exact location of the fire. The station would preempt any broadcasting with announcements such as "we interrupt this program to inform you that the Bristol Fire Department is currently responding to a fire call, and this emergency is being brought to you through the courtesy of [the name of the insurance company]." The listener had to wait until the end of the advertisement before the specific location of the fire was disclosed. Ironically, the announcer would then caution people about not following the fire trucks, as if to believe nobody would.

Except for the brief revival when Charlie Bowman and His Brothers recorded for Columbia in 1928 and 1929, the Bowman brothers string band pretty much dissolved. There was very little interest in keeping it going, as it required finding a replacement for Charlie, who served as their leader. That is not to say that the boys quit playing music altogether; they just did it less formally than when they were part of a four-brother group. Elbert was definitely the most active, and Argil was the least. Elbert Bowman's children remembered his playing guitar and banjo with various musicians while the family lived on Fairview Avenue in Johnson City. As time went on, he began to play the banjo more and the guitar less. He would host jam sessions in the living room of his house with such musicians in attendance as Roby Chinouth (fiddle), Lonnie Durham (banjo), "Blue" Friday (fiddle), Walter Bowman (banjo and fiddle), and Argil Bowman (guitar). Charlie also dropped in on the sessions when he was in Johnson City.

On a Saturday night in 1937, Elbert and three of his sons, Billy, Dalton, and Jake, were on the stage of the Tennessee Theatre in downtown Johnson City. They were billed as Elbert Bowman and String Band. This was the same theater where Bert Pouder had convinced Charlie to participate in his first onstage fiddle contest. It was now under new ownership and no longer named the Deluxe Theatre. Others on the stage that night included the Tennessee Ramblers, Margaret Harrison (song and dance), Dorothy Morelock (taps), Gee and Ed (songs), Nat Johnson (with his lightning feet), and Bill Toohey (master of ceremonies). The Ramblers consisted of "Dad" Fiddlin' Sievers (the leader) and his son Mark, the three Rainey Brothers, Willie Sievers Sharpe, and comedian Kentucky Slim. The featured movie was *Lawless Lands,* starring cowboy great Johnny Mack Brown, and chapter 12 of the action-packed serial *Black Coin,* starring Ralph Graves, Ruth Mix, and Dave O'Brien.[6]

Charlie's tenure with Dwight Butcher's WAGA Radio Gang was transitory. Soon he would again form his own band and begin touring and playing his fiddle all over the southern states.

Chapter 13

CHARLIE'S BUCKLE BUSTERS

With Fiddlin' Charlie Bowman now living in Atlanta and legally separated from his wife, Fannie moved her family from the old log house to Johnson City in 1938. Surprisingly, the structure, which was about 120 years old, and the land still had a mortgage on it. Charlie's brother, Walter, assisted Fannie with selling it to a Roscoe Fitzgerald family. The old home place stood another twenty years until the new owners built a dwelling behind it and had it demolished. Fannie first purchased a residence on East Fairview Avenue in Johnson City, similar to the one she and Charlie rented in Bristol. This meant the family had indoor plumbing once again, including hot and cold running water and a commode that made everything go away.

While this move was transpiring in Johnson City, Charlie formed yet another band in Atlanta that he named Charlie Bowman and His Buckle Busters, borrowing the name of his former group. Since the Hill Billies/Buckle Busters had been disbanded for about five years, it is interesting that Charlie called his new band by this name instead of Charlie Bowman and His Hill Billies or Charlie Bowman and His Blue Ridge Ramblers.

The new Buckle Busters consisted of Lang Howe (accordion), Happy Smith (guitar and yodeler), Eddie King (saxophone and comedy), Eva Smith (guitar, banjo, and vocals), Lillie Leatherman (guitar and vocals), Hilda Rainwater (guitar, peppy singer, and yodeler), and Charlie Bowman (leader, emcee, and fiddler). For a brief time, Jennie sang and yodeled with her dad's new group, as well as played fiddle and accordion. Her diary shows that she joined them on January 1, 1938, appearing first at the Strand Theatre in Covington, Georgia, and touring with them for about five months. She left the group on June 5 after an appearance at the Roanoke Theatre in Roanoke, Virginia. While there is a gap in her diary between late 1931 and early 1938, she continued recording the same type of information as when she was with the Ramblers. The last entry read "went home from here, June 5th." Charlie was so proud of his newly formed band that he had large photographs made of them and sent to his children in Tennessee. After a New Year's engagement in Covington, Georgia, the group undertook an eleven-day continuous engagement at Chattanooga's Bonita Theatre. The news-paper articles touting their shows, including one titled simply "Buckle Busters," must have been an encouragement to them:

> Charlie Bowman's "Buckle Busters," now playing the Bonita Theatre, have been acclaimed the best stage attraction to play this house. This aggregation of instrumentalists and singers entertain every minute they are on the stage. The act is clean—nothing risqué in the entire reper-toire, and Charlie Bowman, the very able master of ceremonies, keeps it that way. The act has played Loews Circuit in the New England States and more recently has been at the Capital Theatre in Atlanta.[1]

As noted by this ad, the one trait that characterized these shows, as well as any of those managed by Charlie, was their family orientation. There was no profane

Charlie Bowman and His Buckle Busters. *Top row, left to right:* Lang Howe, Happy Smith, Charlie Bowman, Eddie King; *front row, left to right:* Eva Smith, Lillie Leatherman, and Hilda Rainwater. Jennie Bowman Cain Collection.

language, suggestive comments, or even sarcasm. This is evident from the title of a newspaper column in Smithfield, Virginia, proclaiming their April 27 and 28 performances "A Clean Show":

> Charlie Bowman and his Buckle Busters have just finished a two days engagement at the Smithfield Theatre. The show was clean and very entertaining each member being versatile doing specialties.
>
> Cousin Eddie played a mean hillbilly sax and is the comic with the show. Smiling Jack played a mean guitar, sings and backs up the gang with his hot hillbilly rhythm playing. Miss Hilda Rainwater sings cowboy and mountain songs and yodels like nobody's business and also plays guitar. Miss Jennie Bowman played the accordion, fiddle, also sings harmony with Miss Hilda.
>
> Charlie Bowman is manager and master of ceremonies with the show. He plays fiddle or any of the string instruments and novelty instruments such as balloon, washtub, broom, handsaw or what have you. The comment on the Buckle Busters was great, and the people in and around Smithfield feel indebtedness to Smithfield Theatre for being able to secure such an attraction.[2]

Charlie must have been delighted with the response to his new band. The package the theaters formulated to attract customers was a carryover from vaudeville featuring a live act, a full-length movie, a two-reel comedy, a cartoon, and even a multichapter serial. After the energetic group performed at the Franklin Theatre in Rocky Mount, Virginia, on May 30 and 31, a local newspaper commented on their performances:

> The lovable star of "Kid Galahad" will be seen in a fast moving story of the prize ring in the featured attraction at the downtown Franklin Theatre tonight (Friday) and Saturday when Wayne Morris and June Travis appear in "The Kid Comes Back." Added are Chapter 5 of "Flash Gordon" and an Oswald cartoon. "Love, Honor and Behave" with Wayne Morris and Priscilla Lane, to be shown as a special one-day attraction Sunday, is a fun-filled comedy with two sprightly youngsters which is rated "tops" in entertainment. Also a two-reel comedy and a cartoon.
>
> Because Charlie Bowman and His Buckle Busters state troupe was so outstanding and pleased so completely, the manager of the Franklin Theatre has yielded to the many requests to hold this clean, peppy little stage company over for next Monday (court day) and Tuesday. Their act consists of good playing, yodeling, singing, and good clean fun. Charlie Bowman is a versatile player who makes a broomstick talk. And the girls are young, pretty, and pleasing musicians.

In addition to the stage show Monday and Tuesday, there will be shown on the screen Jack Luden and his dog Tuffy in "Stage Coach Days" together with Chapter 8 of "Secret of Treasure Island."[3]

Jennie, who had the habit of keeping the words to her songs close at hand in case she required them, sang, yodeled, and played the accordion. (An alphabetized list of the seventy-three song titles she kept in her notebook appears in Appendix C.) She also sang the "Audience Song" with her father. She would sing the first three lines of each verse, and her dad would add the fourth, or "punch" line, which brought immediate laughter from the audience. Both individuals sang the final verse in unison:

Jennie:
There sits a man right back there,
About the 5th row and about the 3rd chair,
He's tall and lean, not much hair on his head.

Charlie:
You can't grow hair where the brain is dead.

Jennie:
There sits a woman right back there,
About the 10th row and about the 8th chair,
She's so fat she can't be beat.

Charlie:
She bought one ticket, but she's usin' two seats.

Jennie:
There sits a couple right down there,
About the 4th row and about the 8th and 9th chairs,
I can tell the girl something she don't know.

Charlie:
The boy borrowed the money to bring her to the show.

Jennie:
There sits a man right back there,
About the 12th row and about the 15th chair,
He's got a mustache so long and stout.

Charlie:
He looks like he swallowed a mule
And left its tail stickin' out.

Jennie and Charlie in Unison:
We wrote this song the other day,
We didn't aim to sing it this way,
We hope you enjoyed it and had a lot of fun,
We thank you folks our song is done.[4]

CHARLIE'S BUCKLE BUSTERS

While vaudeville began to wane in the early 1930s, many theaters continued to show movies interspersed with live entertainment. By the end of the decade, Westerns had become increasingly popular at many of these theaters. One poster heralds Charlie and His Buckle Busters performing at a showing with Gene Autry and Smiley Burnette in the 1937 *Rootin' Tootin' Rhythm*. According to the advertisement, the band was "held over again by special request." Strangely, Gene Autry is playing second fiddle to Charlie and his band; the Buckle Busters are the main attraction in large letters at the top followed by "also Gene Autry" in smaller letters at the bottom.[5]

Charlie often referred to his playing as "sawing on the old fiddle." He could just as well have said "sawing on the old saw," because he could play a saw as well as a fiddle. Playing the saw requires skillful coordination between manipulating the bow, bending the saw, and simultaneously pulling the end up to form a double "S." If a higher pitch is desired, the saw is bent toward the floor; for a lower pitch, it is bent away from the floor. Because of its appealing sound and uniqueness, the musical saw became a regular at performances.[6]

Advertisements for Charlie Bowman and His Buckle Busters. Jennie Bowman Cain Collection.

When Jennie stopped playing with her father's band in mid-1938, she returned to performing at numerous events in Upper East Tennessee. A clipping from a 1938 newspaper shows that by entering a contest at the Strand Theatre in Kingsport, Tennessee, she could have won a trip to WSM radio in Nashville, followed by a guest spot on Fred Allen's "Town Hall Tonight" radio show in New York:

> Frank Taylor and his Novelty Jug Band will travel to Nashville on March 24 to compete in the Tri State finals of Amateur contest sponsored by Crescent Amusement Company, it was announced last night, following their triumph in the Strand Theatre's finals. The Ross Trio from Bristol placed second while Miss Jennie Bowman won third honors with her accordion. Last night's performances climaxed the series of Amateur contests staged each Saturday night by the Strand Theatre. Frank Taylor and his Jug Band took the audience by storm with their comedy, jokes, and mountain music. More that five encores were necessary before the audience would let them go.
>
> The Jug Band is composed of Frank Taylor, leader; Mack Riddle, comedian and T. T. Beggerley, fiddlin'. Taylor's dancing and jug novelties along with Riddle's comedy led the applause, while Beggerley's fiddlin' furnished harmony and rhythm for the trio's antics. The Tri-State winners composed of participants from Alabama, Tennessee and Kentucky will be heard over radio station WSM, while in Nashville. The grand prize in Nashville is a trip to New York and an audition on Fred Allen's "Town Hall Tonight" program. The prizes for last night's contest were $25 to Frank Taylor and His Jug Band, $15 to the Ross Trio, and $10 to Miss Jennie Bowman. W. J. Reach also presented Frank and his band with a certificate of merit from WSM with the privilege of an audition at any time.[7]

Known as "Frank and Mack," Taylor and Riddle often performed in the local area. Johnson City businessman J. Norton Arney frequently booked the boys to play for local civic clubs, using such madcap descriptors as "The Boys from Way up Thar," "As Batty As a Belfry," and "The Craziest Pair in the State with Their Big Troupe of 15 Entertainers."[8]

After coming off the road, Jennie remained active, appearing briefly with Jack Pierce, a former member of the Blue Ridge Ramblers who was playing with the Oklahoma Cowboys. On January 5, 1939, her group performed at the local high school auditorium in Keenburg, Tennessee (just north of Elizabethton). The next two days found them on the stage of the Sevier Theatre in downtown Johnson City. Such local exposure resulted in their securing a contract for daily broadcasts over local radio station WJHL.

Hilda Rainwater Henry recalled her association with Charlie Bowman and His Buckle Busters in a 2004 interview:

> I was with the Buckle Busters in 1938 and worked with them barely a year. When Charlie came to see if I would go with him, he promised my mama and daddy he would really take care of me. They felt like they could trust him for me to go away from home. He was the first group that I went on the road with. I played on the radio with some of the groups, but not on the road. I joined the band in Atlanta. Most of our travels were in North Carolina, South Carolina and Tennessee. We played one date in Virginia. I was outgoing then and always laughing, meeting everybody and smiling.

Hilda commented on her boss's character while performing with his band:

> Charlie was a mighty good person, and what he said he would do, he did. He would look after the girls in his group as if they were his own daughters. He kept in contact with what was going on all the time. We had a good group, and we weren't thinking about anything but just rehearsing and putting on the show. One thing I always remembered about Charlie was when we first started on the road. We didn't make much money from the show dates until we got to the theatres. If anybody did without anything, Charlie would go out and bring something back. I kept noticing that he wasn't taking anything for himself; he would feed us, and he would do without if he didn't have enough money for all of us to eat.
>
> I never saw anything unkind come out of Charlie. I never heard him say any harsh words; he was never harsh with anyone in his group. If they weren't doing exactly what he thought they should do, he would just talk to them. What he did, he did with all his heart. He put everything he had in it. He was the same Charlie off the stage as he was on the stage. The fiddle was his first love.

The retired entertainer spoke of the type of music that was featured in their concerts:

> We played mostly just country music; that was Charlie's request. He preferred some good plain down-to-earth country music. When we went on the air, we didn't try to add anything to it. Wherever we went, we always had good reception. Charlie would tell us before we went on the stage, "I want everybody to act like you are enjoying it because if you act like you are enjoying it, they [the audience] will enjoy it too." Charlie told me

he needed me to teach the rest of them how to smile. It was the hardest thing for Lillie to go on stage and smile while she was entertaining.

We went to so many small towns and places. We traveled in two cars. The band was in one and we had a driver. Charlie was in the other, and he would go ahead as a booker of show dates. I remember one show that we played in a town where Roy Acuff was playing. Someone later called and said that many of the crowd that was supposed to be going to hear Roy Acuff came over to our show. Our show outdrew him. I always remembered how just a little group like us outdrew Roy Acuff.

Charlie always dressed country; most of his shirts were striped. He liked to wear country looking shirts and overalls. He could play his fiddle and make it sound like a reed organ. Charlie was a good country fiddler; he played mostly country tunes. One night I remember when we were on stage, I heard this racket backstage and he was bringing out a tub and he played it like a bass fiddle. It had but one string on it.

Charlie let Eddie do most of the comedy in the act. He and Eddie had a skit they would do; Charlie played the straight man. Eddie was always forgetting his lines and messing up Charlie. He would just make something up causing us to get tickled at him. I had a lot of fun playing in that group because they were just home folks; I was a little cowgirl and dressed like a little "farmerette" from Georgia. I sang such songs as "Colorado Blues" and "I Wanna Be a Cowboy's Girl." There was another little girl that came with us about the time I came home from Charlie's group. Her name was Bertha Tyner. She was from North Carolina. She sang country songs too and did some yodeling.

Hilda was asked if Charlie ever made reference to his family back in Tennessee:

Charlie was very quiet about his family except Jennie. I didn't know too much about his family, but I did know that sometimes he would have mood swings. He seemed to be depressed about something and feeling low. He didn't want to be around anyone. He just wanted to be alone for a while, and then he would just get really involved. I knew something was bothering him, but I didn't know what. When Jennie came on the show, he seemed so happy, and I could sense a bond between them. Charlie seemed to be very happy when Jennie came on the show. She was a very sweet girl, very likable person, favoring her daddy a lot. The first time I met Jennie was in Johnson City when she came to one of our shows. Jennie was good on the accordion. She would stay a little bit at a time with the band and then she would go home; she didn't just stay there all the time. I think it was because of her husband. He couldn't stay on the road with her.

The Buckle Buster singer of yesteryear related how she became homesick and decided to leave the band and come off the road:

> Later, I got homesick and told Charlie I wanted to come home. He tried to get it out of me to promise that I would come home a little while and then come back with the group. I had it in my mind that I really didn't like to be on the road and be away from home a lot. I loved everyone in the group and we got along just fine. It wasn't for me to stay away from home too long.[9]

Not long after Hilda quit traveling with the band, Charlie sent her a letter dated July 25, 1938, from the Milner Hotel in Roanoke, Virginia, while he was performing with the Buckle Busters. In spite of Charlie's pleas, as noted in this letter, she remained with her family in Georgia:

> Dear Hilda: I like you a lot and do miss you on the show. I am going to make some changes on the show soon, and I want you to come and join me again. I will send you a ticket to come on and will take the best care of you I possibly can financially and otherwise. We are later going to work Georgia and Alabama as we have some real good territory down there, and you will be close home. I still have Lil, Eva, Happy, also Eddie Lang. I am playing Roanoke again 28–29–30 July but I changed the name of the show for this date to the Blue Ridge Music Makers.
>
> I expect to have a girl show sometime later on, and you said you would get you a girl partner and rehearse for a sister team. Did you do this yet? I'd like for you to get a girl with dark hair as near your size as possible that can sing harmony with you and play some instrument and would be glad if she could tap, and be sure she can smile. You can drill that into her. You know what it takes. I have 100% confidence in you and would always treat you as I have in the past. I hope you are interested. Well give my regards to all and let me hear from you immediately.[10]

Charlie Bowman and the Buckle Busters performed from January 1938 until about the end of the year. When the half-century-old showman dissolved the Buckle Busters in 1939, he was never again the leader of his own band.

Chapter 14

THE RICE BROTHERS GANG

In 1939 Charlie Bowman joined the Rice Brothers Gang. Anyone tuned to Shreveport, Louisiana's CBS Radio affiliate, KWKH, 1130 AM, at seven o'clock on the morning of June 16, 1940, would have heard these words: "Howdy folks. This is Hoke Rice speaking atcha . . . for 'Postle Paul, 'Tenn-O-See' Charlie, and Cicero."[1] Hoke was the leader of the Rice Brothers Gang, an act that he and his younger brother, Paul, started during 1935 in Roanoke, Virginia. Charlie's association with the group began soon after he moved from Atlanta to Shreveport, Louisiana. Whether it was the Rice Brothers or KWKH that brought Bowman to Shreveport is not known, but he joined the group in late 1939 and soon began working with them on this station. The Rice Brothers Gang consisted of Scott Wilson (announcer), Cicero Merneigh (bass, fiddle, and comedy), Hoke Rice (manager, emcee, and guitar), Paul Rice (known as 'Postle Paul, guitar, and yodeler), Cricket Walters (hot fiddle), Lonnie Hall (violin), Reggie Ward (bass fiddle), and Eddie Hurd (clarinet and saxophone). While the act began small, it enlarged within ten years to as many as ten performers and bookings up to eight weeks in advance. Hoke Rice would eventually make about 250 recordings for a variety of record companies under such names as Hoke Rice, The Rice Brothers Gang, the Rice Brothers and Their Gang, and Hoke Rice and His Gang. As Charlie had done with his Buckle Busters group, the fiddler had photo prints made of his new band and sent to his children in Tennessee.

Hoke's radio career began in 1925 when he teamed up with champion fiddler Clayton McMitchen. He later joined several groups, working in thirty-two states before forming his own band. His brother, Paul, was four years younger and had the curious nickname "Mama's Little Man." Scott Wilson was a seasoned young announcer when he joined the gang. He made several guest appearances on their show during the time he was acting as master of ceremonies on KTBS's "Hi Neighbor!" The Rice Brothers came to Shreveport in late 1939 from the Village Barn, a popular café in Greenwich Village.[2] The boys occasionally played music with the old Skillet Lickers gang. Hoke's formula for success was to play and sing something between hillbilly and popular. His group was formed with the

The Rice Brothers Gang. *Left to right:* Charlie Bowman, Paul Rice, Reggie Ward, Scott Wilson, Cricket Walters, Hoke Rice, and Eddie Hurd. Jennie Bowman Cain Collection.

express intention of specializing in that type of music. After intensive preliminary rehearsal, Hoke auditioned for KWKH's directors and was immediately assigned an early morning spot on the air, and they played to a steadily increasing audience throughout the winter.

Within two weeks, the highly successful act was shifted to a more auspicious time on the KWKH morning schedule. Fan demand, however, was so insistent that the group soon had the unique distinction of being the only KWKH act regularly scheduled twice daily, first in the early morning and then during the noon hour. Fan mail became so voluminous that it required a stenographer working eight hours a day just to read and sort it. This outpouring of support proved to the station that their rural listeners preferred these radio hillbillies above swing bands and symphonic broadcasts.[3] The station soon discovered that the best time to feature this kind of music was early in the morning while people were getting ready to go to work. This is evidenced in the Monday, February 12, 1940, early morning lineup for KWKH from the *Shreveport Times*:

5:30	The Sunshine Boys
6:00	The Carter Family
6:15	Happy Dan's Radio Folks
7:00	The Carter Family
7:15	Rice Brothers and Their Gang
7:30	The Arizona Ranch Girls
12:00	Rice Brothers and Their Gang[4]

Four months later, on Tuesday, June 18, 1940, KWKH's radio schedule showed a slightly different lineup; oddly enough, the popular Carter Family was dropped from the early morning lineup:

5:30	The Breakfast Cabaret
6:00	United Press News
6:05	The Breakfast Cabaret
6:15	Arthur Smith and His Dixie Liners
6:45	Happy Dan's Radio Folks
7:00	Rice Brothers and Their Gang
7:15	Morning Melodies
7:35	The Arizona Ranch Girls[5]

With all its success, the act continued on this schedule until Hoke's commercial commitments confined his activities to one broadcast a day. Although the Rice Brothers Gang and five other groups played their music during this daily two-hour slot, it was not enough to satisfy the musical appetites of KWKH listeners. Consequently, the six mountain music acts were transported by bus and limousine to towns all around the radio's listening area for one-night performances in schools and churches, with each act traveling to a different town. These personal appearances gave the station's eager fans an opportunity to meet their radio heroes in person. As if six nights a week on the road were not enough, the six acts were combined for the Saturday Night Roundup on the stage of the Shreveport Municipal Auditorium before two to three thousand people. They played such popular songs as "Nobody's Darling but Mine," "You Are My Sunshine," "Cripple Creek," "Fast Train," and "Fox Chase."

Hoke and his gang accomplished something short of amazing on June 16, 1940. After performing less than ten months on the air, their show was put on the South Central Quality Network, allowing them to be heard on four additional southern radio stations: WWL in New Orleans, WSMB in New Orleans, WMC in Memphis, and KARK in Little Rock. Counting KWKH, the Rice Brothers Gang was heard at different times during the day on five radio stations. Tuesday through Saturday, they were on WWL and WMC at 6:45 A.M. and WSMB at 7:45 A.M. (rebroadcast by electrical transcription). On Tuesday, Thursday, and Saturday they were on KARK at 6:45 A.M. This was in addition to broadcast appearances Monday through Saturday at 7:00 A.M. on KWKH. These additional outlets gave them a wide listening audience.[6] The group's success was in its versatility of style, as the members could be countrified "hillbillies" one moment and sophisticated "mountain Williams" the next. People loved their flexibility.

Two of the Rice Brothers Gang's most memorable sponsors included Grove's Tasteless Chill Tonic and Black-Draught Laxative. The former, the sponsor of the South Central Quality Network, was a sweet tonic with granulated quinine added. A pharmacist, E. W. Grove of Paris, Tennessee, developed it in 1878. The other sponsor, Black-Draught Laxative, was "a liquid purgative consisting of an infusion of senna with sulfate of magnesia and extract of liquorice." Charlie Bowman described it as "a syrupy sweet spicy laxative that will literally clean out your innards."

KWKH advertisements for the Rice Brothers Gang. Jennie Bowman Cain and Bob Cox Collections.

Dean Schmitter, producer of the show, worked so long with the Rice Brothers Gang that he gradually became an integral part of the act—similar to "The Johnson Wax Program with Fibber McGee and Molly" of the mid-1930s to the late 1950s, in which their announcer, Harlow Wilcox (known on the airways as "Waxy"), was incorporated into the show, often sparring with Fibber while simultaneously plugging the sponsor. Dean engaged in rapid-fire sparring with madcap "Tenn-O-See" Charlie, who described the suave Mr. Schmitter as "corny." Dean wrestled with the station clock throughout the Rice Brothers regular morning shows to get the gang on and off the air at the required time. He once commented that Charlie Bowman was the only man he knew who could make faces over the air and delay a program in so doing. Dean rarely got a break because where Charlie Bowman left off 'Postle Paul, known as "Mama's little man," continued. Most of Schmitter's verbal abuse toward the fiddler usually missed its mark, with Charlie getting in the last lick—by design of course.[7] Charlie kept several of his comedy routines (see appendix D), all of which were performed with "Peewee" (Cicero Merneigh). Because they were neatly typed, it is thought that some of these routines were read on their broadcasts.

While Charlie was performing with the Rice Brothers Gang, another potential cash flow prospect came along. He and singer/songwriter Bobby Gregory

Paul Rice and Charlie Bowman in a comedy routine on KWKH. Jennie Bowman Cain Collection.

teamed up to write "When the Flowers Bloom Again in the Springtime." Bobby wrote the melody and Charlie composed the lyrics.

> Once we strolled thru the garden,
> When flow'rs were in bloom,
> And our hearts they were happy and gay,
> But there soon came a day,
> When we two had to part,
> And I'll always remember that day.
>
> *Chorus*
> When the flow'rs bloom again the springtime,
> And the birds start in to singin' their refrain,
> I'll be thinkin' of you then my darlin',
> And be longin' to see your sweet face again.
> Thru that garden,
> Where our hearts never knew an hour of pain,
> When the flow'rs bloom again in the springtime,
> I'll be coming back to you again.

Charlie received three letters showing the difficulty they had with this song. The first arrived on April 25, 1940, from Helen Jacobson of the American Academy of Music:

> Dear Mr. Bowman . . . Enclosed you will find contracts and Canadian Assignments covering your composition, "When The Flowers Bloom Again In The Springtime," which we have just accepted from Bobby Gregory. Will you be good enough to sign your name wherever your initials appear and return all copies to us immediately for completion here? As soon as they are executed, your copy will be returned to you. Your prompt attention would be appreciated.[8]

A second letter came to Charlie that same day from Bobby Gregory:

> Dear Friend Charlie . . . I finally got around to fixing up that song lyric to "When The Flowers Bloom Again In The Springtime," and it turned out to be a pretty nice number, and a good song for recording, so I wish you would try to get the Rice Brothers to record it on their next session as you said you would. Enclosed you will find the contracts and manuscript copy of [the song]. So do your best to get it recorded down there.[9]

The contract attached to the letter specified royalties amounting to "two cents for each complete pianoforte copy sold and paid for and not returned in the United States and Canada. 25% of all net royalties received by you for your own use and benefit from the reproduction on phonograph records and music rolls, in the United States and Canada." Based on this February 11, 1948, letter received from Bobby Gregory eight years later, it appears that nothing materialized concerning this song:

> Dear Charlie . . . Received your letter in reference to the song, "When the Flowers Bloom Again in the Springtime," the song we placed with Exclusive Publications a long time ago. Nothing was ever done with the song, as it was never published. A couple of the Hoke Rice tunes were published, and the others were left unpublished. A while back, I tried to get the songs back from the publisher but was unsuccessful, but will try again soon. I will write you if I can get the tune back, and in case I get down in your neighborhood, I will drop by and see you.[10]

There is no indication that the Rice Brothers Gang or any group ever recorded it. Therefore, this project appears to have been merely a long wait for something that never materialized.

While Charlie was a part of the Rice Gang, he became reacquainted with Fiddlin' Arthur Smith. As previously noted, the two fiddlers once shared the same stage one night in Erwin, Tennessee, when inclement weather forced them to combine their concerts. In 1940 they shared the KWKH microphone. Smith and his band, the Dixie Liners, went out over the airways at 6:15 each weekday morning. Like the Rice Brothers Gang, each member of Smith's group had colorful nicknames: Fiddlin' Arthur Smith (leader, fiddler), Gale "Curley" Daniels, Perry "Sheik" Clisbee, Fred "Bashful" Vincent, and Jango "Fire Cracker" Barnette.[11]

While the former Hill Billie fiddler was playing with the Rice brothers in Louisiana, Fannie was making plans to purchase another house in Johnson City. On February 21, 1940, she and Pauline jointly purchased a house on Myrtle Avenue just a couple of blocks from their Fairview Avenue residence. She and Fannie lived there eighteen years until her death in March 1958, Pauline lived there for sixty-four years, until she passed away in December 2003. The family was pleased with the new abode, within view of beautiful Buffalo Mountain. Fannie's new kitchen was much larger and had three stoves—wood, gas, and electric. However, she had too much experience cooking on an old-fashioned wood stove to switch to the newer models.

In 1941, the Rice Brothers continued their success by issuing *The Rice Brothers Song Folio,* which contained eleven of their own songs: "When Love Gets Hold of Your Heart," "Stardust Range," "Tears in My Heart," "Careless Love," "I Will Miss You Tonight Little Darling," "Jumping Judy," "Dry Your Eyes Little Girl," "Dust on the Prairie," "Did You," and "Please Don't Stay Away." "Jumping Judy," an instrumental, was cowritten by Charlie and Hoke. The folio also had a list of thirty-four of the fifty recordings the Rice Brothers Gang produced in three separate sessions between June 13, 1938, and April 27, 1941, for Decca Records as part of their 5500–6000 Country and Western series.[12]

Even though Charlie was a member of the gang at this time, he did not participate in any of these recordings. The gang's sound had begun to migrate heavily toward a Western swing flavor, which included a steel guitar, clarinet, harmonica, guitar, fiddle, and bass. Charlie was an old-time fiddler, with not a hint of wanting to transform into a western swing fiddler.

National exposure came to the group when the popular annually produced *Hillbilly Hit Parade of 1940* (published in early 1941) featured them on the cover. While the other four musicians in the group are shown in coats and ties, Charlie is appropriately wearing his hillbilly checkered shirt and bib overalls. The magazine also ran a short article about the group, telling how the gang made personal appearances nightly and stayed booked up five to eight weeks in advance. Other artists on the cover of this magazine included Arizona Red (Ed McBride), Floyd Tillman, and Roy Hall and His Blue Ridge Entertainers. Featured in the article was "Gonna Raise the Ruckus Tonight," one of the two songs that Charlie and His Brothers had recorded in October 1928 when Columbia Records' "Uncle Fuzz" came to Johnson City.[13]

In 1941, fifty-two-year-old Fox Hunt Charlie left the Rice Brothers Gang and returned to Atlanta, where he soon married twenty-five-year-old Ruth Sewell. News of their union quickly spread to Gray Station, where it was not well received by family members or friends. Some resented the fact that his new bride was younger than his oldest daughters, Pauline and Jennie. Also, some held on to the hope that the love flame between Charlie and Fannie was still flickering and just needed to be refueled. However, his marriage to Ruth seemed to confirm that it had truly been extinguished. While Ruth had no children from her previous marriage, within a year she and Charlie adopted her sister's daughter, Mary Lou Blackstock, when she was only a few weeks old. Charlie now had a new family, but unlike with his first one, this time he stayed home and did not leave them to entertain on the road. When he did perform, he took his wife and daughter along.

In 1943 Charlie's good friend and former Dwight Butcher Gang performer, Ernie Hodges, who had become a music critic for the *Atlanta Constitution,* got Charlie a job with his employer. Not long into his new profession as a printer, Charlie began having trouble with his right arm; his doctor informed him that he needed to have a bone surgically removed from it. In a letter sent to his brother Alfred's daughter, Hazel Reaves, he mentioned the operation: "I'm not able to work but am improving. I may soon be able to do light work, but doctors said it would take a year for my arm to get entirely well so I will have to take it easy for a while."[14] After the surgery and a full year of rest, Charlie had not recovered to his satisfaction and he resigned from his printing job. He continued to play his fiddle sparingly on stage, relying more heavily on his skills as master of ceremonies and comedian. By 1945, he and fellow musician Lowell Johnson began playing gigs in the Atlanta area.

In 1945 Charlie, Ruth, and Mary Lou moved to Johnson City. It is not known why, but Jean recalled they had been constantly "burning the road up between Johnson City and Atlanta." Perhaps the East Tennessee area offered more opportunities for the aging fiddler to wind down his career or possibly he just wanted to be closer to his first family. Charlie and Ruth initially rented a house in Johnson City adjacent to Jennie and Staley on Hamilton Street; they soon relocated near Gray Station, just a short distance from the old log house. For the next five years, Charlie entertained anywhere and everywhere he could find an opportunity, regardless of the compensation. One such venue was the Smoky Mountain Jamboree, a weekly stage show held each Saturday night in the auditorium of City Hall in downtown Johnson City.

Ironically, this hall was just across the street from the Deluxe Theatre where Charlie had participated in his first fiddle contest twenty-one years prior. With Jennie, he appeared on eight consecutive Saturday nights in 1946, beginning on March 9 and ending on May 4. Charlie retained the handwritten performance notes he used on stage (see Appendix D). These scribbles were not meant to make sense to anybody but him, and some of the jokes are blatantly obvious, while others appear obscure. The bulk of this humor was pure corn, but as hillbilly material it was meant to be that way. Charlie was a natural-born comedian who could take a scenario that really was not very humorous and make it uproarious by "putting himself into the joke."

One of the selections Charlie played on his fiddle was his favorite gospel song, "Nearer My God to Thee." Jasper remembered that his dad had a different way of playing this hymn. He loosened the bow hairs and slid

Advertisements for the Smoky Mountain Jamboree and the Big Burley Warehouse Barn Dance. Jennie Bowman Cain Collection.

COMING!

CHARLEY BOWMAN

and Daughters, PAULINE and JENNIE
and Son HOWARD BOWMAN

WITH

Comedian Bert Bence

AND

TED, the Girl who Plays the One-string
Fiddle.

WILL APPEAR AT THE

JONESBORO COURTHOUSE

Saturday Night, August 31

RING OUT THE OLD YEAR—
RING IN THE NEW—AT THE

GALA NEW YEAR MIDNITE FROLIC

● 11 P. M. SATURDAY NITE ●

VAUDEVILLE

and

. 2 BIG FEATURES .

SEVIER THEATER

PARKER BROTHERS Jamboree

Presenting

Famous Stars Of Radio And Stage

The Five Parker Brothers

ALSO

HONEYSUCKLE JONES - - The Funniest Black-face in Captivity
MISS JENNIE BOWMAN - - Accordion Player and Vocalist Suberb

ALL APPEARING IN PERSON AT

GRAYS STATION FAIR

BIG BURLEY
WAREHOUSE

Tuesday Night
March 8th

9 until 12

HARRY MEADE'S
East Tenn. Mountaineers

featuring

JENNIE BOWMAN
Piano Accordion

Charlie's and Jennie's Upper East Tennessee appearances. Jennie
Bowman Cain Collection.

them over the strings, with the wood part of the bow under the fiddle. Slowly, he would drag the bow over the strings, producing a beautiful organlike sound. This song was later played at Charlie's funeral, but on an organ, rather than a fiddle.

Charlie made haste in getting Mary Lou on the stage with him, incorporating her into his acts at the local high schools and theaters when she was barely four years old. She would quietly sit on the front row until her dad introduced her to the audience, at which time she would get up out of her seat, walk up on the stage, sing her song, and then quietly return to her place on the front row. The only song she remembered singing is one of Tennessee's state songs, "Tennessee Waltz." She believed he was trying to convert her into another Shirley Temple, but she preferred to dance. Mary Lou eventually prevailed, becoming a dancer who performed all over the country and earned numerous awards. Meanwhile, Ruth sold tickets at the front door. Mary Lou recalled a couple of comedy routines that Charlie often performed on stage, which she characterized as good clean fun. One of them involved the use of a pair of size forty woman's bloomers. He always wore big baggy overalls on stage, and what people didn't know was that his front pockets were not only deep but also connected. Charlie often pretended to be looking for something in one of his pockets and kept pulling objects out. The crowd would be amazed at how many things he would have in his "pocket." Finally, he would pull out a pair of woman's bloomers, which were bigger than a kitchen table. He would then hold them up for the audience to see, which immediately brought laughter and an abrupt end to the gag.

Charlie saved additional handwritten jokes that he used. The date and place are not known, but they are probably from the Smoky Mountain Jamboree:

> *1-* Bought a goat and skunk. They sleep with him. How about the smell? He said to heck with em. They would have to get used to him.
> *2-* Teacher called for silence. So quiet you can hear a pin drop. Way back in house. Said let her drop.
> *3-* Do you know why a goose stands on one foot? No, why does he stand on one foot. If he raises the other one he'd fall.
> *4-* Monkey joke. Saw tree full of monkeys.
> *5-* Was awful mad. Said I said he was a blabber mouth idiot. I don't know how they found it out.
> *6-* I can't see, I can't see. Why can't you see? Had my eye's shut.
> *7-* Do you know the difference between a corset and a garbage can? No, what's the difference? None. They both gather the waist.
> *8-* My brother's name was Dick. He got awful sick. Doctors took him fishing.[15]

Another comedy routine that Mary Lou remembered involved Charlie playing a small mouth harp that was only a couple inches long. While he was playing it, someone would come up behind him and slap him on the back, saying, "How are you doing, Charlie Bowman?" He would then "swallow" the harp and when he took a breath the harmonica would sound. The other person would then push on Charlie's stomach, causing a different and louder sound to come out of the harmonica. As the person pushed on different areas of Charlie's stomach, the harmonica played a tune. Charlie included this popular skit in many of his comedy routines.[16]

Between 1947 and 1950, Charlie mostly played with friends and neighbors in jam sessions. At sixty, he knew that his performing days were behind him. But little did he know he was about to be rediscovered by a new generation of old-time music lovers.

Charlie Bowman, circa 1940. Pauline Bowman Huggans Collection.

Charlie's Resting Years
1947-1962

Roll on buddy (roll on buddy),
Don't you roll so slow (roll so slow),
Baby how can I roll (baby how can I roll),
When the wheels won't go?
Charlie Bowman's "The Nine Pound Hammer"

Chapter 15

CHARLIE'S FIDDLE RESTS

By 1950 a poor economy had made performing at local schools almost futile. These shows were simply not bringing in enough cash for Charlie and Ruth to meet their financial needs. Interest in hillbilly music was waning and would soon suffer even more from rock and roll, which would redefine popular music. In an effort to improve their economic situation, Charlie and Ruth opened a chenille shop located between Johnson City and Jonesboro, but this venture failed. Consequently, the couple began discussing the possibility of moving back to Atlanta, where they believed they could earn more income. Charlie, who was now sixty-one-years-old, knew that going back on the road professionally was no longer an option.

The three of them moved to Union City near Atlanta, where they opened a small combination general merchandising shop and grocery store appropriately named Charlie Bowman Groceries & Meats. Reminiscent of Lige Adams's old country store in Gray Station, it stocked about anything a person would want—clothing, shoes, groceries, flowers from their own hothouse, shrubbery, hog and cow food, plus chenille bedspreads left over from their business venture in Tennessee. What began as a moderately profitable business soon evaporated within a few short years. Interstate 95 opened nearby, taking traffic away from Union City and, consequently, away from the store. Another problem was that large chain supermarkets began to open, forcing the smaller mom-and-pop grocery stores out of business.

Jasper worked in his father's store for about nine months, serving as meat cutter and produce purchaser. Ruth virtually ran the store and tried to make it profitable, but Charlie showed little interest in its operation. The bland lifestyle he was now experiencing in Union City was a far cry from the lively encores he received playing all over the country with some of the finest string bands of the 1920s–40s. In an effort to boost declining sales in their store, Charlie and Ruth allowed their customers to buy items on store credit with the understanding that they would cash their monthly checks at the store and pay off their outstanding debt. This arrangement was a win-win proposition for both parties. As an added attraction to further entice customers, they maintained a small zoo behind the store, which provided a location for his Saturday night impromptu jam sessions. There were a few small animals, including squirrels, rabbits, a monkey, and even a black snake. The local chief of police, who appreciated Charlie's kind of music, regularly played in this unusual backyard.

On September 28, 1950, Charlie received a typed postcard from Jim Walsh of Vinton, Virginia, giving him some much needed encouraging news:

> Dear Charlie: Have just come to work at WSLS [Roanoke, Virginia] and found your welcome letter waiting. I shall be glad to write an article about you and send it to the Sunday Johnson City Press-Chronicle. I'd like to have one or two good photos of you—clear snapshots might do—to send along with the article. Pictures can be either as you appear now or when you were recording. If you have anything of the sort—of you alone or with some of your fellow musician—please send it along to me. I'll write a letter. Jack Reedy was my good friend when I lived in Marion, Va. He is now dead. Am also going to write features for the Johnson City paper about my visit to Thomas A. Edison's laboratory at West Orange, N.J., where I was master of ceremonies. Best of luck to you, and I hope I can give you some publicity that will be helpful.[1]

For the next five years, Charlie continued hosting jam sessions, eventually moving them from his backyard zoo to his living room. Fortunately, reel-to-reel tape recording technology allowed him to record the majority of these gatherings. Although most of these tapes were lost after he died, one survived. On the recording, Charlie speaks about leaving Gray Station in October 1935 and making his home in Atlanta. He further mentions that he had not performed much since his arm operation twelve years prior (dating the tape to about 1955). Charlie attempted unsuccessfully to convince Ruth to speak on the tape. He comfortably assumes the role of master of ceremonies with his good friend and fellow fiddler Laurel Johnson, along with two other men whom he referred to as Mr. Haynes on guitar and Mr. Norman on banjo. Both were quite talented instrumentalists. Charlie bragged on the three of them for their generosity in playing at no cost at hospitals and nursing homes for elderly people. They played eight songs on the tape: "Cumberland Gap," "Katie Hill," "Earl's Breakdown," "Foggy Mountain Breakdown," "Billy in the Lowground," "Rocky Pallet," "I Don't Love Nobody," and "Nobody's Business." Charlie commented that Frank "Dad" Williams often played the old tune "Billy in the Lowground." Then he asked the group to play a favorite tune of his, "Dusty Miller," but they were reluctant since they had not played it in a while. He says of Laurel Johnson, "If you ever get him started [fiddling], the only way to stop him is like those big farm wagons like we used to have where you pull that big pole down to lock the wheels." Charlie jokes that

"Laurel Johnson could play a fiddle for six months straight without stopping." Referring to his own baritone voice, he modestly described it as sounding like a log containing a knot making its way through a sawmill.

Charlie recorded this session specifically for his old Hill Billie co-fiddler Tony Alderman. He talks directly to his former band member throughout the tape, trying to persuade him to come to Atlanta for a visit and even giving him his phone number. Charlie had visited Tony at his Galax, Virginia, home numerous times and had spent the night once with his parents, whom he called very nice people. The tape suggests a strong bond between two old-time fiddlers. It is not known how many, if any, trips Tony made to their Union City home.

In the summer of 1957, Howard threw a party for his father in Johnson City. The now retired fiddler made everyone feel welcome by circulating himself to all who attended, even the younger children, greeting them with his deep voice and his charismatic personality. The party concluded without Charlie playing his fiddle or displaying some buckle buster comedy. He obviously considered himself a family member, not the guest of honor. This was the last time most of Charlie's relatives saw him alive.

Dark days were on the horizon for the veteran fiddler. He realized that the old days were passing by as, one by one, he began to learn of the death of his siblings. Alfred, the oldest, died on Father's Day, 1956, followed by his sister Mary in 1958. However, three outlived him: Walter died in 1967, Elbert in 1982, and Ethel in 1985. On March 11, 1958, the sixty-eight-year-old retired performer received word that Fannie Mae had passed away in Johnson City, just two months shy of her seventy-second birthday. This was especially excruciating to Charlie despite the fact that she was no longer his wife. Without hesitation, he came to Johnson City from Union City by himself to attend her funeral, as he wanted to be alone.

Fannie had requested that she not be viewed at a funeral home, but instead in the living room of her Myrtle Avenue home. He quietly slipped through the front door into the crowded living room, where the many mourners in the room quickly spotted him. Pauline took him by the hand and escorted him to the casket. Charlie whispered to her, "She's as beautiful as she always was." Jean remembered her father looking at his first wife for what seemed to be an eternity. It was as if wanted to remain with her and not leave her this time. This was a dark and gloomy moment for Charlie as his mind, no doubt, drifted back to the choices he made in 1925, 1931, and again in 1935 to leave his family and seek the bright lights of the vaudeville stages. At this very emotional moment, Charlie's fiddle meant very little to him. Perhaps the words to his composition "Roll On Buddy" came to mind, this time with lyrics in the past tense: "I had a good woman just the same . . . Fannie Bowman was her name."[2] Or maybe he thought of another of his compositions, "Is This Goodbye Forever?"

I learned to love you but I have lost,
I can't forget you darling, no never,
With tear dimmed eyes I will clasp your hand,
Knowing this is goodbye forever.[3]

Fannie's body was transported from her home in Johnson City to the Gray Station Methodist Church for her funeral and subsequent burial in the adjoining Gray Station cemetery. At her memorial service, the church was packed full of people, with an overflow crowd standing outside. Just prior to family friend Pastor Glenn Garber's preaching, Charlie quietly slipped into the back pew without making eye contact or speaking to anyone. Jean remembered that one of the songs sung at her mother's funeral was very appropriate: "Well Done." Family and friends sent 101 floral wreaths to her gravesite, and Fannie's grave marker, provided by her oldest son, Lester, read simply "Our Mama."

Many years later when Pauline was asked if she thought Fannie still loved Charlie right up to the end, her answer in a choked-up voice was "Yes, I do." She was then asked if she thought Charlie still loved Fannie to the end, and her quick emotional answer was the same. Indeed, there is physical evidence that the flame between Charlie and Fannie never truly went out. Fannie's grave marker does not say "Fannie Mae Mohlar" (her maiden name) or "Fannie Mae Ferguson" (her first husband's name). Instead, it says "Fannie Mae Bowman." Mary Lou remembered Charlie mentioning Fannie repeatedly, and there was no doubt in her mind either that he always loved her. Coming to her funeral was his way of saying goodbye to his hardworking and dedicated wife.

The year 1958 marked not only the death of Fannie and his sister Mary but also the demise of the old log house in Gray Station—and his right leg. Although diabetes ran in the family—his mother had died of it—he had never been diagnosed with the disease. After his amputation, Charlie stayed indoor much of the time in his wheelchair. However, Charlie had too much internal energy and fortitude to allow the loss of a leg and confinement to a wheelchair to stop him entirely. Instead, he used the carpentry skills of his youth to make items for sale. A list of such items and their prices are revealed in a handwritten note he kept:

> Well Lamps: $3.00, Ox Yokes: $1.25, Pencil Holders: $.30, Flower Planters: $1.25, Whatnots: $1.75, Bobby Pin Holders: $.30, Small Rocking Chairs: $.50, Small Ox Yokes: $.50, Coca Cola Bottle Lamps: $1.00, Jug Lamps: $1.00, Flower Pot Lamps: $1.00, Wood Spool Lamp: $1.00 and Wine Bottle Lamps: $1.00.[4]

In 1959 Charlie bought stock in a recording company known as the National Recording Corporation (NRC), which had been formed by Atlanta radio personality, Georgia Tech football broadcaster, and 1984 Country Music Disc Jockey

Hall of Fame winner Bill Lowery. By this time, records were progressing from the larger breakable 78-rpm format (with a small hole in the middle) to the smaller unbreakable 45-rpm disc (with a large hole in the center). The NRC facility, though not state of the art, attracted country music newcomers such as Bill Anderson, Joe South, Ray Stevens, Jerry Reed, Roy Drusky, Razzy Bailey, Gene Vincent, Mac Davis, and others. They hung around the studio begging the sound engineers to let them record anything.[5] Unfortunately for Charlie, the old-time string band music that he had known and played all his life was no longer in vogue.

By this time, a new Elvis (Elvis Presley) had emerged on the scene, but in no way did he resemble the old Elvis (Elvis "Tony" Alderman). Unlike the old Elvis, the new one did not play a fiddle, wear bib overalls, buck dance, engage in buckle-busting comedy, or sing old-time music. Instead, the hip-swinging crooner sang rock and roll music. By Charlie's standards, this handsome young man was a dismal failure, and he would have nothing to do with his music. He felt the same way about another former Sun Records recording star sent to his house to audition for a record contract with NRC. After the young blond's performance in Bowman's living room, Charlie's assessment was that he had no talent, looked and acted like a wild man, and pounded his piano so hard he nearly ruined it—vetoing Jerry Lee Lewis's desire to record for NRC. Nevertheless, Lewis autographed one of his Sun records for Mary Lou, whose opinion of the singer differed immensely from her father's.

Over the years, Charlie became friends with Mr. H. P. Van Hoy, who in 1924 founded the Union Grove Fiddlers Convention in Union Grove, North Carolina. He ran this gathering until 1969, when his son, Harper A. Van Hoy, began operating it. It is now called the Fiddlers Grove Ole Time Fiddlers and Bluegrass Festival. Charlie attended its thirty-fifth fiddler's convention in 1959 with Ruth and Mary Lou. To his pleasant surprise, he met Tony Alderman there, who was no doubt startled to see the aging and wheelchair-bound Charlie. Gone were the days of the duo bowing their fiddle while fingering the other's. Although his life was fast drawing to a close, Charlie was about to receive one last breath of fresh air before taking his final bow.

Chapter 16

THE AGING FIDDLER REDISCOVERED

In 1960 Charlie became the focus of several noted country music historians, musicians, and collectors. Visitors to his Union City home included such notables as Archie Green, Mike Seeger, Dorsey Dixon, and Ed Kahn. Their more-than-casual interest revitalized Charlie, and he began corresponding with some of the same people he had known in his performing days, as well as some young newcomers who had heard his records. Lonnie Blush, a performer with whom he had once shared the stage, wrote to him on May 18, 1960:

> Hello Charlie: It has been many a year since I have had any news of you,
> but hope you remember me. Last night, we put on a show for the boys
> in the Hospital at Walter Reed, and we had the Happy Hicks on the
> show. We began talking backstage, and Tony Alderman mentioned that
> he had been talking to you a short while ago. He said that you would
> like to hear from some of us so I thought I would dash off a few lines
> to you. After the show, about fourteen of us went to a place called the
> 823 Restaurant in Washington DC and who do you think was there?
> Another old friend of yours—Fran Trappe. He was playing accordion
> with a piano team called the Heintze Brothers. He sends his regards to
> you and promised to drop you a few lines. Charlie, I often remember
> some of the good times we had and some of the old boys like you,
> Lonnie, the Hopkins Boys and Old King Tut. It was a lot of fun. Most
> of the boys are out of the entertainment field with the exception of Tony
> and myself and, of course, some of them have passed away. Hope this
> finds you in good health and if you get a chance drop me a few lines.
> As Every Your Friend, Lenny Blush.[1]

Like Charlie, Tony Alderman never abandoned the music he loved. He later moved to Maryland, where he formed a group called the Over the Hill Gang. On October 25, 1983, Tony and his group were on their way to give a free concert at a nursing home in Maryland when, as they pulled into the parking lot, he complained that he didn't feel well and was experiencing chest pains. A nursing home attendant rushed him to a nearby hospital, but it was too late to save him. Tony succumbed to a heart attack at the age of eighty-three.[2]

By the early 1960s, and after several years of rock and roll music, a new generation of folk music lovers arrived on the scene, including the Kingston Trio; the Chad Mitchell Trio; Peter, Paul and Mary; the Limelighters; the Weavers; Joan Baez; and Bob Dylan. While in truth they sounded nothing like the Hill Billies, they played acoustical string music. However, a new generation of young musicians, such as Mike Seeger, catered to the old-time music sound heard on their parents' and grandparents' 78-rpm records. Music historians took their tape recorders into the Appalachian region to locate some of these people, reminiscent of what Ralph Peer and Frank Walker did in the 1920s. Many of the old-time musicians were not only alive but still playing music. A few of them were invited to the Newport Folk Festival of the early 1960s, which added even more interest to this musical genre. These music-collecting pioneers did country music an invaluable service by locating and preserving the old 78s, which would not be around today otherwise. Today, these records are stored in such locations as the American Folklife Center of the Library of Congress in Washington, D.C., and at the University of North Carolina Southern Folklife Collection in Chapel Hill.

In the October 1960 edition of *Hobbies: The Magazine for Collectors,* Jim Walsh's article on Vernon Dalhart mentioned Charlie and included photographs of Charlie, Jennie, and Pauline.

> Another folk musician who remembers with pleasure more than one meeting with Dalhart is 71-year-old Charlie Bowman, who lost a leg in recent years and now lives a shut-in life in Union City, Ga. Charlie began making [Columbia, Brunswick, and Vocalion] records as fiddler for Al Hopkins' Buster Busters and as leader of Charlie Bowman and his Brothers in the 1920s when he lived in Johnson City, Tennessee. He says he won more fiddling awards than any other competing musician. Charlie also has two daughters, Pauline and Jennie, who made Columbia records in their teens, and as their fond father says, "were for years the best-known kids in East Tennessee." Charlie wrote the following letter to me. "I knew Dalhart very well—met him in New York on one of my recording dates and several occasions later. He was a very nice fellow to talk to, and was a good mouth harp player and singer—very serious about his recording work along with Carson Robinson. I have sat in the studio with him while he was recording."[3]

The following letter, dated October 9, 1960, is typical of the fan mail Charlie received after the article was published in *Hobbies* magazine:

> Charlie Bowman: Dear Sir, I was reading in a Hobbies magazine about you being a champion violin player. There is nothing on earth that I

love more than old dance tunes played by a violin. My favorites are Schooldishes Waltz, polkas and square dances. Lively music that takes you off your feet. I noticed in your write-up that you recorded for Columbia, Vocalion . . . [and Brunswick] Records. . . . I was happy to read about you and your two daughters, Jennie and Pauline. Would appreciate it very much to hear from you. Obliged, Phillip Van Derplas.[4]

While Charlie is noted for writing and performing "East Tennessee Blues," "The Nine Pound Hammer," "Roll on Buddy," and "CC&O No. 558," over the years he composed more than twenty-one more songs. It is not known how many, if any, of them, were ever performed in public, but it is known that none were ever recorded. They were, however, typed out and kept in a loose-leaf notebook. While some of these limericks might have been written earlier, it is believed that most were composed after the *Hobbies* article was published in late 1960. They included the following:

"Is This Goodbye Forever?" "Emery's Fast Ride," "It Was Springtime," "No War for Me," "Mother, It's Only Me," "I Can't Say Good-by," "My Railroad Shack," "Ain't Dat a Shame?" "Southern Blues," "Ain't Goin' to Happen More," "Mean Old Blues," "Things Ain't the Same," "My Rolling Mill," "Sad and Blue," "It's Autumn," "She's Cheating on Me," "Mother's Love," "She Was My Love," "She Went Away," "Shimmy Shake and Dance," "A Hobo's Song" (penned by Ruth), and "Come Here Brownie."[5]

The December 1960 edition of *Disc Collector,* with Woody Guthrie on the front cover, ran a one-page article titled "Meet Charlie Bowman." It gave a brief synopsis of Charlie's career and ended with these words: "Charlie is a shut in and would like to hear from any member of *Country Directory* or *Disc Collector.*"[6] The article then gave Charlie's Union City, Georgia, address and ended with "To Be Continued," indicating plans to do a series of articles about him. This same publication also contained information about the deaths of A. P. Carter on November 7 and Johnny Horton on November 12.[7] Between *Hobbies* and *Disc Collector* magazines, the floodgates of mail opened, giving Charlie an indication of just how important his musical career had been.

Charlie received a letter from Joe Nicholas, the editor of *Disc Collector,* dated October 15, 1960:

Dear Mr. Bowman: My good friend Mr. Jim Walsh of Vinton, Virginia sent me an article on you to publish in my journal *Disc Collector.* First of all, I'd like to tell you about my journal. I started this journal back in 1950 for the purpose of getting all the collectors of country or hillbilly records together in one club where they could swap records, histories on the old country artists, photos, etc. Today, the club is worldwide with members in every country you could possibly name. I have a personal collection of records numbering over 14,000 plus hundreds of books, radio song folios, photos and a bunch of other material.

I am hoping someday to turn it over to the Library of Congress, or some other archive that will save it. I would really like to have a story on your recording career, or any information at all you wish to give me. Did you ever record any material that wasn't issued? I hope you don't mind my printing the article on you that Jim Walsh sent in. This is just the material we need badly, and my members will be glad to see an article on you. Today your old records are all collector's items and hard to come by, usually the only way they can be gotten is on tape. Respect-fully, Joe Nicholas.[8]

Charlie replied to Joe's correspondence on November 28, 1960, with a com-bined letter and autobiography he titled "About Charlie Bowman." He sent a condensation of his career—growing up on an East Tennessee farm, working the vaudeville stages with the Hill Billies and Blue Ridge Ramblers, and moving to Atlanta and working the southern and western states. He attached to his letter a partial discography of his records with the Hill Billies, Charlie Bowman and His Brothers, and the Bowman Sisters:

Dear Joe: You mentioned my friend Jim Walsh. I haven't met him in person but hear from him often for several years. He is a great fellow. With what I'm sending you now and what he sent you on me will be glad for you to use it. Maybe you can get a story out if it. Hope so. Of all the recordings I worked on, I haven't got a single copy—have some on tape. Thanks a lot for sending me *Disc Collector*. I got a lot of pleasure out of them and will appreciate copies of any magazine pertaining to artists of old time music. Jim Walsh had been sending me *Hobbies* for several months. He gave me and my daughters nice write up in October issue of *Hobbies*. If I have written you anything you can use will appreci-ate seeing it in print. I'm a shut-in and will be glad to get any kind of reading material to help me pass the time away. Am sending you a list of records I help make. If you use this give Al Hopkins all [the credit] you can. He was one of the greatest hill billie singers and piano players, he was great. He died many years ago in a car accident. I'm very glad that my career as an old time fiddler was very successful. I have played in 22 states but had to give it up. As I told you, I am a shut in, use wheel chair. I enjoy getting letters. It helps me to while away the time. Respt yours, Fiddlin Charlie Bowman.[9]

Charlie's letter writing campaign achieved international status when he began corresponding with John Edwards of Cremorne, Australia, who had devoted himself to collecting old-time hillbilly music of the period between 1923 and 1941. In his endeavors, Edwards became a leading authority on the subject. He corresponded with as many of the old record artists as he could and acquired a sizable number of records, photographs, biographies, and other related items from that period. John was especially attracted to Charlie and the various groups with whom he performed. This twenty-eight-year-old country music historian's work was important to him; thus, in late 1960, he had his lawyer prepare a will defining the placement of his vast collection upon his death. Little did he realize how soon this legal document would be required. On Christmas Eve 1960, he was killed in an automobile wreck near Sydney.[10] Ironically, John never visited the United States. His mother, Irene Edwards, devastated over the loss of her son, wanted to carry on his unfinished work and became active in transferring John's collection to the United States. His scores of friends helped her establish the John Edwards Memorial Foundation. Eugene Earle, an avid collector of old-time country music, served as the cofounder and president. Other officers of the organization included Archie Green (first vice president), Fred Hoeptner (second vice president), D. K. Wilgus (secretary) and Ed Kahn (treasurer). The collection was eventually transported to the Southern Folklife Collection at the University of North Carolina in Chapel Hill. Irene Edwards continued to correspond with some of the people John had communicated with, including Charlie. Eugene Earle wrote a later to Charlie from New Milford, New Jersey, dated March 18, 1961:

> Dear Mr. Bowman: Forgive me for not writing to you sooner. I received your letter from Mrs. Edwards, enclosing your latest letter to John. I do not presently have John's collection, and it will probably be a few months before they will be sent. I know that John was obtaining a good bit of historical information on you and the other artists you knew. I plan to complete the book John was preparing, and after I receive his files, I may have some questions for you. I have always enjoyed your music, and the music of Al Hopkins band, and would like to have as much info as possible to include in the book. I'm sure that in the short period that you have corresponded with John, you found out what a wonderful person he was. His death was tragic, indeed, and I personally will miss his wonderful letters. I will be keeping in touch. Perhaps I can meet you someday. I had a wonderful visit with another old-timer you know, Tom Ashley. We recorded him and others in the area, and issued a Folkways LP Record. Regards, Eugene W. Earle.[11]

While Tony Alderman did not appear to write many, if any, letters to Charlie or to visit him in his home, it is known that the two friends frequently talked by telephone. Charlie wrote his co-fiddler two short letters in the spring of 1961. In the first correspondence, he expressed his regret at missing the previous

Galax fiddle convention, saying that he had just received a letter that week from Mr. Vanhoy. Tony had sent him a tape of the convention music, which, Charlie indicated, he and his friends enjoyed immensely.[12] In the second note, Charlie requested a tape of some of their Hill Billie recordings to send to Joe Nicholas in Michigan.[13]

On April 27, 1961, Mike Seeger, a founding member of the old-time string band the New Lost City Ramblers, went to Charlie's Union City home to record an interview with him. Devoted to singing and playing traditional mountain music of the southern United States, Mike sings and plays the banjo, guitar, fiddle, mandolin, jaw harp, French harp, quills, dulcimer, autoharp, and other instruments. He has produced more than sixty recordings for six different record labels.

Charlie received a letter from country music historian Archie Green, at the University of Illinois, Champaign, Illinois, on May 18, 1961:

> Dear Charlie: Thanks very much for your note, which came today. I have been in touch with Tony Alderman and have prepared a long reply to his tapes, photographs, etc. As you'll read in the copy to you, I'm leaving for California for two weeks time. When I return I'll get in touch with both of you. Also, I'll send the article to your friends. Thanks again for your splendid help and interest in "our" project. Cordially, Archie Green.[14]

Archie attached a copy of the lengthy letter he wrote to Tony dated the same day. Tony was living in Washington, D.C., at the time.

> Dear Mr. Alderman: I am deeply in your debt for your generosity in sending me tapes, photographs and letters. My impulse was to respond at once, but I held off until I could listen to each tape twice. Now that I have assimilated the material you sent, I can make a decent reply. I promise you, and Mr. Bowman, too, that I shall write a long scholarly article on the contribution of the Original Hillbilly Band. There are some youngsters who honor the old-time music by preserving the records. Others issue little fan magazines on the music. Still others are bringing the music to new audiences via current L-P recordings. My task is to document the material, events, and personalities for serious journals and, I trust for future students. Since I wrote last, my "Coal Discography" has appeared. I sent one each to both you and Mr. Bowman. I believe that it will demonstrate my interest in the music and the depths of my research.
>
> My purpose in writing today is chiefly to convey thanks and to pass on my article. In a few days I have to go out to San Francisco on Library business. When I get back I shall finish a long article on the Carter Family. With that out of the way, I'll dig into the story of how hillbilly music

was named. At the moment, Mr. Alderman, I'll refrain from questions. Perhaps while I'm out on the Coast you'll have time to make copies of the Coolidge clipping, contract, etc. that you described in the tapes. In the meantime, I have put out a few questions to others on the dates of Fiddling John Carson's and Henry Whitter's early recording. Quite soon, I feel I'll have all the jigsaw pieces together.

I might indicate that in my opinion your first released Hillbilly record were Okeh: 40294 "Silly Bill," "Old Time Cinda," 40336 "Cripple Creek," "Sally Ann," 40376 "Old Joe Clark" and "Whoa! Mule." These were in the 1925 Okeh Catalog. . . . I don't think it'll be too difficult to run down the actual recording and release dates for these first three records. If these were, in fact, the first records you made and we pinpoint the recording date we'll know just when the Peer conversation took place.

There is one time sequence that needs clarification. It deals with John Rector's single Victor record. The session that preceded your actual recording date with Peer at Okeh (1923 Dodge). Was an unsuccessful session Rector arranged by telegram at Victor? Am I correct in assuming that your gang went up twice; once for an unsuccessful session at Victor and once for a successful one at Okeh? If this is true how much time separated the two sessions? Also, you say that Rector made one Victor record. Was this before he went up with your group? If so the sequence would be at least three trips: (A) Rector for one Victor record, (B) The whole gang at Victor, (C) The whole gang at Okeh.

But enough for problems that can be taken up later. I do not want to close without thanking you for your extreme kindness in cooperating with Mr. Mike Seeger and Mr. John Cohen of the New Lost City Ramblers. They are East Coast boys. I am from San Francisco. Yet I knew them well. You are right, Mr. Alderman, when you say that they are introducing hillbilly music to college audiences. I might add that they are doing a fine job.

This has been a long letter, and I have enjoyed writing it. I am sending a carbon of it to Mr. Bowman since we seem to be in on a three-way partnership to bring the Original Hillbilly band story back to life. I shall be happy to hear from both of you after you look at the coal list. Sincerely, Archie Green, Librarian.[15]

Three months after mailing this letter to Charlie, Archie kept his word. He came to Union City on August 10, 1961, for an interview.

Charlie and another country legend, Dorsey Dixon, became good friends over the years. Dorsey and his brother, Howard, were well known in the country music field as the Dixon Brothers. They were singers and songwriters, with Dorsey playing the fiddle and Howard the acoustical steel guitar. Dorsey wrote numerous letters to Charlie that were neatly printed by hand, such as one sent from E. Rockingham, North Carolina, dated October 13, 1961:

> Charlie: Your real nice letter came today. I'm enclosing the new poems I wrote about John Edwards, "The John Edwards Foundation," and my late brother Howard titled "Howard's Church Life." Hope you'll enjoy reading them a lot. You spoke of not hearing from Eugene Earle. I'm afraid he's loaded with work trying to get the book ready that he and John were working on at the time of John's death. The last time I heard from him was shortly after Archie Green and Ed Kahn's visit here with me. I heard from him through Mrs. Edwards in a letter. He was looking to get John's collection material for the book any day. It seems he was having custom's troubles. Best Regards, Dorsey Dixon.[16]

Dorsey's concerns about writing the poem were quickly answered in a letter he got from Irene Edwards in Australia dated October 15, 1961:

> Dear Mr. Bowman: It must have been very enjoyable being able to talk with Mr. Archie Green and Mr. Ed Kahn. They are fine people. I had letters from both about a week ago. They must have covered great distances in their travels and how interesting it must have been. Mr. Dixon certainly is a good writer. I get lots of delightful letters from him and just recently he sent me a tape recording with the song he wrote about John and about his brother, Howard. There were other songs on it as well. He is very gifted to be able to compose as he does. Although I had heard his records when John was here, it came as a surprise to hear his voice again. It is so strong and melodious. He records amazingly well. I hope Mr. Dixon was able to accept the kind invitation you gave him to visit you. I think you would have lots of fun talking about old times and perhaps playing and singing together. John appreciated everything, the smallest kindness pleased him, and he was grateful. He was born in 1932 at the height of the depression and so of necessity, was brought up the hard way, but I really think it is the best way. I do sincerely hope that Gene Earle, Archie Green, and Ed Kahn will be able to carry out their plans for the Memorial Foundation. There will be a terrible amount of work involved but they are clever and competent people and if it is at all possible to do it they will. Yours very sincerely, Irene Edwards.[17]

Financed by Eugene Earle, Dorsey paid a visit to Charlie's Union City home in November 1961 to conduct a taped interview with the expert fiddler. During their dialogue, Dorsey reminisced about a song he wrote called "The School House

THE AGING FIDDLER REDISCOVERED

Fire," which was a true story regarding a 1923 Cleveland, South Carolina, tragedy that claimed the lives of seventy-six children. Later, Howard set the words to the tune of "Life's Railway to Heaven." Many of their songs reflected the God-fearing hardworking people in the textile mills where both Dorsey and Howard worked. Dorsey once made a profound statement to Charlie. Mike Seeger had visited them both on separate occasions without telling them that he was an accomplished musician. This modesty of remaining silent about his musical talents impressed the two of them. Dorsey remarked that Mike was an example of something his father always taught him—"A loaded wagon doesn't rattle."[18] Charlie and Ruth were delighted to have Dorsey spend a few days in their home. It was during this visit that Dixon played his guitar and sang several songs, including one he had written about John Edwards from a poem he composed titled "The John Edwards Foundation." Irene Edwards requested that Dorsey put the poem to music. Within a couple months, she composed a letter to Charlie:

> Dear Mr. Bowman: I appreciate very much getting your photograph and the calendar, which is most interesting to have. How John would have loved to see them. May I say what a pleasant and good-looking young man you were. How sad it is that we all have to grow older but it is good to have happy memories to look back on. I was most pleased to know that Mr. Dixon visited with you and that he enjoyed it so much. It was kind indeed of Mr. Earle to send you a tape of your recordings; yes, he certainly must be a wonderfully kind person and very clever too. I read in a magazine here where Mrs. Jimmie Rodgers had died in November from cancer. Did you know of Jimmie Rodgers? He was one of John's very favorite artists. When you mention Al Hopkins as your leader, would that be Al Hopkins and His Buckle Busters? John had the following recordings by them if you are interested—"Buck-Eyed Rabbits"/ "Bristol Tennessee Blues," "Sweet Bunch of Daisies"/ "Daisies Won't Tell," "Marosovia Waltz"/ "Polka Medley," "Cluck Old Hen"/ "Black Eyed Susie," "Blue Ridge Mountain Blues," "Cinda"/ "Sally Ann," "Whoa, Mule"/ "Johnson Boys," "Roll On the Ground"/ "Ride That Mule" and "East Tennessee Blues" (as the Hill Billies). Would it be you who played the fiddle on these? I still weep whenever I look at John's catalogue; it is so beautifully done and such a monument to his industry and research. I have just received an offer from a well-known sculptor here to do a bas-relief panel of John for the university in the States where his collection goes. Yours sincerely, Irene Edwards.[19]

Charlie's health continued to decline in early 1962. Many of the people with whom he had corresponded suspected the worst when he failed to promptly answer their letters. Dorsey Dixon was especially worried, which he expressed in a letter dated May 5, 1962, just two weeks before Charlie died. It is doubtful that Charlie ever read it:

> Dear Charlie: I knew something was wrong. I was fixing to write Ruth to see if I could hear from you. Bless your heart Charlie and thank you so much for your short letter. I was getting more and more distressed about you. I know you didn't feel like writing the letter I received just a short while ago, but you'll never know how much it meant to me. I do hope the doctor will be able to give you something for relief from pain. Charlie, I do hope this letter will find you lots better. Don't worry yourself trying to write a long letter to me when you're in pain. Just a line or two so I can hear from you once a month. Take it easy Charlie. If I don't hear from you in a reasonable length of time, I'll write you again. Take care of yourself and write again when you feel like it. Your Old Friend, Dorsey Dixon.[20]

Chapter 17

TIME TO "ROLL ON BUDDY"

As Charlie Bowman's health deteriorated dramatically, he realized that his time was short. The words he wrote for his song "The Nine Pound Hammer" became very real to him, and he must have thought to himself, "How can I roll when the wheels won't roll?" Charlie's "nine pound hammer" had become a little too heavy not because of his size but because of his health. Other lines from his songs most likely came to mind also: "I'm going on the mountain and I ain't coming back, no I ain't coming back."

Charles Thomas Bowman died in the early morning hours of Sunday, May 20, 1962, at Atlanta's Saint Joseph Infirmary, just two months shy of his seventy-third birthday. Several of his children were en route to see him when they learned of his impending death, but the end came before their arrival. Only Mary Lou and Ruth were at his bedside when he took his final breath.

His passing did not go unnoticed by old-time music fans. His obituary appeared in numerous magazines and newspapers around the country, including the very popular *Variety Magazine*:

> Charles Bowman, 72, one of the leading exponents of country style music in the 1920–30s, died May 20 in Atlanta. Known as "The Champion Fiddler of East Tennessee," he was said to have won more fiddling competitions than any other performer of his era. He headed a group, Charlie Bowman & His Brothers, which made Columbia records and was principal fiddler for Al Hopkins & His Buckle Busters on Brunswick and Vocalion labels. With his daughters, Jennie and Pauline, who had a singing act, he traveled extensively in vaudeville. He had been in poor health since having a leg amputated in 1958. Survived by his wife, five sons, and six daughters.[1]

The local *Johnson City Press-Chronicle* also acknowledged his passing:

> Atlanta, Ga.—Charles T. "Fiddlin'" Charlie Bowman, 73 of Union City, Ga., formerly of Gray Station, died [at 1 A.M.] yesterday in St. Joseph's Hospital, Atlanta. Well-known for many years as a musician, Bowman

had won national fame with his fiddling. He had his own band for years, and he played for the late B. Carroll Reece the first time he ran for election. Bowman was a native of Washington County and had been a carpenter. He had made his home in Union City for the past ten years.[2]

Charlie's funeral service was held at the Union City Methodist Church on Tuesday, May 22, with a total attendance of 165 family members and friends. Several old-time music performers were among the mourners, including Ernie Hodges, Laurel Johnson (who served as a pallbearer), and Eddie King. Family members at his funeral included one brother and one sister, six of his and Fannie's ten children, and, of course, Ruth and Mary Lou. By this time, all of his old Hill Billie band members were deceased, with the exception of Tony Alderman, who was not present.

No old-time music was played that afternoon. Conspicuously absent were fiddles, banjos, guitars, ukuleles, slide guitars, pianos, harmonicas, accordions, buckle busting comedy, buck dancing, brooms, saws, washtub basses, underfeed furnaces, and thick balloons. There were no sounds of a hound dog chasing a fox through the Tennessee hills, no train trying to get a stubborn donkey off the railroad tracks, no sound of Fogless Bill's CC&O train engine whistle, and no gobbler or bantam hen cackling in a barnyard scenario. Instead, the program was a bit brief and very somber, with no special singing. The music consisted of only three gospel songs: "I Won't Have to Cross Jordan Alone," "Just One Rose Will Do," and Charlie's favorite gospel song, "Nearer My God to Thee." This last song wasn't rendered the way Charlie had played it with the fiddle bow hairs loosened and drawn over the top of the strings; instead, the music emulated from a plaintive church organ.[3] Ruth had Charlie's remains laid to rest at the nearby Holly Hill Memorial Park in Fairburn, Georgia, not on East Tennessee soil, where he would have preferred. Unlike the words "The Nine Pound Hammer," his tombstone wasn't made out of number nine coal, but instead was a flat granite marker provided for by his oldest son, Lester, with this brief inscription:

> Charles T. Bowman
> Fiddlin' Charlie
> Born Washington Co. Tenn
> 1889–1962

Soon after her husband died, Ruth packed her belongings and moved to California, but not before doing the unthinkable. She rid herself of much of Charlie's collection of memorabilia from his many travels and performances. What was of monetary value was sold for whatever she could get out of it, and what she could not sell was discarded. Ruth took Charlie's most prized possession, the fiddle that won him so many fiddle contests and that he used when he played with the Hill Billies, to a local pawn shop in Atlanta and hocked it for an undeterminable amount of cash. The large trunk containing the fiddler's various costumes that he wore while performing on stage also promptly disappeared. Had she saved these items, they would have become invaluable artifacts to music historians, collectors, and museums. Mary Lou rescued what she could of Charlie's remaining items. Fortunately, she was able to retrieve photographs, songs, letters, and one of Charlie's fiddles that was hand-made and given to him by Laurel Johnson. Not salvaged, however, was Charlie's large collection of reel-to-reel tapes made at his home while he was an invalid and his collection of postmarks from his many fan letters.

Dorsey Dixon sent one final letter to the Bowman home, offering a final tribute to his old friend and fellow musician. It consisted of a ten-verse poem:

> Charlie Bowman went to sleep
> To get a needed rest
> He had braved the battles of life
> And finally stood the test.
>
> The tone of Charlie's fiddle
> Has blessed the hearts of man
> Leading all stringed instruments
> In the Bowman Brothers band.
>
> The sound of his old fiddle
> Was a thrilling sound to hear
> When Charlie led the Bowman band
> In places there and here.
>
> The music sank into our heart
> And banished all our woe
> When the Bowman Brothers played
> And Charlie pulled the bow.
>
> People came from far and wide
> To places where they went
> To listen to Charlie pull his bow
> And happy times they spent.
>
> But Charlie Bowman left one day
> For a bright and sunny land
> God needed our old timer
> To lead another band.
>
> Charlie laid his fiddle down
> And put his bow away
> We'll listen to him play again
> But God needed him that day.

His music much more thrilling
His tone will be just fine
His fiddle will have more power
Than the one he left behind.

So we should not be selfish
Our hearts should not be sore
Charlie will lead another band
On Heaven's golden shore.

Charlie plays his music
With the angels there on high
And we can listen to him play
In that sweet by and by.[4]

Chapter 18

ALIVE THROUGH HIS MUSIC

Charles Thomas Bowman's legend lives on to this very day. "East Tennessee Blues," "The Nine Pound Hammer," and "Roll on Buddy" can be heard daily both on old-time and bluegrass radio stations all over the world. A trip to a local library will find his name in volumes of books written on the subject of old-time music, and he has been featured in numerous magazines and newspapers.

On August 8, 1963, Archie Green and Ed Kahn interviewed Elbert Bowman at his home in Johnson City. This meeting focused on the role Charlie's youngest brother played as part of Charlie Bowman and His Brothers string band, as well as his involvement with the Hill Billies' recording session with Brunswick and Vocalion in New York City. Of particular historical importance is how Elbert created the sounds of the nine-pound hammer on his banjo. Elbert's family carried on the Bowman tradition by singing and playing popular, western swing, gospel, old-time, and bluegrass music. One son, Billy Bowman, became the steel guitar player for the legendary Bob Wills and the Texas Playboys between 1950 and 1958 and was later inducted into the International Steel Guitar Hall of Fame (see appendix D).

Charlie received arguably his biggest honor when he was inducted into the North American Fiddlers Hall of Fame in Osceola, New York, on July 28, 2001, almost thirty-nine years after his passing. This event took place in the foothills of the Appalachian Mountain range, not in the Great Smoky Mountains, but in the Adirondack Mountains approximately 760 miles northeast of East Tennessee. On that special night, Charlie joined forty-one other American and Canadian fiddler giants, including Chubby Wise, Johnny Gimble, Buddy Spicher, Eck Robertson, John Carson, Doc Roberts, Gid Tanner, Lowe Stokes, Randy Howard, Howdy Forrester, Bob Wills, Tommy Jackson, Clayton McMitchen, Kenny Baker, Mark O'Connor, Arthur Smith, Clark Kessinger, Roy Acuff, and Benny Martin.[1] Ironically, the 2002 winner was also a Tennessean, old-time longbow fiddler Ralph Blizard of Blountville, Tennessee, whose parent's home Charlie had frequently visited.

The stated goal of the North American Fiddlers Hall of Fame is "to honor every fiddler who has ever made hearts light and happy with the fiddle's lifting music." There can be no hesitation that Charlie provided this over his quarter of a century of entertaining others. Listening closely to old-time Appalachian-style music or its cousin, bluegrass music, one can hear the influence of Charlie's unique fiddle sound.

The local Washington County, Tennessee, Council unanimously issued a declaration proclaiming July 26, 2004, as "Charlie Bowman Day," and the Tennessee Historical Commission in Nashville, Tennessee, approved an official state historical marker for "Fiddlin' Charlie Bowman." On August 12, family members and friends dedicated the marker in a ceremony on Roscoe Fitz Road, not far from the spot where Charlie and Fannie raised their family. Present at the dedication ceremony were several state and local politicians. The historical marker read:

> Fiddlin' Charlie Bowman, 1889–1962. Charlie Bowman, Hall of Fame
> fiddler, recording artist, vaudeville performer, and writer of *Nine Pound
> Hammer* and *East Tennessee Blues,* toured with the Hill Billies and other
> music groups, once performing for President Calvin Coolidge. Two
> daughters, Jennie and Pauline, were among the first sister act recorded
> in the country music genre. Charlie and brothers Elbert, Walter, and
> Argil played for Congressman B. Carroll Reece's campaigns. Charlie and
> his wife, Fannie, reared 12 children in a log house on Roscoe Fitz Road.[2]

During the years preceding his death, Charlie often commented that he felt it was a shame the way popular music had changed. Rock and roll had relegated hillbilly music to the sidelines. Charlie always believed hillbilly music would eventually come back. He would have been pleased to read this letter from a fan, which arrived eight months after his death:

> Dear Mr. Bowman: I found your address in a magazine and wanted to
> drop you a note and wish you a Merry Christmas and let you know that
> you haven't been forgotten. I have several of your old records and enjoy
> them a lot. I really appreciate the kind of music you recorded and wish
> people would still record it. I read that you are a shut-in and wonder
> if you possibly have a tape recorder? I have two good ones and could
> send you copies of your old records (if you don't have them). I would
> like very much to talk to you on tape and most of all, get some pictures
> of you as you now are and of the band you had when recording (if you
> have any now). If you're unable to write, I would greatly appreciate your
> getting someone in your family to drop me a line.[3]

As Bob Taylor, governor of Tennessee, said on April 24, 1889, three months before Charlie was born: "Happy is the home where fiddles and fiddlers dwell and nearest to Heaven is the church where fiddlers and singers blend their music in hymns of praise to Almighty God. . . . there is no reason why the virtuoso and the fiddler should fall out. Let the nightingale sing in his realm, and let the cricket sing in his. We will all play together on golden fiddles in the 'sweet bye and bye.'"[4]

AFTERWORD
Archie Green

A journey across the continent, west to east, reverses expected routes. If accompanied by a parallel adventure in cultural exploration, the linked trails hold promise of continuous reflection. In 1940, I had begun two decades working as a shipwright and building tradesman in California. After 1960, acquiring a folklorist's tools, I studied and wrote about the expressive life of American workers. Returning home to San Francisco in 1982, I gained some perspective on my dual trips through land and lore.

On August 10, 1961, Ed Kahn, a graduate student at UCLA, and I visited Charlie Bowman at his home in Union City, Georgia. Previously, I had immersed myself in unraveling the origin of commercial hillbilly music. Bowman had participated in the early band that named the idiom; his recollection of people, places, and recording events added to the story. Additionally, he helped me immensely to comprehend the interaction of European and African elements in Appalachian music. Some findings of our Union City visit appeared in the *Journal of American Folklore* (1965) and in *Only a Miner* (1972); I'll not repeat their substance here.

Rather, I shall reflect on our meeting with Bowman, its intentions, and what residue of meaning I now extract after reading Bob Cox's manuscript. To begin, no singular model surfaces in relating a musician's story. Cox views Bowman from within the extended clan as he balances the latter's commitment to career over that of family obligation.

Charlie Bowman was not the first music maker to be pulled away from wife and children by the demands of the road; nor will he be the last. Cox's book, juxtaposed with my individual reaction to it, illustrates one of the gulfs between biographer and reader. Along with other country music fans (we denominated our special form alternately as "Appalachian," "old time," or "hillbilly"), I knew nothing of Bowman's family or his background in Gray Station, Tennessee.

Perhaps it might interest readers to know that a California youngster on first hearing radio and phonograph country songs in the mid-1920s thought that he had encountered cowboy music. My actual exposure to the Southland—the consciousness of discovery—came on a World War II troop train to a Navy boot camp in old Virginia. In John Henry's Big Bend Tunnel in the West Virginia mountains, I knew that I had entered a land previously known via songs and stories. With training completed, I visited the Virginia state capitol in Richmond to feel the power of Confederate imagery firsthand. Thus, my transition in distinguishing cowboy balladry from string-band numbers stretched out over the decades and much geography.

By the time of my 1961 visit with Charlie Bowman, I had heard enough Appalachian music to appreciate its contours, but had yet to grasp its complexity. Many performers helped in this growth in understanding; here, I focus arbitrarily on Bowman. In regards to him, I asked why "hillbilly," a term of semantic elasticity, had been applied to this musical genre. Further, in its defining function of simultaneously sentimentalizing and denigrating rural life, was it not commenting on bedrock ambivalence in American identity?

Writing in the spring of 2006, it is easy to be disturbed by the divisions among our nation's citizens—political, social, and moral. To the extent that music serves as one mark of personal and group identity, it can be studied for its role in society. I am unaware of Charlie Bowman's own views about the large meaning attributed to his career. Did he reflect on the conflict between family life and professional demands? How did he measure success or failure in his ventures?

Certainly, the emergence of rock at the end of his performing life threatened him. As best he could, he reiterated his loyalty to the old-time country music at which he excelled. Seemingly, he did not offer any critical opinions on these matters. We find little mention in Cox's narrative of Bowman's views on ethical problems in his era. Did he support Franklin Delano Roosevelt's New Deal? Did he encounter any of FDR's art projects? Did he go beyond general southern ideas on race relations? How conscious was he of issues now placed under the rubric "political culture"?

In my study of the hammer-song complex in *Only a Miner,* I noted Charlie Bowman's contribution to the classics "Nine Pound Hammer" and "Roll on Buddy." While in his East Tennessee teenage years (1903–1905), crews of black laborers built the CC&O Railroad near his home. Like other mountain boys who grew up in an Anglo-American ballad and fiddle tradition, young Charlie found fascinating the strange singing of the black crews then engaged in blasting, drilling, grading, spiking, tamping, and related chores. He retained some memory of these functional work chants, putting fragments into new compositions in recording studios in the 1920s.

We still sense something of Bowman's discovery during his formative years of an exotic music when we hear his hammer songs performed by contemporary bluegrass bands. I am aware of an unstated premise in my retrospective thoughts on a visit in 1961. I believed then (and to this day) that contextual data enhanced appreciation of an expressive art form. Put simply, one could enjoy Merle Travis or Bill Monroe without having any knowledge of Charlie Bowman. However, even a few facts about the latter deepened response to the former.

This assertion cannot be demonstrated empirically. Do we expect all those who listen to "Nine Pound Hammer" or "Roll on Buddy" to be equally curious about their origin? Of course, our underlying question touches the rationale for any writing about music. Without a belief in the utility of my essays and books, I could not have translated my single meeting with Bowman into published commentary.

From my present vantage point, I look back at decades of effort following a trade and related intellectual activity. The cowboy songs heard in childhood, I now denominate "vernacular music." (This tag's history appears in my essay "Vernacular Music: A Naming Compass," *Musical Quarterly,* Spring 1991.) This bin is broad enough to hold Charlie Bowman's earliest hammer-song recordings, as well as his final radio performances with the Rice Brothers' Gang at Shreveport, Louisiana.

Without delving into technical analysis, I need only cite two of the Rice hits— "You Are My Sunshine," " Nobody's Darling But Mine"—to suggest the range of Bowman's repertoire. Students may use different labels or name other numbers. The underlying problem remains. Where do we place those songs that echo our largest experiences? For myself, I can report that both "Nine Pound Hammer" and "You Are My Sunshine" had touched me deeply independent of my meeting with Bowman. Yet after my visit with him, and upon reading Cox's manuscript, these pieces gained an extra edge for me.

At this juncture, I deal not only with an individual artist's reach in performance sources and styles, but also with evolution in commercial country music. Charlie Bowman made his prime mark as a fiddler. Bob Cox documents Bowman's contributions to a complex musical genre that changed substantially within the fiddler's lifetime.

The evolution (or devolution) of country music was not a cultural or historical abstraction to Charlie Bowman. In blunt terms, each new mode or stylistic shift made the old-time fiddler less employable. The interaction of aesthetics and economics is also seen in Bob Cox's detailed treatment of Charlie's daughters Jennie and Pauline. While still in their teens, they appeared on Columbia Records as the Bowman Sisters. Later, they joined H. M. Barnes's Blue Ridge Ramblers, a hillbilly vaudeville-circuit and recording troupe.

Where do the Bowman sisters fit in country music's continuing narrative? Were they pioneers embracing new sounds, or did they represent individuals unable to accommodate to an industry's unrelenting demands? I think of Jennie and Pauline as marchers in a sinuous parade including Samantha Bumgarner, Molly O'Day,

Dolly Parton, and the Dixie Chicks. To the extent that this parade analogy is apt, we still have to assign meaning to its purpose and ultimate direction.

In retrospect, I served as one part of a diverse group of 1960s enthusiasts (cultural guerrillas) who "rediscovered" Charlie and his peers in their final years. We brought some of them to concert or festival audiences, and presented others via films, books, journal articles, sound recordings, and museum exhibits. Our motives were as varied as our explorations: romantic, nostalgic, hortatory, idealistic, reformistic, transformative, liberating.

My journey to Bowman's last home crossed the North American continent. It also contributed to a key (and still open) question as to music's role in bridging differences in large society. We want hymns to hail "One Nation, One People," yet we guard jealously the unique compositions that speak to plural identities.

Balladry, lyric songs, and instrumental tunes together serve divergent aims. A nation that spans time zones and includes disparate groups may honor select artistic forms as it dishonors other representations. A given musical piece may symbolize the large community's character while it remains comprehensible, or even dangerous, to rival citizens.

At this late date, I can only speculate about Charlie Bowman's thoughts in 1961 on meeting a few folklore students and musical performers. For myself, I felt then, as I do now, that his fiddle tunes, work chants, blues, and ballads might substitute as an elixir—take a drop of the magic potion and be healed of national and personal ills.

APPENDIX A
Record Discography

Codes: C (Charlie), E (Elbert), W (Walter), A (Argil), J (Jennie), P (Pauline), N (No Bowman family member).

VOCALION/BRUNSWICK RECORD SESSIONS

The following information was taken from a three-CD set, *The Hill Billies: Al Hopkins and His Buckle Busters* (Document Records, DOCD 8039, 8040, 8041 [1999]), containing the group's complete recorded works from Okeh, Brunswick, and Vocalion Records, with liner notes by Charles Wolfe.

April 30–May 1, 1926, New York City

Mountaineer's Love Song, C, Vocalion 5115
Cripple Creek, C, Vocalion 5115
Long Eared Mule, C, Vocalion 5116
Mississippi Sawyer, C, Vocalion 5116
Old Joe Clark, C, Vocalion 5117
Silly Bill, C, Vocalion 5117
Hickman Rag, C, Vocalion 5118
Possum up a Gum Stump, Cooney in the Hollow, C, Vocalion 5118

October 21–23, 1926, New York City

East Tennessee Blues, C, Vocalion 5016, Brunswick 103
Governor Alf Taylor's Fox Chase, C, Vocalion 5016, Brunswick 106
Fisher's Hornpipe, C, Vocalion 5017
Blue-Eyed Girl, C, Vocalion 5017
Betsy Brown, C, Vocalion 5018
Kitty Wells, C, Vocalion 5018
Sally Ann, C, Vocalion 5019, Brunswick 105
Kitty Waltz, C, Vocalion 5019, Brunswick 106
Cackling Hen, C, Vocalion 5020
Donkey on the Railroad Track, C, Vocalion 5020
Texas Gals, C, Vocalion 5021
Going down the Road Feeling Bad, C, Vocalion 5021

Sourwood Mountain, C, Vocalion 5022
Ragged Annie, C, Vocalion 5022
Round Town Girls, C, Vocalion 5023, Brunswick 103
Buck-Eyed Rabbits, C, Vocalion 5023, Brunswick 104
Walking in the Parlor, C, Vocalion 5024
Cumberland Gap, C, Vocalion 5024
Cinda, C, Vocalion 5025, Brunswick 105
Bristol Tennessee Blues, C, Vocalion 5025, Brunswick 104

May 12–14, 16–17, 21, 1927, New York City

Hear Dem Bells, E, Vocalion 5173, Brunswick 181 and 189
Sweet Bunch of Daisies, CE, Vocalion 5178, Brunswick 174
Daisies Won't Tell, CE, Vocalion 5178, Brunswick 174
Black-Eyed Susie, CE, Vocalion 5179, Brunswick 175
Cluck Old Hen, C, Vocalion 5179, Brunswick 175
Georgia Buck, N, Vocalion 5182, Brunswick 183
Baby Your Time Ain't Long, CE, Vocalion 5182, Brunswick 183
Oh Where Is My Little Dog Gone? C, Vocalion 5183, Brunswick 187
Wasn't She a Dandy?, E, Vocalion 5183, Brunswick 187
Darling Nellie Gray, E, Vocalion 5186, Brunswick 185
Sleep Baby Sleep, C, Vocalion 5186, Brunswick 185
Coming 'Round the Mountain, CE, Vocalion 5240, Brunswick 181
Blue Ridge Mountain Blues, CE, Brunswick 180
Down to the Club, C, Brunswick 184
The Nine Pound Hammer, CE, Brunswick 177
Whoa, Mule, CE, Brunswick 178
Echoes of the Chimes, C, Brunswick 180
Boatin' up Sandy, CE, Brunswick 182
Johnson Boys, CE, Brunswick 178
The Fellow That Looked Like Me, E, Brunswick 184
C.C. & O. No. 558, CE, Brunswick 177
Ride That Mule, CE, Brunswick 186
Bug in the Taters, CE, Brunswick 182
Roll on the Ground, CE, Brunswick 186
When You Were Sweet Sixteen, N, Brunswick 176
Down the Old Meadow Lane, N, Brunswick 176

December 20–21, 1928, New York City

Gideaon's Band, N, Brunswick 295
Old Dan Tucker, N, Brunswick 295
Old Uncle Ned, N, Brunswick 300

West Virginia Gals, N, Brunswick 318
Blue Bell, N, Brunswick 300
Carolina Moonshiner, N, Brunswick 318
Polka Medley (Intro: Rocky Road to Dublin, Jenny Lind), N, Brunswick 321
Marosovia Waltz, N, Brunswick 321
Wild Hoss, N, Brunswick 335
Medley of Old Time Dance Tunes (Intro: Soldier's Joy, Turkey Buzzard, When You
    Go a Courtin'), N, Brunswick 335

COLUMBIA RECORD SESSIONS
Information obtained from Columbia Record labels.

October 16, 1928, Johnson City, Tennessee
Roll on Buddy, CEWA, Columbia 15357 D
Gonna Raise the Rukus Tonight, CEWA, Columbia 15357 D
My Old Kentucky Home, CEWAJP, Columbia 1473 D
Swanee River, CEWAJP, Columbia 15473 D

February 20, 1929, Johnson City, Tennessee
Moonshiner and His Money, CEWA, Columbia 15387 D
Forky Dear, CEWA, Columbia 15387 D

October 23, 1929, New York City
Railroad Take Me Back, CJP, Columbia 15621 D
Old Lonesome Blues, CJP, Columbia 15621 D

AMERICAN RECORD SESSIONS
Information obtained from Jennie Bowman Collection (in author's possession).
None of these records are believed to have been released.

April 22, 1931, New York City
Lonesome Blues, CJP, American 10575
The Railroad Boomer, CJP, American 10576
When the Leaves Turn Green, CJP, American 10577

APPENDIX B
Jennie Bowman's Tour Diary

TOURING WITH THE BLUE RIDGE RAMBLERS

1931

Jan. 12, Princess Theatre, Mt. Hope, West Virginia

Jan. 13, Town Theatre, Slabfork, West Virginia

Jan 14–15, Lyric Theatre, Oak Hill, West Virginia

Jan. 16–17, Princess Theatre, Mt. Hope, West Virginia

Jan. 19–24, Charleston, West Virginia

Jan. 26–27, Warner Theatre, Chillicothe, Ohio

Jan. 28–31, Laray Theatre, Portsmouth, Ohio

Feb. 1–7, Keith Albee Theatre, Huntington, West Va.

Feb. 9–10, Auditorium Theatre, Marietta, Ohio

Feb. 11–14, Ritz Theatre, Clarksburg, West Va.

Feb. 16–21, Penn Theatre, Uniontown, Penn.

Feb. 22–24, Capital Theatre, Wheeling, West Virginia

Mar. 7–10, Gates Theatre, Brooklyn, New York

Mar. 11–13, Orpheum Theatre, New York, New York

Mar. 18–20, Pitkin Theatre, Brooklyn, New York

Mar. 21, Stanley Theatre, Bridgeton, N.J.

Mar. 23–24, State Theatre, Newark, Delaware

Mar. 25–26, Everette Theatre, Middletown, Delaware

Mar. 28–31, Triboro Theatre, Astoria, L.I., New York

Apr. 1–2, New Theatre, Elkton, Maryland

Apr. 3–4, Capital Theatre, Dover, Delaware

Apr. 5, Steel Pier, Atlantic City, N.J.

Apr. 6–8, Park Theatre, Reading, Pennsylvania

Apr. 9, Metropolitan Theatre, Philadelphia, Penn.

Apr. 10, Globe Theatre, Philadelphia, Penn.

Apr. 11, Broadway Theatre, Philadelphia, Penn.

Apr. 13, Opera House, Centerville, Maryland

Apr. 15, High School Auditorium, St. George, Delaware

Apr. 16, High School Auditorium, Philadelphia, Penn.

Apr. 17, Auditorium Theatre, Philadelphia, Penn.

Apr. 18–24, Loew's Metrop. Theatre, Brooklyn, N.Y.

Apr. 30–May 2, Loew's Strand Theatre, New Brittain, Conn.

May 3, Apollo Theatre, Atlantic City, N.J.

May 4–5, YMCA Auditorium, Coatesville, Penn.

May 6, Alamedy Theatre, Lebanon, Pennsylvania

May 7–9, Capital Theatre, Shamokin, Penn.

May 11–15, Colonial Theatre, Lancaster, Pennsylvania

May 18–19, Colonial Theatre, Phoenixville, Penn.

Aug. 8–11, Publix Lawler Theatre, Amherst, Mass.

Aug. 12, Amherst Theatre, Amherst, Massachusetts

Aug. 13–15, York Theatre, Athol, Massachusetts

Aug. 16–18, Orpheum Theatre, Gardner, Massachusetts

Aug. 22–29, Broadway Theatre, Springfield, Mass.

Aug. 31, Sept 1–2, Crown Theatre, New London, Conn.

Sep. 3–5, Strand Theatre, Stanford, Connecticut

Sep. 8–9, Ideal Theatre, Springfield, Vermont

Sep. 10–11, Capital Theatre, Winchester, Mass.

Sep. 12, Opera House, Ludlow, Vermont

Sep. 14, Town Hall, Woodstock, Vermont

Sep. 15, Star Theatre, Bellowsfalls, Vermont

Sep. 16–17, City Theatre, Bidderford, Maine

Sep. 18–24, Strand Theatre, Portland, Maine

Sep. 25–27, Opera House, Bath, Maine

Sep. 28–30, Park Theatre, Rockland, Maine

Oct. 5–9, City Opry House, Waterville, Maine

Oct. 11–16, Bijou Theatre, Bangor, Maine

Oct. 17–20, Temple Theatre, Houlton, Maine

Oct. 21–23, Paramount Theatre, Fort Fairchild, Maine

Oct. 24, Star Theatre, Westbrook, Maine

Oct. 26–29, Park Theatre, Barre, Vermont

Oct. 30–31, Palace Theatre, St. Johnsburg, Vermont

Nov. 1–3, Merrimac Theatre, Lowell, Massachusetts

Nov. 4, Stafford Springs, Conn.

Nov. 5–7, Colonial Theatre, Haverhill, Mass.

Nov. 9, Town Theatre, Windsor Locks, Conn.

Nov. 10–11, Community Theatre, North Attleboro, Mass.

Nov. 14–15, Plaza Theatre, Northhampton, Mass.

Nov. 16–18, Auburn Theatre, Auburn, Maine

Nov. 19, Strand Theatre, Rumford, Maine

Nov. 20, Livermore Falls, Maine

Nov. 21, Rex Theatre, Norway, Maine

Nov. 24, Strand Theatre, Willimantic, Conn.

Nov. 25–27, Palace Theatre, Middletown, Conn.

Nov. 30–Dec. 1, Flynn Theatre, Burlington, Vermont

Dec. 2–3, Orpheum Theater, Woodsville, N.H.

Dec. 4–5, Premier Theatre, Littleton, N.H.

Dec. 7–9, Capital Theatre, Concord, N.H.

Dec. 10–12, Fitchburg Theatre, Fitchburg, Mass.

Dec. 16, High School Auditorium, Smyrna, Del.

Dec. 18–19, Oxford Theatre, Philadelphia, Pa.

Dec. 21, High School Auditorium, St. George, Delaware

Dec. 25–26, Victoria Theatre, Mahanoy, Pennsylvania

Dec. 27, Clemonton Theatre, Clemonton, New Jersey

1932

Jan. 1–3, Majestic Theatre, Bridgeton, New Jersey

Jan. 4–5, Opera House, Charleston, West Va.

Jan. 6–7, Imperial Theatre, Brunswick, Maryland

Jan. 9–15, State Theatre, Harrisburg, Penn.

Jan. 16, Auditorium Theatre, Lewistown, Penn.

Jan. 18–20, Rialto Theatre, Lewistown, Penn.

Jan. 21, Huntington, Penn.

Jan. 22–23, Trivoli Theatre, Frederick, Maryland

Jan. 25–26, Strand Theatre, Covington, Virginia

Jan. 27–28, Lyric Theatre, Beckley, West Virginia

Jan. 29–30, Bollington Theatre, Norton, Virginia

Feb. 1, Plaza Theatre, White Sulphur Springs. W.V.

Feb. 2, New Theatre, Tazewell, Virginia

Feb. 3, Wytheville, Virginia

Feb. 4–6, Princess Theatre, Mt. Hope, West Virginia

Feb. 8–10, Paramount Theatre, Bristol, Tennessee

Feb. 11–13, Strand Theatre, Knoxville, Tennessee

Feb. 15–17, Paramount Theatre, Charlottesville, Va.

Feb. 18–20, Paramount Theatre, Newport News, Virginia

Feb. 22–23, Culpeper, Virginia

Feb. 24–27, Suffolk, Virginia

Feb. 29–Mar. 1, Harrisonburg, Virginia

Mar. 2–3, Masonic Theatre, Clifton Forge, Virginia

Mar. 4–5, Appollo Theatre, Martinsburg, West Va.

Mar. 6–8, (No appearances, Got caught in blizzard)

Mar. 9, Leesburg, Virginia

Mar. 10–12, Maryland Theatre, Hagerstown, Maryland

Mar. 14–15, Capital Theatre, Winchester, Virginia

Mar. 16–17, Arcade Theatre, Waynesboro, Penn.

Mar. 18–19, Burke Theatre, Cumberland, Maryland

Mar. 21, S. Cumberland, Maryland

Mar. 22, Moorefield, West Va.

Mar. 23–24, Westminster, Maryland

Mar. 26, Colonial Theatre, Bethlehem, Penn.

Mar. 30, Auditorium Theatre, Kennett Square, Penn.

Mar. 31 / Apr 1–2, Frankford Theatre, Frankford, Penn.

Apr. 4–5, Plaza Theatre, Philadelphia, Penn.

Apr. 8–9, Broad Theatre, Souderton, Pennsylvania

Apr. 10, Mt. Ephraim, N.J.

Apr. 11–17, Capital Theatre, Scranton, Pennsylvania

Apr. 18–20, American Theatre, Pittston, Pennsylvania

Apr. 21–23, Shenandoah, Penn.

Apr. 25–27, Carbondale, Penn.

Apr. 28–30, Binghamton Theatre, Binghamton, New York

May 1–7, Fays Theatre, Philadelphia, Penn.

May 11, (The Ramblers Switch to Smalley Time Circuit)

May 11, Community Theatre, Catskill, New York

May 12, Cobleskill, New York

May 13, Fort Plain Theatre, Fort Plain, New York

May 14, Glens Falls, New York

May 15–17, Johnstown, New York

May 18–19, Cooperstown, New York

May 20, Walton, New York

May 21–22, Stamford, New York

May 23–24, Hamilton, New York

May 25–27, Sidney, New York

May 28, Fort Plain Theatre, Fort Plain, New York

May 29–30, Delhi, New York

May 31–Jun. 1, Margaretville, New York

Jun. 2–3, Middleburg, New York

Jun. 4–6, Little Falls, New York

Jun. 11, Tannersville, New York

Jun. 13–18, State Theatre, Middletown, New York

Jun. 20–21, Park Theatre, Cobleskill, New York

Jun. 23–25, Playhouse Theatre, Hudson, New York

Jun. 27–29, Kingston Theatre, Kingston, New York

Jul. 1–2, Temple Theatre, Kane, Pennsylvania

Jul. 4–6, Temple Theatre, Wellsville, New York

Jul. 7–Nov. 13, (4–month vacation)

Nov. 14–15, Buchanan Theatre, Buchanan, West Va.

Nov. 16, High School Auditorium, Radford, Virginia

Nov. 17–18, Charlottesville, Virginia

Nov. 19, High School Auditorium, Fincastle, Virginia

Nov. 20–22, Grand Theatre, Ronceverte, West Va.

Nov. 23, High School Auditorium, Union, West Virginia

Nov. 24, White Sulphur Springs, W.V.

Nov. 25–26, Grand Theatre, Covington, Virginia

Nov. 28–29, Granada Theatre, Bluefield, West Virginia

Dec. 1–2, Lincoln Theatre, Marion, Virginia

Dec. 3, Shenandoah Theatre, Abington, Virginia

Dec. 5–6, Victory Theatre, Saltville, Virginia

Dec. 8–9, Orphium Theatre, N. Wilkesboro, N.C.

Dec. 10, Palace Theatre, Taylorsville, N.C.

Dec. 12–13, Pastime Theatre, Boone, North Carolina

Dec. 14, High School Auditorium, Blowing Rock, N.C.

Dec. 15, Banner Elk College, Banner Elk, N.C.

Dec. 16–17, New Theatre, Tazewell, Virginia

Dec. 21–22, Star Theatre, Richland, Virginia

Dec. 23, High School Auditorium, Mountain City, Tenn.

Dec. 30, County Courthouse, Jonesboro, Tennessee

TOURING WITH CHARLIE BOWMAN AND HIS BUCKLE BUSTERS

1938

Jan. 1, Strand Theatre, Covington, Georgia

Jan. 5–15, Bonita Theatre, Chattanooga, Tennessee

Jan. 22, Ritz Theatre, Roanoke, Alabama

Jan. 29, Ritz Theatre, Sylacauga, Alabama

Feb. 5, Ritz Theatre, Roanoke, Alabama

Feb. 9, President Theatre, Manchester, Georgia

Feb. 12, Ritz Theatre, Scottsboro, Alabama

Feb. 14–15, Villa Rica Theatre, Villa Rica, Georgia

Feb. 17, Brookhaven Theatre, Atlanta, Georgia

Feb. 18, Palace Theatre, Guntersville, Alabama

Feb. 19, Ritz Theatre, Guntersville, Alabama

Feb. 26, Pastime Theatre, Phoenix City, Alabama

Apr. 1, Palace Theatre, Guntersville, Alabama

Apr. 2, Ritz Theatre, Guntersville, Alabama

Apr. 14, High School Auditorium, Ranburne, Alabama

Apr. 18–19, Vance Theatre, Henderson, North Carolina

Apr. 20–21, State Theatre, Clarksville, Virginia

Apr. 22–23, Weldon Theatre, Weldon, North Carolina

Apr. 25–26, Franklin Theatre, Franklin, Virginia

Apr. 27–28, Smithfield Theatre, Smithfield, Virginia

Apr. 29–May 2, Weldon Theatre, Weldon, North Carolina

May 4, Pastime Theatre, Murfreesboro, N.C.

May 6–7, Weldon Theatre, Weldon, North Carolina

May 8, Dixie Theatre, Scotland Neck, N.C.

May 9–10, Majestic Theatre, Tarboro, North Carolina

May 12–13, New Theatre, Plymouth, North Carolina

May 14, Richard Theatre, Ahoskie, North Carolina

May 15, Dixie Theatre, Scotland Neck, N.C.

May 17–18, Majestic Theatre, Tarboro, North Carolina

May 19–20, Palace Theatre, Windsor, North Carolina

May 21, Louisburg Theatre, Louisburg, North Carolina

May 22–23, Nash Theatre, Spring Hope, N.C.

May 24–25, Franklinton, N.C.

May 27, Stone Theatre, Bassett, Virginia

May 28–29, Dolly Madison Theatre, Rocksboro, N.C.

May 30–31, Franklin Theatre, Rocky Mount, Virginia

Jun. 2–4, Roanoke Theatre, Roanoke, Virginia

(Went home from here, June 5th)

Information from the Jennie Bowman Cain Collection (in author's possession).

APPENDIX B

APPENDIX C
Jennie Bowman's Songbook

The following is a collection of songs performed by Jennie Bowman while touring. She wrote all of these songs by hand and kept them in a notebook to be used to practice the words just before she sang them in a performance. From the Jennie Bowman Cain Collection (in author's possession).

Any Old Time
The Apple Tree
The Audience Song
Birmingham Jail
Black Mountain Trail
Blow Yo' Whistle Freight Train
Budded Roses
Colorado Blues, Cowboy's Dream
Darling Think of What You've Done
Days of Long Ago
Down on the Old Plantation
Dream Mother
Drifting and Dreaming
East Bound Train, Echoes from
    the Hills
The End of Memory Lane
Freight Train Blues
God Bless My Darling
Gonna Lay Down My Old Guitar
Hey, Hey, I'm Memphis Bound
The House at the End of the Lane
I Can't Say Goodbye
The Little Old Church in the
    Valley
I Love You Best of All

I Want to Be a Cowboy's Sweetheart
I'm a Shanty in Old Shanty Town
I'm Following the Star
If You Will Give Me Your Love
In the Mountains of Virginia
Lamplighting Time in the Valley
Left My Gal in the Mountains
Little Shoes
Lonesome Blues
Mellow Mountain Moon
The Mississippi Blues
Moonlight and Roses
Moonlight on the Prairie
My Blue Ridge Mountain Home
My Ohio Home
Oklahoma Blues
On the Sunny Side of the Rockies
Please Don't Be Angry
Please Don't Talk About Me When
    I'm Gone
Queen of the Blue Ridge
Railroad Booker
Ramshackle Shack
Red River Valley
Rio Grande Sweetheart

Roll along Kentucky Moon
She No Longer Belongs to Me
Slipping Around
The Smelt Song
The Spell of the Moon
There's a Mother Always Waiting
  for You
There's An Old Trail
Tired of Me
Trouble in Mind
Twenty-One Years
Valley of the Moon
Wabash Moon
Wait for the Wagon

Waiting for a Train
We Live in Two Different Worlds
When It's Night Time in Nevada
When It's Roundup Time in Heaven
When It's Springtime in the Rockies
When the Moon Comes Over the
  Mountain
When the Sun Goes Down Again
Where the Silvery Colorado Wends
  Its Way
Winking At Me
Yes I Know
You're the Only Star in My Blue
  Heaven

APPENDIX D
Charlie Bowman's Comedy Routines

The following were comedy routines used by Charlie Bowman during his many performances. Now contained in the Charlie Bowman Collection (in possession of Charlie's youngest daughter, Mary Lou Weibel of Fayetteville, Georgia), some are typed in complete form; others are handwritten, often with key words that provided Charlie an outline of the upcoming show. It is believed the typed ones were read over KWKH, Shreveport, Louisiana, during their radio shows.

THE RICE BROTHERS

First Act

Peewee: Hoke, Isn't Tennessee Charlie supposed to work with us tonight?

Hoke: Sure, isn't he here?

Peewee: No, he failed to show up.

Charlie [from the audience]: No, I never failed to show up, but I'm not working 'til I eat.

Hoke: Eat, eat, eat is all I've heard out of him for the past three weeks, Peewee.

Charlie: Yeah! Eat, eat, eat is all I've heard for three weeks, I never get anything and man, I'm hongry.

Peewee: Well, Tennessee Charlie, Hoke and I have decided we need you to work tonight and we'll send and get you something to eat. Now, what do you usually eat?

Charlie: Breakfast, dinner, and supper more than anything else.

Peewee: No, I mean what kind of food do you want to eat?

Charlie: Oh, am I gonna get to eat?

Peewee: Yes, soon as you tell us what you want.

Charlie: Well, I want some, ah— No, I don't want none of that. Get me some, ah— No, I believe I'll change it to, ah—

Peewee: Well, what do you want (very angry)?

Charlie: I want a whole slop barrel full of chitlins for man, I'm hungry!

Peewee: Chitlins, you don't even know what chitlins are.

Charlie: Why anybody knows what chitlins is.

Peewee: Well what are chitlins?

Charlie: That's a hog's inner tubes. Anybody knows that.

Peewee: Will you please come up here. Hoke and I want to talk to you.

Charlie: I don't want nobody to see me talking to you and Hoke.

Peewee: Why?

Charlie: They might think I'm lowdown, too. But that's all right I'll come [Charlie makes for the stage].

Peewee: Hoke, I think something ought to be done for Tennessee Charlie. I think he's really sick.

Hoke: He couldn't be because he wants to eat all the time.

Peewee: I think he's got a tapeworm.

Charlie: No, I've got no tapeworm. I used to have a tapeworm but since I went to work for the Rice Brothers, he starved and walked out on me. I'm so hongry I'm all puffed in—I'll be back after I eat. [Charlie exits].

Peewee: Hoke, I see Tennessee Charlie is bound to eat so I guess you'll just have to take over and give the folks some music.

[The Rice Brothers and Gang perform two musical selections]

Charlie: I've come back to talk this thing over with you. Now what I want to know is how much are you gonna pay me if I work.

Peewee: Well just how much salary do you want?

Charlie: Salary! I don't want none of that dad blamed stuff a'tall.

Peewee: Why don't you want any salary?

Charlie: [Thinking he meant celery]: Cause I eat some one time and it made my chest hurt.

Peewee: Oh, I mean how much pay would you want?

Charlie: How much will you gimme?

Peewee: I will give you three and a half a day.

Charlie: I'll take it. I'm done a working right now.

Peewee: Wait a minute. Now that means three meals and a half a dollar a day. In other words, I pay you a half dollar and throw the meals in myself.

Charlie: Just gimme the half dollar and I'll throw the meals in myself. [pause]. Naw!, I won't do that, that's not enough. Would I get a raise after I work awhile?

Peewee: Sure, if your work's good enough.

Charlie: Aw, I knowed there was a ketch to it. [Disgustedly]. I'm gone.

Peewee: Wait a minute, I've got one more offer to make you.

Charlie: What is it?

Peewee: If you'll work, I'll pay you what you're worth.

Charlie: That settles it. I won't work that cheap for nobody.

Second Act

Peewee: Charlie, I'm going to move. I'm very dissatisfied with my rooming house.

Charlie: What's wrong with it?

Peewee: I'm sure I heard two rats fighting in my room last night.

Charlie: How much do you pay for your room?

Peewee: I only pay two dollars a week.

Charlie: What the heck do you expect for two dollars a week—a bull fight?

Peewee: Say, Charlie, I want to tell you about my new clock that I bought. It will run six months without winding.

Charlie: Golly, gee—whizzle-de-bum. Shet your mouth wide open—How long do you reckon it would run if you'd wind it?

Peewee: Come here Charlie, I want to tell you about my grandfather. He lived to be 90 years old and never used glasses. What do you think of that?

Charlie: Huh! That's nothing. My grandfather lived to be a hundred and ten and he always drank out of bottles.

Charlie: Peewee, I bet I can guess how old you are.

Peewee: How old am I?

Charlie: I'll say [pause] . . . I say you're 50.

Peewee: You're right. How did you know that?

Charlie: Well I got a brother that's 25 and he's just half crazy.

Peewee: You think you're so smart. How much is 6 and 4?

Charlie: It is 12.

Peewee: No. Charlie, It's 11.

Peewee: No [pause] . . . Why don't you try 10?

Charlie: It can't be that 'cause 5 and 5 is 10.

Peewee: Aw—let me try you on another one. I'm going to lay 4 eggs here [points]. 4 eggs there and 4 eggs over there. Now how many eggs would I have?

Charlie: You would have 12. But I don't believe you can do it. Go ahead and try it.

Peewee: Now let cut out the foolishness. I want a little information.

Charlie: I can tell you anything you wanna know.

Peewee: I'm having trouble with my goldfish. They are turning red. What can I do about it?

Charlie: Poor fish—I guess if they'd put you in a bowl of water without a bathing suit, you'd turn red too.

Charlie: Peewee, do you know why a corset and a garbage can are alike?

Peewee: No, I believe not. Why?

Charlie: They both gather the waist.

Charlie: Peewee, is it correct to say—I'm is 21 years old, or I am 21 years old.

Peewee: I am 21 years old.

Charlie: That's what I thought.

Charlie: Is it correct to say I is good looking or I am good looking.

Peewee: I am good looking.

Charlie: That's what I thought. Is it correct to say I'm is a fool or I am a fool.

Peewee: I am a fool.

Charlie: That's what I thought.

Third Act

Charlie: Hey, Peewee, I wanta show you a picture of my grandfather, we was talking about awhile ago.

Peewee: [Looks at picture then at Charlie]—Charlie you are a much better looking man than your grandfather was.

Charlie: Ha. I gotta right to be. I'm a later model.

Peewee: Say Charlie, are you married?

Charlie: Am I, man I've been married.

Peewee: If your wife should die would you marry again?

Charlie: Naw—I think I'd take a rest.

Peewee: Well, does your wife depend on you?

Charlie: She shore does. If I didn't find jobs for her she's starve to death.

Peewee: Does your wife always think of your happiness?

Charlie: Yeah, she hired a detective to check up on it. But after all, I'm happier for the past three weeks than I've been in my life. I'm getting a salary now.

Peewee: Getting a salary—I didn't know you had a job.

Charlie: I haven't but my wife has.

Peewee: Say Charlie, she tried to divorce me the other day, for talking.

Charlie: Why Can't a man talk if he wants to?

Peewee: Shore, but I was talking in my sleep.

Charlie: Say, Peewee, somebody told me that you are one of the smartest men in the South. They said you could even understand all animal languages.

Peewee: That me, all right. What do you want to know?

Charlie: When a dog barks, and a pig grunts, and a cow bawls, do you know what they are saying?

Peewee: Sure, didn't I tell you I understand all animal languages.

Charlie: Oh yeah! Well I want you to do me a favor. The next time you see a skunk, ask him what the heck is the big idea!

Charlie: Hey, Peewee, will you lend me a quarter to get where my family is?

Peewee: Sure I will, where is your family?

Charlie: They're at the movies.

Peewee: I can't see why a big strong man like you would be begging. Why don't you look around for work?

Charlie: I can't look around. I've got a stiff neck.

Peewee: Well Charlie, I'm going to give you a quarter, not because you deserve it, but because it really pleases me.

Charlie: Why don't you give me a dollar and really enjoy yourself?

Peewee: Say, how long have you been out of work?

Charlie: I don't know. I can't remember whether I was born in 1888 or 1889.

Peewee: I should think you would be ashamed to beg in a place like this.

Charlie: Don't apologize for it Peewee. I've seen worse.

Charlie: Oh! I just heard a new joke in the audience. Let me tell it to you.

Peewee: All right, let's have it.

Charlie: Here goes, once there were two traveling salesmen.

Peewee: Whoa. You can't tell that here because it is a dirty joke.

Charlie: I'm gonna tell it anyway.

Peewee: No your not. My wife's in the audience.

Charlie: Ha! Ha! Ha! It don't make any difference. She's the one who told it to me.

Peewee: Charlie, there's one thing I notice when Cicero and his wife have a fight. Cicero always manages to come out ahead.

Charlie: That right, I believe in a man running his own home.

Peewee: Yeah, but every time he comes out ahead she's right behind him with a club.

Charlie: My brother had very bad luck. Just as his business was turning the corner, the crash came.

Peewee: That's too bad. What was his business?

Charlie: He was a taxi driver.

SMOKY MOUNTAIN JAMBOREE
Johnson City, Tennessee, City Hall Auditorium

March 9, 1946: 1- Ensemble: Too Young To Marry. 2- Jennie: T For Texas. 2- Goin Fishing. 3- Looks Like A Dog Got Feather's On It. 4- Sets Under Bed At Night. 5- Maggie - Novelty Fiddle. 6- Ragged Underwear. 7- Jennie - Any Old Time. 8- Spell Boy, Girl, Cat, Male Or Female. 9- Police Song. 10- Pants Off.

March 16, 1946: 1- Ensemble- Cacklin' Hen. 2- Jennie Song- Paper Bag. 3- Joke- How many ribs has a monkey got. Take off shirt and count. 4- Joke- How long can a person live without brains. How old are you? 5- Novelty Whistle- Rotterdam. 6- Joke- How many kinds of milk are they? How many faucets? 7- Jennie Song. 8- (Chas) To look at me you'd think I'm from the country. 9- Chas- If woman keeps getting dresses shorter in 5 years, I'm moving here to stay. 10- Chas Song- There are styles make you happy. Want to get off and hide. 11- Chas & Eddie- Slight of hand (bloomers).

March 23, 1946: 1- Ensemble. 2- 200 a month-2 months, vacation with pay, taste tester, castor oil. 3- Jennie Song. 4- Nose runs feet smells (built upside down). 5- Novelty Fiddle- Bag pipe. 6- Human body, head, arms, legs, spinal column, brains, head on one end, sit on other. 7- My little brother got awful sick. Rushed him to the doctor. Awful quiet. 8- Jennie Song. 9- My picture when I was a baby. Bald headed little rascal. You got upside down. 10- Charlie & Jennie- Make song to rhyme. 11- Jennie- Mary had a little lamb. 12- Charlie- I had a girl friend and her name was Nellie. 13- Fiddle. 14- Announcements- After Mon, Tue, Wed. 15- Suit case- to pups.

March 30, 1946: 1- Ensemble- Dill Pickle Rag. 2- Guessing weight Job at stock yard. Chicago. How much does this one weigh? First hog I missed in 2 years. 3- Jennie's song. 4- New bug called kiss bug. Kissed 4 girls at Bristol. They died. 5- Broom fiddle. 6- Went to doctor. Coat on tongue. Vest and pair of pants. 7- Too many in bed. 8- 9 Lb Hammer. 9- Visit country cousin. Baseball. Slid into what I thought was 1st base. 8- Jennie's song. 9- Charlie- Eddie, what difference is there between a hobo, a tramp, and a bum? Hobo will work. Tramp might. Bum won't work. Ha ha. How long have you been a bum? 10- Suit case. She is in there.

April 6, 1946: 1- Ensemble- Hickman Rag. 2- I moved. I now live on Petticoat Avenue just inside the outskirts. 3- Perfume 50 dollars an ounce, moth balls 25 cents a bushel. 4- Jennie's song. 5- Say the stork came to my house again today. How many does that make? On 1st trip, stork had long legs. Now looks like a duck. After today stork won't bring anymore babies. Airplane- 1-1 seater, 2-2. 3-3. Going home just saw Zeppelin go over my house. 6- Kissed every lady in the house. Missed one. See you after show. 7- Fiddle: Nearer My God to Thee. 8- Saved girls life. Nail in plank. 9- On farm, raised goats. Goat has no nose. How does he smell? Terrible. Brought goat home. Sleeps with me. How about the smell? Let him get used to me. 10- Jennie's song.

April 13, 1946: 1- Ensemble- Sally Ann. 2- I'm is a fool. 3- Two traveling salesmen. 4- Jennie's song. 5- Fell like woman's stocking. Knee high. Plum full. 6- Put in pie don't eat. (teeth). 7- Fiddle. 8- Kidnap. Hold for ransom. Man outside got shot gun. 8- Charles- Broadcast in the mtn's of Va. 9- Jennie's song.

April 20, 1946: 1- Ensemble. 2- Three great men never born. Uncle Sam. Santa Claus. Charles McCarthy. 3- Jennie's song 4- Austin car joke. 5- Long and tall blind mule. 6- Fiddle- Old Joe (Clark). 7- Brother getting married. 8- The way to spell chicken.

May 4, 1946: 1- Ensemble. 2- To buy a cow or a bicycle. 3- If I had a face like yours. 4- Soap and water. 5- Jennie's song. 6- Retailing dogs without license. 7- Fiddle. 8- How many sides to anything. Jennie-2 sides to everything. 9- Changes pants for every occasion.

APPENDIX E
Billy Bowman's Accomplishments

About the time Fiddlin' Charlie Bowman was concluding his association with the Hill Billies, Billy Marshall Bowman, son of Elbert and Gladys Bowman, was born on October 30, 1928, in Washington County, Tennessee. In his early teen years, he began showing a preference for western swing music, unlike the musical genre of his father and uncle. He first learned the dobro, playing with various groups in and around Bristol. However, Knoxville was actually the site of his initial full-time employment in music. While a youngster, he got his brother's guitar and put a dinner knife under the strings to raise them from the neck and used a Listerine bottle as a slide. He became infatuated with the resultant sound of it—the sound of steel. Billy was once quoted as saying that western swing music must be born in you. He often remarked that he was born pattin' his foot. When he performed in shows around the country, the entertainer always looked out at his audience, and if he saw somebody pattin' the floor, he would say, "Well, we're gonna do all right." If he didn't, he would remark, "Uh, oh. We're in trouble."

On WNOX's Midday Merry-Go-Round and Tennessee Barn Dance in the mid-1940s, Billy performed in a country group headed by Johnny Wright, husband of legendary Kitty Wells, and Eddie Hill. During part of this stay, two of his brothers, Buddy and Jake, were his fellow band members. In the early 1940s, three of Billy's brothers, Weldon, Jake, and Buddy, traveled for a short time with Knoxville's blind evangelist, J. Bazzel Mull, as singers in his evangelistic campaigns. The reverend and his son came to the Bowman home for dinner one evening. Mr. Mull needed someone to read the Bible for him, so Weldon "became his eyes." In appreciation, J. Bazzel gave young Weldon an autographed Bible.

When Johnny Wright and Eddie Hill broke up, Eddie moved some of the musicians, including Billy, to Memphis, where they played mostly jazz and pop on WMPS radio and in various clubs. Soon, Billy found himself on the stage of Nashville's Grand Ole Opry with Paul Howard and the Arkansas Cotton Pickers. It was during this time that Billy achieved his first national exposure; as an eighteen-year-old, he played steel guitar on a million seller, "Shenandoah Waltz," for country singer Clyde Moody (King Records, 1947). Billy performed on the

Opry in the Ryman Auditorium from 1947 to about 1949. He did not like playing at this former church building because he said he could not hear himself playing while performing on the stage. Neither did he care for the large bags of sand in the ceilings that were put there for fire protection, confessing that he was always worried that one might fall on his head. Because the Opry's management frowned upon the lively western swing played by the Cotton Pickers, Howard was forced to move his organization to Shreveport, Louisiana. This fortunate move brought about an opportunity for Billy to audition for the world-famous bandleader and fiddler, Bob Wills. This event, which occurred in Oklahoma City in 1950, was the beginning of his eight-year tenure with the reputed "King of Western Swing" and his legendary Texas Playboys.

Billy wrote and cowrote several songs, mostly instrumentals for the steel, two of which are "B. Bowman Hop" and "Midnight in Amarillo." To date, these have captured the attention of stylists from sixteen nations, notably Holland, Japan, and England. Billy's tunes have been recorded by such renowned steel players as Maurice Anderson, Vic Ashmeade, Cindy Cashdollar, Jimmy Day, Pete Drake, Buddy Emmons, Lloyd Green, Pete Mitchell, Tommy Morrell, Herb Remington, Bill Stafford, and even fiddler Dale Potter. Billy's long-time friend, Barbara Mandrell, performed these songs on her syndicated television show. More recently, his compositions have been played on *A Prairie Home Companion,* a weekly production of Public Radio International, hosted by popular humorist Garrison Keillor. Die-hard fans of Bob Wills's music can recognize Billy's singing as well as his instrumental work; his high tenor voice with the Bob Wills trio (Billy Jack Wills, Jimmy Widener, and Rusty McDonald) on "Faded Love" (MGM, 1950) is claimed by many musicologists as the primary ingredient that made this song a hit. Additionally, Billy was lead vocalist for Wills on "With Tears in My Eyes" (MGM, 1953), written by his ex-boss, Paul Howard, who graciously consented to Billy's transfer from his own Cotton Pickers to Wills's band. He also sang in various Texas Playboy trios.

After leaving Wills, Billy had brief stints with Billy Walker, Hank Thompson, and former Texas Playboy Lew Walker. These short-lived jobs had ceased by 1960 when his career was relegated to semiretired status, with his returning to East Tennessee, where he appeared on local weekly television shows. Shortly thereafter, Billy moved to his final residence in Columbia, South Carolina, where he played in local clubs and did some session work on recordings. Until physically and mentally unable to continue, he participated in three annual events as a musician: "Bob Wills Days" in Turkey, Texas; the International Steel Guitar Convention in St. Louis, Missouri; and the Smoky Mountain Steel Guitar Jamboree in Knoxville, Tennessee.

By late 1988, although Billy was still in great demand for public appearances and recording sessions, his failing health necessitated a dramatic decline in his playing; he was simply incapable of honoring a majority of the invitations. Nevertheless, a few weeks before his passing, he was making plans to perform at a Texas Playboy reunion in Pawhuska, Oklahoma, and to record under his own name again (for the first time since 1957)—two of the dreams he never was privileged to realize. After a six-month battle with cancer, Billy died in 1989. In spite of the brevity of Billy's full-time career, which lasted a little over twelve years, he was the recipient of many accolades and distinctive honors. He was inducted into both the International Steel Guitar Hall of Fame in St. Louis and the Western Swing Society Hall of Fame in Sacramento. Billy was also recognized by two state legislatures, Oklahoma and California, for his contributions to music.

As a musician, Billy was much more popular—and esteemed for his creative riffs on such recordings as "St. Louis Blues," "Doin' the Bunny Hop," "Texas Blues," "I've Got a New Road under My Wheels," "The End of the Line," "I Laugh When I Think How I Cried Over You," "Hang Your Head in Shame," and several peppy instrumentals by Bob and the band. In recent years, some of his most artistic work has been rereleased on compact discs, including a few live radio broadcasts from Pasadena, California, that originally aired in the 1950s.

Although Billy Bowman died relatively young, his music lives on in a new generation of talented pedal steel guitarists.

For the above information, I am indebted to Dr. James Bowman, whom I interviewed on July 14, 2000, in Johnson City, Tennessee.

NOTES

1. A FIDDLER'S FIRST NOTES

1. Samuel Cole Williams, *History of Johnson City and Its Environs* (Johnson City, TN: Watauga Press, 1940), 9.
2. G. R. McGee, *A History of Tennessee* (New York: American Book Co., 1899), 248.
3. Peter Zimmerman and Peter Coats, *Tennessee Music—Its People and Places* (San Francisco: Miller Freeman Books, 1998), 175.
4. Joyce Cox and W. Eugene Cox, *History of Washington County, Tennessee* (Johnson City, TN: Overmountain Press), 818.
5. State of Tennessee Historical Marker for Daniel Boone in Boones Creek (no longer standing).
6. State of Tennessee Historical Marker for Buffalo Ridge Baptist Church (located in Gray, Tennessee, at new church site several miles from original church).
7. Dorothy Hamill, "Of Many Things: Conversation Piece," *Johnson City (TN) Press-Chronicle,* May 1, 1960.
8. E. S. Depew, "In Memoriam: Samuel Bowman," *Jonesboro (TN) Herald-Tribune,* undated clipping. Bob Cox Collection, West Columbia, SC.
9. Arthur Loesser, *Humor in American Song* (New York: Howell, Soskin, Publishers, 1974), 52.

2. FANNIE'S FIDDLER BEAU

1. "I Can't Say Goodbye," written by Charlie Bowman. Charlie Bowman Collection (in possession of Charlie Bowman's youngest daughter, Mary Lou Weibel, Fayetteville, GA).
2. Charlie Bowman, taped interview by Dorsey Dixon, Union City, Georgia, Nov. 1961. Southern Folklife Collection, Univ. of North Carolina, Chapel Hill.
3. Dorothy Hamill, "Remember the Good Old Days and the Bowman String Band," *Johnson City Press-Chronicle,* Feb. 4, 1960.
4. "Arkansas Traveler," lyrics accessed at Lyrics for Traditional Bluegrass and Early Country Music, http://bluegrasslyrics.com/all_song.cfm-recordID=sp089.htm.
5. Ibid.
6. Pete Seeger, *American Favorite Ballads* (New York: Music Sales Corp., 1980).

3. BIRTH OF A STRING BAND

1. Alan Lomax, "Folk Song Style," *American Anthropologist* 61, no. 6 (1959): 41.
2. *A Fiddler's Convention in Mountain City, Tennessee: 1924–1930 Recordings,* County Records #525. A supplemental booklet by Joe Wilson, included with this recording, identifies all the performers in the famous photograph.

3. Handwritten log of all the fiddle contests Bowman won before turning professional. Charlie Bowman Collection.
4. Kelley Kirksey, (former) President of the Federation of Old-Time Fiddling Judges, "Old-Time Fiddling: How to Understand and Appreciate It, Learning to Listen" (n.p., n.d.).
5. "Reece Death Recalls Bowman String Band," *Jonesboro Herald and Tribune*, June 7, 1961.
6. Charles Wolfe, *The Devil's Box: Masters of Southern Fiddling* (Nashville and London: Country Music Foundation Press and Vanderbilt Univ. Press, 1997), 53.
7. Classified ads, *Johnson City (TN) Chronicle*, Aug. 17, 1929.
8. *The Talking Machine World* 20, no. 6 (1924): 181.
9. Wolfe, *The Devil's Box*, 9–10.
10. Ibid., 203–16.

4. A HILLBILLY HILL BILLIE

1. *(Lexington Park, MD) Enterprise*, Sept. 26, 1974. I am grateful to Jennifer Cutting of the American Folklife Center at the Library of Congress, Washington, DC, for bringing this source to my attention.
2. Ibid.
3. Ibid.
4. *The Hill Billies: Al Hopkins and His Buckle Busters* (Document Records, DOCD 8039, 8040, 8041 [1999]); this 3-CD set containing complete recorded works from Okeh, Brunswick, and Vocalion Records with liner notes by Charles Wolfe.
5. Ibid.
6. *(Lexington Park, MD) Enterprise*, Sept. 26, 1974.
7. Charlie Bowman, interview by Dixon.
8. Quoted in *A Dictionary of Americanisms on Historical Principles*, ed. Mitford Mathews (Chicago: Univ. of Chicago Press, 1951), 808.
9. Charlie Bowman, taped interview by Archie Green and Ed Kahn, Union City, GA, Aug. 10, 1961. Southern Folklife Collection, Univ. of North Carolina, Chapel Hill.
10. *A Fiddlers Convention in Mountain City, Tennessee: 1924–1930 Recordings*, 2–3. Supplemental booklet identifies all the performances in the famous photograph.
11. Ibid., 3.
12. Ibid., 2.
13. Information written on the back of a photograph. Jennie Bowman Cain Collection (in possession of Bob Cox, West Columbia, SC).
14. Selma Jeanne Cohen, *International Encyclopedia of Dance: A Project of Dance Perspectives* (Oxford: Oxford Univ. Press, 1998).
15. "Fiddlers Contest at Mountain Is Great Success," *(Bristol, TN/VA) Herald Courier*, May 5, 1925.
16. Alan Lomax, *The Folk Songs of North America in the English Language* (Garden City, NY: Doubleday & Co., 1960), 230–31.
17. "Hill Billies Capture WRC," *Radio Digest Programs Illustrated* (Chicago: Radio Digest Publishing Co.), Mar. 6, 1926.
18. Charlie Bowman, interview by Green and Kahn.
19. Starr family to Washington, DC, radio station WRC, Jan. 10, 1926. Charlie Bowman Collection.

20. *(Columbus) Ohio State Journal,* Jan. 10, 1926.
21. "Hill Billies Capture WRC, Boys from Blue Ridge Mountains Take Washington with Guitars, Fiddles, and Banjos; Open New Line of American Airs," *Radio Digest Illustrated,* Mar. 26, 1926, 5, 24.
22. "Hill Billy Fiddler Is to Aid in Contest," *Washington (DC) Times,* Feb. 2, 1926.
23. "Hill Billies Capture WRC," 24.
24. "Hill Billy Fiddler Is to Aid in Contest."
25. "Meet Charlie Bowman," *Disc Collector Magazine: The Country Record Collectors Bible,* no. 16 (1960): 3.
26. John Lambert to Al Hopkins, Feb. 21, 1927. Charlie Bowman Collection.
27. A theater flyer for Sunday, Apr. 11, 1926, showing the Hill Billies as part of a nine-act bill for the Keith-Albee Vaudeville circuit. Charlie Bowman Collection.
28. Elkins Theatre advertisement, Elkins, WV, July 17–18, 1928. Charlie Bowman Collection.
29. "Personnel of Hill Billies Is Given Play Here Friday," *Johnson City Staff–News,* Sept. 8, 1927.
30. Anthony Slide, *The Encyclopedia of Vaudeville* (Westport, CT: Greenwood Publishing, 1994).
31. Ibid.

5. RECORDING IN THE BIG APPLE

1. *The Hill Billies–Al Hopkins and His Buckle Busters.* A complete discography can be found in Appendix A.
2. Ibid.
3. "Donkey on the Railroad Track," The Hill Billies, Vocalion Records #B5020, lyrics taken from record.
4. "Fiddle Tunes of the Old Frontier: The Henry Reed Collection," traditional fiddle tunes performed by Henry Reed of Glen Lyn, VA. American Folklife Center, Library of Congress, Washington, DC.
5. Loesser, *Humor in American Song,* 52–53.
6. Elbert Bowman, taped interview by Archie Green and Ed Kahn, Johnson City, TN, Aug. 8, 1963. Southern Folklife Collection, Univ. of North Carolina, Chapel Hill.
7. "Governor Alf Taylor's Fox Chase," The Hill Billies, Vocalion Records #A5020, lyrics taken from record.
8. Dr. Bob Taylor to the author, July 29, 2005, after learning about the Hill Billies' recording of "Governor Alf Taylor's Fox Hunt on 'Buffalo Mountain.'"
9. "Cackling Hen," The Hill Billies, Vocalion Records #B5020, and "Cluck Old Hen," The Hill Billies, Vocalion Records #B5179, lyrics taken from records.
10. "The Nine Pound Hammer," Al Hopkins and His Buckle Busters, Brunswick Records #177A, lyrics taken from record.
11. Elbert Bowman, interview by Green and Kahn.
12. Archie Green, *Only A Miner: Studies in Recorded Coal-Mining Songs* (Urbana: Univ. of Illinois Press, 1972), 346.
13. Tom Hodge Column, *Johnson City Press,* Sept. 25, 1984.
14. "CC&O No. 558," Al Hopkins and His Buckle Busters, Brunswick Records #177B, lyrics taken from record.
15. Lyrics to "Emery's Fast Ride." Charlie Bowman Collection.

16. Lyrics to "My Railroad Shack." Charlie Bowman Collection.
17. Charlie Bowman, interview by Dixon.
18. Bill Malone and Judith McCulloh, *Stars of Country Music: Uncle Dave Macon to Johnny Rodriguez* (Champaign: Univ. of Illinois Press, 1975), 80.
19. Lyrics to Charlie's "Southern Blues." Charlie Bowman Collection.
20. *The Hill Billies: Al Hopkins and His Buckle Busters.*
21. Information obtained from Jennifer A. Cutting, Archive of Folk Culture, Library of Congress, Washington, DC, 2002.
22. Willard Hotel, Nov. 20, 1933, before the Wisconsin Society of Washington, DC.
23. Bill Malone, *Country Music U.S.A.: A Fifty-Year History* (Austin and London: Univ. of Texas Press, 1974), 310.

6. "UNCLE FUZZ" COMES TO TOWN

1. Handout notes from Dr. Charles Wolfe, Birthplace of Country Music Alliance (BCMA) Conference, Bristol, Apr. 2004, covering the 1928 and 1929 Columbia Records sessions of Frank Walker in Johnson City, TN, p. 1. Hereafter cited as "Wolfe, BCMA notes."
2. Ibid., 2.
3. Josh Dunson, Ethel Raim, and Moses Asch, eds., *Anthology of American Folk Music,* (New York: Oak Publications, 1974), 8–17. Includes interviews with Moses Asch and Frank Walker.
4. Ibid.
5. *Johnson City (TN) Press-Chronicle,* June 12, 1942.
6. Wolfe, BCMA notes, 3–4.
7. Ibid., 5–6.
8. "Roll on Buddy," Charlie Bowman and His Brothers. This original song has been released on three labels: Columbia Records #147208, #15357-D (recorded in Johnson City, TN, Oct. 16, 1928); *A Fiddler's Convention in Mountain City, Tennessee: 1924–1930 Recordings;* and *Appalachian Stompdown,* JSP Records (London), ASIN B000DN6CN8, a four-disc boxed set released in February 2006. The quoted lyrics were taken from this recording.
9. David McIntosh, *Folk Songs and Singing Games of the Illinois Ozarks,* ed. Dale R. Whiteside (Carbondale: Southern Illinois Univ. Press), 1974.
10. Patrick Carr, *The Illustrated History of Country Music (by the Editors of Country Music Magazine)* (Garden City, NY: Doubleday & Co., 1979), 41–42.
11. Anne Cohen, of the John Edwards Memorial Foundation, Inc., to Staly Cain, Oct. 20, 1972. Charlie Bowman Collection.
12. "Moonshiner and His Money," Charlie Bowman and His Brothers, Columbia Records #15387-D.
13. Lyrics to "Tennessee Moonshine Song." Charlie Bowman Collection.
14. *Banjo Pickin' Girl: Women in Early Country Music,* Rounder Records #1029. Other artists included on this recording are Eva Davis and Samantha Bumgarner, Roba Stanley, Louisiana Lou, Billie Maxwell, Blue Ridge Mountain Singers, Moonshine Kate, Rubye Blevins (Patsy Montana), Girls of the Golden West, and Coon Creek Girls.
15. E-mail to Bill Knowlton from Dr. Charles Wolfe, Jan. 19, 2004. Copy in possession of Bob Cox, West Columbia, SC.

7. WOPI: OVER THE AIR ON THE STATE LINE

1. "WOPI–8 Years on the Air," advertising brochure, 1937. Jennie Bowman Cain Collection.
2. Maurice Horn, *100 Years of American Newspaper Comics* (New York: Gramercy Books, 1996), 352–53.
3. Fran (unknown) to Jen (Jennie), Nov. 30, 1930, WOPI stationery "Radio Broadcasting Station, WOPI Inc, The Voice of the Appalachians." Jennie Bowman Cain Collection.
4. Ernest J. (Tennessee Ernie) Ford Musical Arrangements Collection, Special Collections, Music Library, University of California at Los Angeles.

8. THE BLUE RIDGE RAMBLERS

1. Tony Russell, "H. M. Barnes Blue Ridge Ramblers," *Old Time Music* (Summer 1975): 11.
2. Ibid.
3. "Songs From Dixie, Old and New," advertisement under the title "Outstanding Records," Brunswick Radio Corp., 78-rpm record sleeve.
4. "Mountain Girls at the Capitol," clipping from unnamed Wheeling, WV, newspaper, mid-February 1931. Jennie Bowman Cain Collection.
5. Russell, "H. M. Barnes Blue Ridge Ramblers," 11.
6. For biographical information on Marcus Lowe, see this page on the Akron (OH) Civic Theatre Web site: http://www.neo.rr.com/Civic/html/marcus_loew_.html. The information on the site is derived from Christine Mendiola, "A History of Loew's Theatre of Akron, Ohio: 1929 to 1965," master's thesis, Univ. of Akron, 1974.
7. "Clarence C. 'Major Mite' Howerton," *The Internet Movie Database,* http://www.imdb.com/name/nm0398116/.
8. Janet Kerr, "Lonnie Austin/Norman Woodlieff," *Old Time Music* (Summer 1975): 9.
9. Ibid., 10.
10. Vaudeville tour diary. Jennie Bowman Cain Collection.
11. Vaudeville tour diary. Pauline Bowman Huggans Collection (in possession of Bob Cox, West Columbia, SC).
12. Allan R. Sutton, *Dime Store Dynasty: The Scranton Button Company Story* (Highlands Ranch, CO: Mainspring Press, 2000).
13. List of radio stations Charlie, Jennie, and the Pauline sisters performed during their vaudeville performances tour. Jennie Bowman Cain Collection.
14. Poem titled "Impressions." Jennie Bowman Cain Collection.
15. Unidentified newspaper article, Lowell, MA, 1931. Clipping in possession of Bob Cox, West Columbia, SC. Bob Cox Collection.
16. Text from Sammy Davis Jr., Recognition Act, 107th Cong., 2nd sess., HR 3628, Jan. 24, 2002.
17. "The Hill Billies Are Here in Person," unidentified newspaper, Huntington, PA, Jan. 21, 1932. Jennie Bowman Cain Collection.
18. Autograph book entry, Mar. 10, 1932, to Pauline and Jimmie from organist Dusty Rhodes. Jennie Bowman Cain Collection.
19. Autograph book. Jennie Bowman Cain Collection. Additional performers included Mabel Brown, Asher M. Brown, A. J. Brown, Sunny Brancy, Marian

Bailes, Marie DeComo, Dick Dixon, Rita Simon, Irene Kyle, Ellie Cerrito, Sonny Roe, Gert Roe, Shad Roe, Jackie Guillet, and Mary Urcan.

20. Photograph book. Jennie Bowman Cain Collection.

9. CHARLIE'S VARIETY FIVE

1. "Artists Usher in New Year at the Majestic: Superior Talent Combined in Midnight Vaudeville Program at Theater," *Johnson City (TN) Chronicle*, Jan. 1, 1932.
2. "Charlie Bowman and His Variety Five," *Johnson (TN) City Chronicle* [1932].
3. "Majestic New Year's Frolic Plays to Crowd," *Johnson City (TN) Chronicle*, Jan. 2, 1935.
4. Photo and article about newcomer "Smiling" Frankie Carle and his new dance orchestra, in an unidentified newspaper, Springfield, MA, June 14, 1940.
5. Anthony Slide, *The Encyclopedia of Vaudeville* (Westport, CN: Greenwood Publishing, 1994).
6. Western Union telegram, H. M. Barnes to Jennie Bowman, Oct. 10, 1933. Jennie Bowman Cain Collection.
7. Western Union telegram, H. M. Barnes to Jennie Bowman, Oct. 17, 1933. Jennie Bowman Cain Collection.

10. CHARLIE'S BLUE RIDGE MUSIC MAKERS

1. Wayne W. Daniel, *Pickin' on Peachtree: A History of Country Music in Atlanta, Georgia* (Urbana: Univ. of Illinois Press, 1990), 124.
2. "Blue Ridge Music Makers Take Station by Storm," *Atlanta Journal* [1935].
3. Ibid.
4. Zimmerman, *Tennessee Music*, 175.
5. Lyrics to "Is This Goodbye Forever?" Charlie Bowman Collection.

11. CHARLIE'S SOUTHERN MOUNTAINEERS

1. Photograph with group names listed on the back. Jennie Bowman Cain Collection.
2. Max Hall, untitled clipping, *Atlanta Georgian*, circa 1937. Jennie Bowman Cain Collection.
3. Ernie Hodges, North Carolina Fiddling, Davis Unlimited Records, DU-33031, album cover notes.
4. Ibid.
5. Daniel, *Pickin' on Peachtree*, 155.
6. "Songs and Poems by the Blue Ridge Hillbillies and Mrs. Marvin P. Hingle." Charlie Bowman Collection.
7. "Rhyme Family Will Appear in Macon Thursday," *Macon (GA) Telegraph and News*, July 5, 1936.
8. Rhyme Money issued by the Georgia Real Estate Taxpayers Association, "15 Mills: Vote for the 15 Mill Amendment." Jennie Bowman Cain Collection.
9. Ibid.

12. THE DWIGHT BUTCHER GANG

1. Daniel, *Pickin' on Peachtree*, 153.
2. Artist profile of Dwight Butcher, 1940, Renfro Valley Barn Dance Web site, http://www.talentondisplay.com/renfrovalleyartists.html.

3. Tour diary. Jennie Bowman Cain Collection.

4. *WLS Family Album, 1950* (Chicago: Prairie Farmer Publishing Co., 1951), 29.

5. "WOPI–8 Years on the Air," 7.

6. *Johnson City (TN) Chronicle* advertisement, Summer 1937.

13. CHARLIE'S BUCKLE BUSTERS

1. "Buckle Busters," *Chattanooga (TN) News,* Jan. 11, 1938.

2. "A Clean Show," *Smithfield (VA) Times,* May 5, 1938.

3. *(Rocky Mount, VA) Franklin News-Post,* June 3, 1938.

4. "Audience Song," performed by Charlie and Jennie Bowman. Jennie Bowman Cain Collection.

5. Gene Autry, *Rootin' Tootin' Rhythm* movie poster, 1937. Jennie Bowman Cain Collection.

6. Jim Leonard and Janet Graebner, *Scratch My Back: A Pictorial History of the Musical Saw and How to Play It* (Santa Ana, CA: Kaleidoscope Press, 1989).

7. "Jug Band Will Go to Nashville," unidentified newspaper clipping, circa 1938. Jennie Bowman Cain Collection.

8. *Johnson City Press,* 1938, several newspaper advertisements. Jennie Bowman Cain Collection.

9. Hilda Rainwater Henry, taped interview by Bob Cox, Aug. 4, 2003.

10. Charlie Bowman to Hilda, addressed from the Milner Hotel in Roanoke, VA, July 25, 1938. Hilda Rainwater Henry Collection (in possession of Hilda and Bartow Henry, Danielsville, GA).

14. THE RICE BROTHERS GANG

1. Hoke Rice, *The Rice Brothers' Song Folio* (N.p.: The Rice Brothers and Their Gang, 1941).

2. *On the Level* (newsletter of radio stations KWKH and KTBS, Shreveport, LA), July 1940.

3. "Hillbillies Are Radio Favorites," *Shreveport (LA) Journal,* Dec. 20, 1939.

4. KWKH radio schedule, *Shreveport (LA) Times,* Feb. 12, 1940.

5. Ibid., June 18, 1940.

6. Program Previews, *Shreveport (LA) Times,* June 18, 1940.

7. *On the Level,* July 1940.

8. Helen Jacobson, American Academy of Music, to Charlie Bowman, Apr. 25, 1940. Charlie Bowman Collection.

9. Bobby Gregory to Charlie Bowman, Apr. 25, 1940. Charlie Bowman Collection.

10. Bobby Gregory to Charlie Bowman, Feb. 11, 1948. Charlie Bowman Collection.

11. Photograph and description, *Shreveport (LA) Times,* Mar. 31, 1940.

12. The songs included "Ain't That Too Bad," "Alabama Jubilee," "At the Close of a Long, Long Day," "Be Careful with Those Eyes," "Cheatin' on Your Baby," "China Boy," "Do Something," "Down Yonder," "Hold Me," "I Cried for You," "I Love My Savior," "In a Shanty in Old Shanty Town," "Is It True What They Say About Dixie?" "I Wish You Were Jealous of Me," "It Made You Happy When You Made My Cry," "Japanese Sandman," "King Cotton Stomp," "Lovelight in the Starlight," "Marie," "Mood Indigo," "My Idea of Heaven," "Nagasaki," "Oh Susannah," "On the Sunny Side of the Street," "On the Jericho Road," "Sugar Blues," "Sweet Someone,"

"They Cut Down the Old Pine Tree," "When I'm Walking with My Sweetness," "Won't You Come Back to Me," "You Are My Sunshine," "You Got That Thing," "You Tell Her Cause I Stutter," and "You've Got to See Daddy Ev'ry Night." *The Rice Brothers' Song Folio.*

13. *Hillbilly Hit Parade of 1940* (New York: Southern Music Publishing Co. and Peer International Corp.), 1941. The Gang became associated with a major country song that would become one of the world's most beloved melodies. While Jimmie Davis is best known for his 1940 Decca hit recording of "You Are My Sunshine," it is 'Postle Paul Rice who is believed to have written this classic. The original Decca record label shows Paul's name just below the title.

14. Charlie Bowman to Alfred Bowman's daughter, Hazel Bowman Reaves, and her husband, Ray Reaves, fall 1943. Bob Cox Collection.

15. Handwritten program notes used during performances. Charlie Bowman Collection.

16. Mary Lou Weibel taped interview by Bob Cox, Fayetteville, GA, Nov. 16, 2000.

15. CHARLIE'S FIDDLE RESTS

1. Jim Walsh to Charlie Bowman, Sept. 28, 1950. Charlie Bowman Collection.
2. Slightly altered lyrics to Charlie Bowman's composition "Roll on Buddy," denoting that Charlie had a good woman in Fannie Bowman.
3. Lyrics to Charlie Bowman's "Is This Goodbye Forever?" Charlie Bowman Collection.
4. Price list of items made and for sale by Charlie Bowman in his grocery store. Charlie Bowman Collection.
5. Information about Bill Lowery's National Recording Corporation is taken from the biography page of *Ray Stevens: The Official Ray Stevens Web Site* (Clyde Records Inc., 1995–2006), http://www.raystevens.com/bio.html.

16. THE AGING FIDDLER REDISCOVERED

1. Lennie Blush to Charlie Bowman, May 18, 1960. Charlie Bowman Collection.
2. "Fiddler Tony Alderman: The Last of the Hill Billies," *(Waldorf) Maryland Independent,* Nov. 4, 1983. I am grateful to Jennifer Cutting of the American Folklife Center at the Library of Congress, Washington, DC, for bringing this source to my attention.
3. Vernon Dalhart, "Favorite Pioneer Recording Artists" (pt. 6), *Hobbies: The Magazine for Collectors,* Oct. 1960, 34–36, 44.
4. Philip Van Derplas to Charlie Bowman, Oct. 9, 1960. Charlie Bowman Collection.
5. Several songs written by Charlie Bowman. Charlie Bowman Collection.
6. "Meet Charlie Bowman," *Disc Collector,* Dec. 1960, 3.
7. Ibid., 4.
8. Joe Nicholas to Charlie Bowman, Oct. 15, 1960. Charlie Bowman Collection.
9. Charlie Bowman to Joe Nicholas, Nov. 28, 1960. Charlie Bowman Collection.
10. Malone, *Country Music U.S.A.,* 355.
11. Eugene Earle to Charlie Bowman, Mar. 18, 1961. Charlie Bowman Collection.
12. Charlie Bowman to Tony Alderman, undated. Southern Folklife Collection, Univ. of North Carolina, Chapel Hill.
13. Charlie Bowman to Tony Alderman, Apr. 20, 1961. Charlie Bowman Collection.

14. Archie Green to Charlie Bowman, May 18, 1961. Charlie Bowman Collection.
15. Archie Green to Tony Alderman, May 18, 1961, Charlie Bowman Collection.
16. Dorsey Dixon to Charlie Bowman, Oct. 13, 1961. Charlie Bowman Collection.
17. Irene Edwards in Australia to Charlie Bowman. Oct. 15, 1961, Charlie Bowman Collection.
18. Charlie Bowman, interview by Dixon.
19. Irene Edwards in Australia to Charlie Bowman, Jan. 17, 1962. Charlie Bowman Collection.
20. Dorsey Dixon to Charlie Bowman, May 5, 1962. Charlie Bowman Collection.

17. TIME TO "ROLL ON BUDDY"

1. Death notice, *Variety Magazine,* June 6, 1962.
2. Death notice, *Johnson City (TN) Press-Chronicle,* May 21, 1962.
3. Charlie Bowman's funeral book. Charlie Bowman Collection.
4. Poem by Dorsey Dixon. Charlie Bowman Collection.

18. ALIVE THROUGH HIS MUSIC

1. The North American Fiddlers Hall of Fame and Museum Institute, advertisement brochure, Osceola, NY.
2. State of Tennessee Historical Marker at the intersection of Rosco Fitz Road and Bobby Hicks Highway, Gray, TN. Marker wording composed by Bob Cox and Dr. James Bowman.
3. Robert E. Nobley to Charlie Bowman, Dec. 18, 1962. Charlie Bowman Collection.
4. Zimmerman, *Tennessee Music,* 175.

INDEX